AF262959

Seeking Revelation

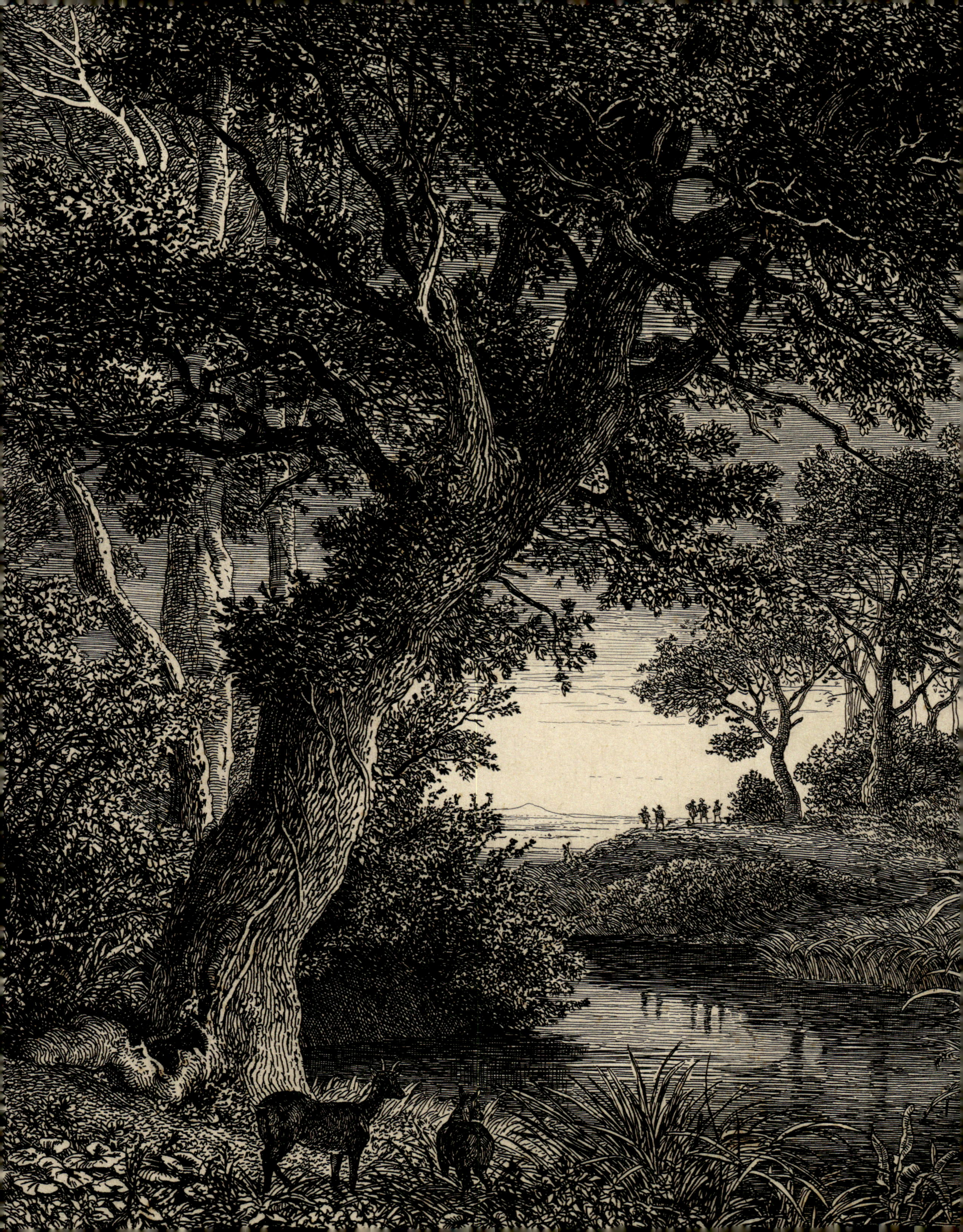

Seeking Revelation

German Romantic Prints and Drawings

Nikki Otten

with contributions by
Cordula Grewe and
Stephanie O'Rourke

Milwaukee Art Museum

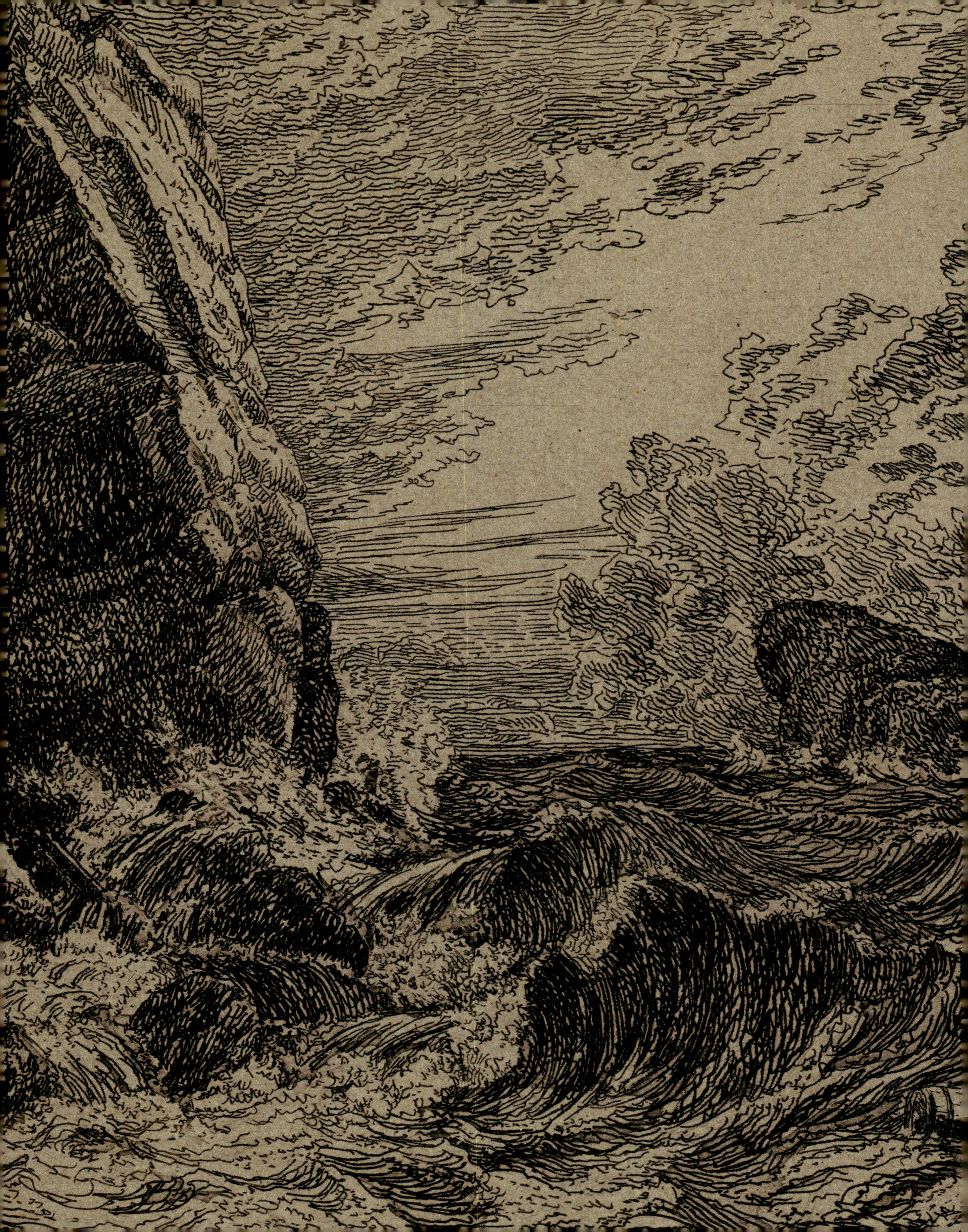

Contents

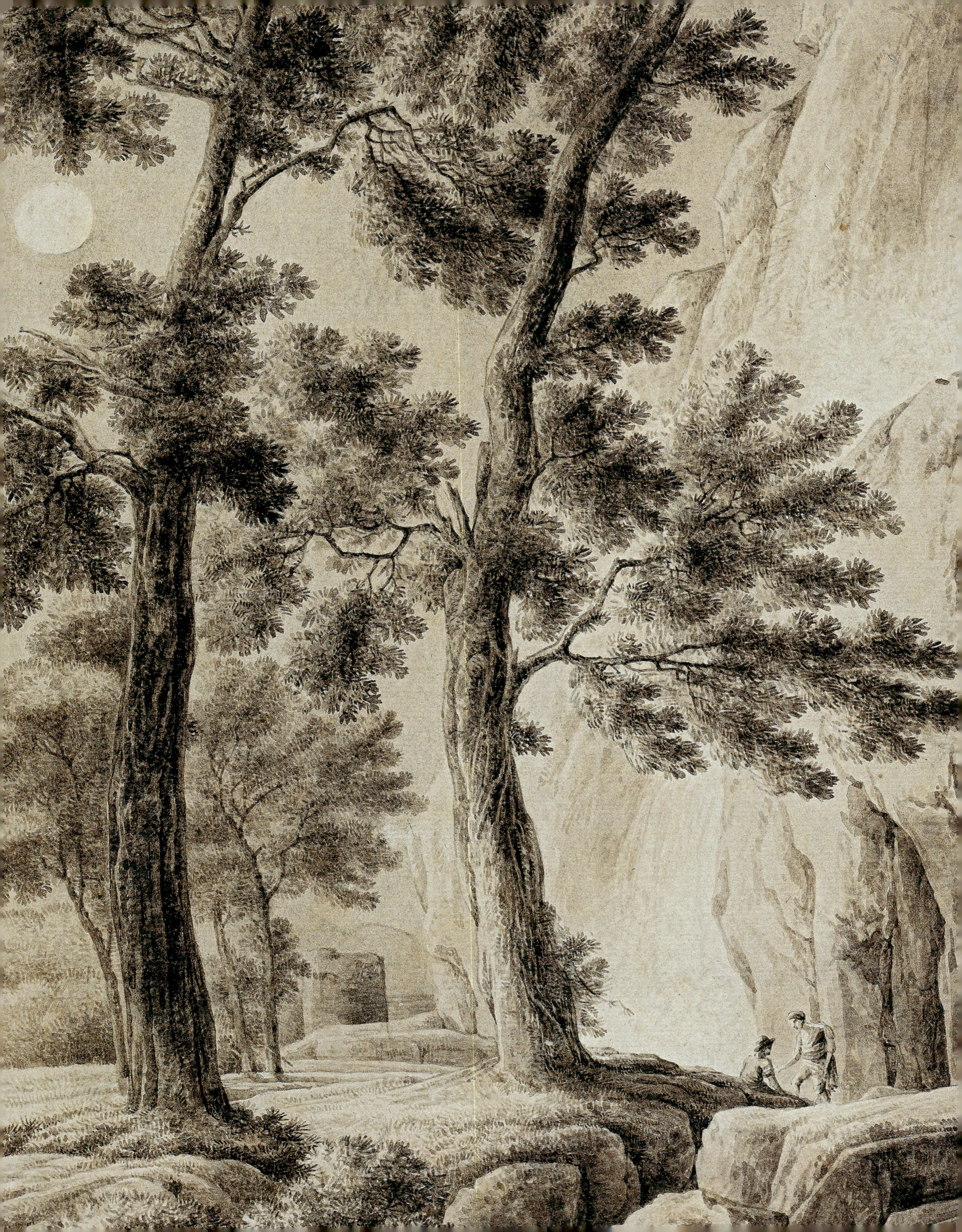

THE FIRST EXHIBITION OF ITS KIND at an American museum in more than a decade, *Seeking Revelation: German Romantic Prints and Drawings* showcases an intriguing and multifaceted movement with special resonance for audiences today. It features the Milwaukee Art Museum's renowned collection of German Romantic works on paper—works by artists who engaged with nineteenth-century Germany's rapidly shifting ideological and social environment. Now, as we live through the unpredictability of the postmodern era, their works offer an example of individuals reconsidering and rebuilding their identities and relationships with each other and the larger world.

Beyond bringing broader awareness to an art movement that is lesser known in the United States, this exhibition recognizes an important period in Milwaukee's past. Many who immigrated to Wisconsin left Germany during the first half of the nineteenth century, and the city still has the highest percentage of German ancestry of any American metropolitan area. This presentation of German Romantic art from the Museum's collection offers our community a moment to reflect on this history and the many civic contributions that have made Milwaukee what it is today.

It is fitting that the Museum's collection offers stellar examples of German art across time. German Expressionism is especially well represented in our holdings: Foundational gifts donated by Mrs. Harry Lynde Bradley and Maurice and Esther Leah Ritz contributed major drawings and paintings by Lyonel Feininger, Ernst Ludwig Kirchner, Wassily Kandinsky, and Gabriele Münter, among others. Marcia and Granvil Specks gave more than five hundred prints by significant figures of German Expressionism in 2000, making the Museum's collection one of the best in the country for this material. Postwar works by artists such as Joseph Beuys, Katharina Grosse, Anselm Kiefer, Sigmar Polke, and Gerhard Richter bring the conversation into the present day through materially innovative processes that engage with memory, history, and society.

Seeking Revelation draws special attention to the Museum's extensive collection of nineteenth-century German art. This strength has its origins in the generosity of collector René von Schleinitz. Born in Germany in 1890, von Schleinitz later immigrated to Milwaukee, where he worked for the manufacturing company Harnischfeger and then in real estate. Between 1962 and 1972, he gave more than three hundred paintings and decorative art objects, including academic genre scenes by artists such as Carl Spitzweg and Ferdinand Georg Waldmüller, as well as Meissen porcelain and Mettlach steins. A memorial fund in his name, established in 1976 after von Schleinitz's death and dedicated to acquisitions of nineteenth-century German art, has allowed for the purchase of most of the works in this exhibition. That fund encouraged prints and drawings

curators at the Museum—first Joseph Ruzicka and later Kristin Makholm—
to make strategic purchases of German Romantic works on paper, which
few museums outside of Germany had at the time. An exhibition curated
by Makholm in 2002, *Romanticism to Impressionism: Nineteenth-Century
German Prints and Drawings from the René von Schleinitz Memorial Fund*,
featured the previous decade's acquisitions.

Now Nikki Otten, associate curator of prints and drawings, has
continued this legacy, bringing her keen passion to deepening and enriching these holdings since her arrival at the Museum in 2018. This publication is the culmination of her years of research and thoughtful analysis of
this compelling movement and the lessons these artists hold for us today.
The catalogue contributes new thinking to the small but growing body of
scholarship about the movement in English while also enriching our
knowledge of the Museum's collection as a whole.

Such projects require generous financial support and the deep
knowledge of staff. I offer my gratitude to Katharine and Sandy Mallin and
to the Milwaukee Art Museum's Print Forum, the supporting sponsors of
the catalogue and exhibition. The IFPDA Foundation and Drs. Peter
Drescher and Karin Madsen Drescher provided generous additional
support. The Museum also extends its sincere thanks to the Visionaries for
their support of the 2026 exhibition program: Mark and Debbie Attanasio,
Donna and Donald Baumgartner, Murph Burke, Bill and Sandy Haack, the
Helmerich Trust, Kenneth and Alice Kayser, Joan Lubar and John Crouch,
and Jeff and Gail Yabuki. The ongoing stewardship and engaging presentation of the collection are crucial to this exhibition and catalogue and at the
core of what we do at the Milwaukee Art Museum. I am grateful to the
staff across the Museum for their care and expertise.

Seeking Revelation serves as a potent reminder that all art was once
contemporary. Artists have a unique capacity to challenge, articulate,
and make sense of issues impacting the world; to search for, imagine, and
express new realities. The artists of the German Romantic period grappled
with fundamental questions of faith and identity. Brought together here,
their innovative works show the value of continuing to seek answers.

Elizabeth Siegel
CHIEF OF CURATORIAL AFFAIRS

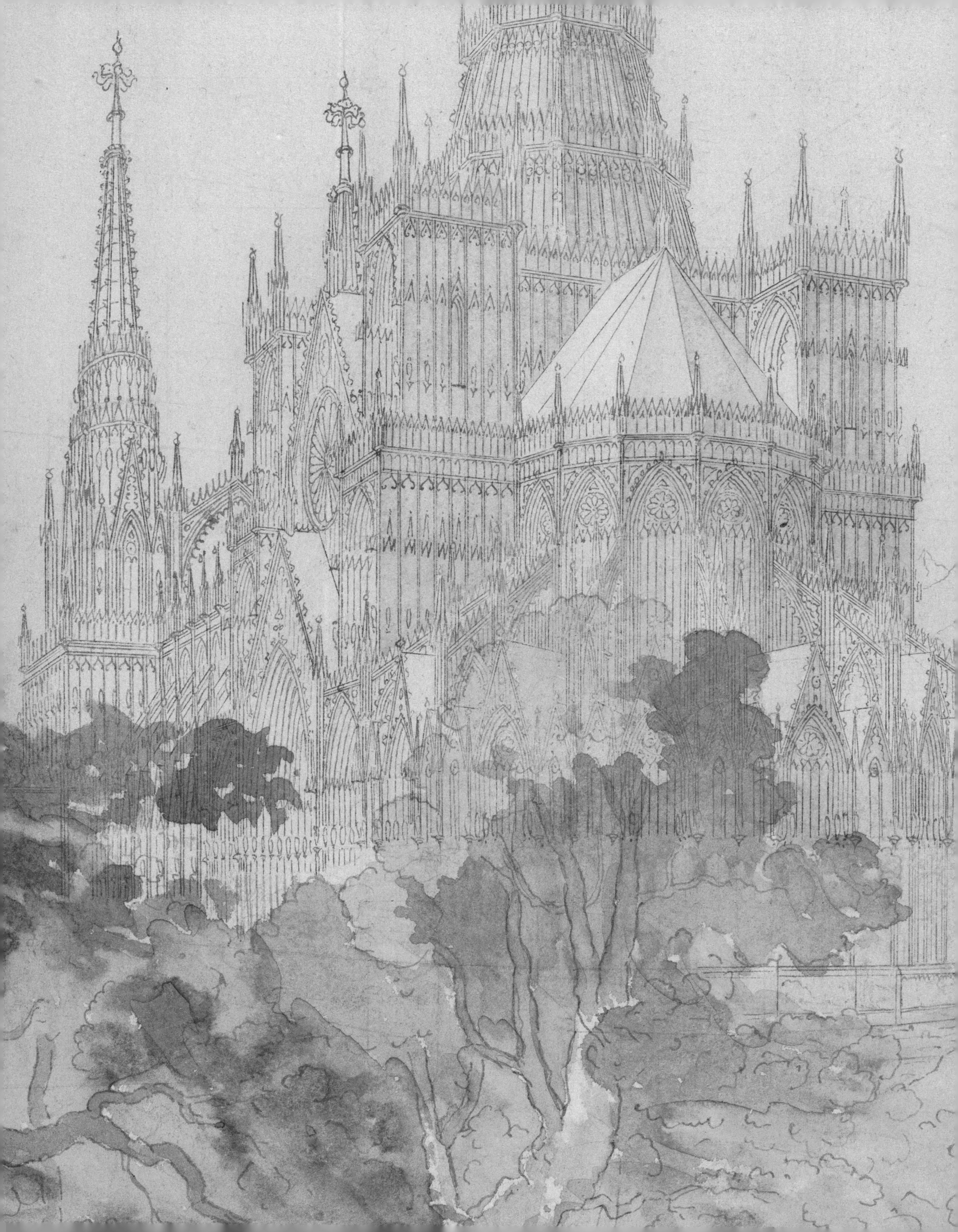

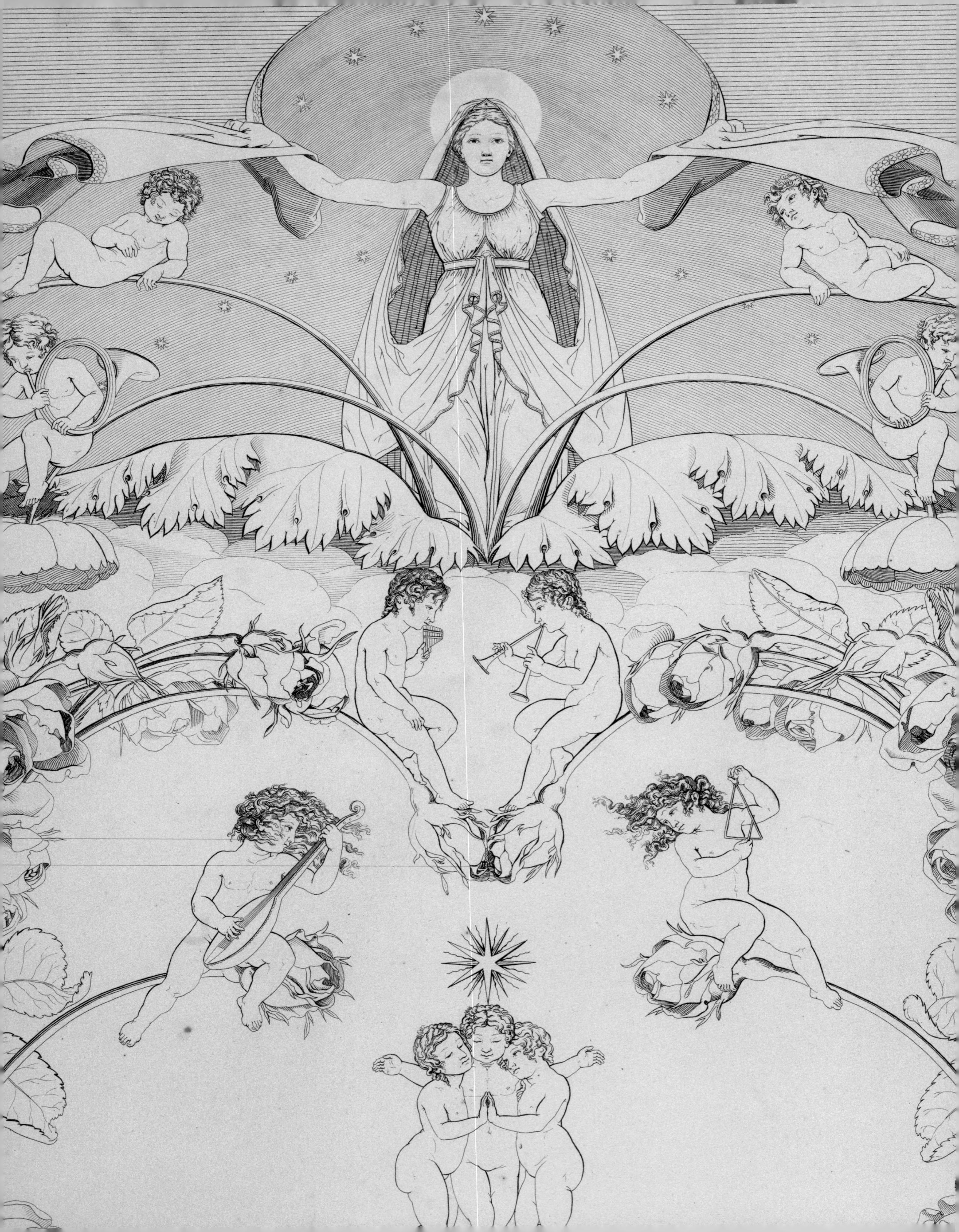

DURING THE GERMAN ROMANTIC MOVEMENT, active from about 1770 to 1850, many artists sought a deeper understanding of universal questions. The French Revolution, Napoleon Bonaparte's invasion of Germany, and challenges to the Enlightenment's emphasis on reason brought decades of upheaval that led artists to reconsider their national identity and sense of self, as well as their relationship to nature and the divine. Through works selected from the Milwaukee Art Museum's collection, *Seeking Revelation: German Romantic Prints and Drawings* examines the approaches some artists used to comprehend and shape their world. Ultimately, even when it did not uncover answers, the act of seeking is revealed as its own reward.

"THE WORLD MUST BE ROMANTICIZED":
DEFINING GERMAN ROMANTICISM

Romanticism resists characterization because it encompasses a wide range of methods, subjects, and styles.[1] The movement spanned literature, music, philosophy, and visual art and assumed different forms in countries across Europe. Some scholars have described Romanticism as a worldview that involved feeling as though something had been lost from contemporary life and must be recovered.[2] Many artists tried to address this loss by exploring ways to repair it in their work. The prominent German writer Novalis (Georg Philipp Friedrich Freiherr von Hardenberg) offered one possibility in his often-cited declaration: "The world must be romanticized. Thus, one finds the original sense again." He explained that to romanticize meant to "give the commonplace a higher meaning, the customary a mysterious appearance, the known the dignity of the unknown, the finite the appearance of the infinite."[3] In this passage, he proposes rediscovering a lost "original sense" by transforming everyday experiences, elevating them and making them new again. For visual artists, romanticizing the world often involved choosing to represent familiar subject matter using styles that imbued it with increased importance or spiritual significance.

Achieving balance between contrasting values was also key to the Romantics, who believed that harmony created beauty.[4] They focused on two opposing pairs in particular: individualism versus community, and reason versus feeling.[5] Aligning these values required constant reevaluation, and this type of ongoing process was fundamental to Romanticism. In a text fragment about poetry, German writer and philosopher Friedrich Schlegel contended, "The romantic kind of poetry is still in the state of becoming; that, in fact, is its real essence: that it should forever be becoming and never be perfected."[6] The act of seeking was Romantic for this very reason: It provided the seeker access to a state of perpetual becoming, a longing that could never be fully satisfied. This endeavor is one aspect that the movement's varied stylistic tendencies have in common.

Introduction and Acknowledgments

Like Romanticism, "German" is not easily defined because Germany did not become a unified country until 1871. At the end of the eighteenth century, German-speaking territories were part of the Holy Roman Empire, which was made up of duchies and other political entities that spanned much of central Europe (fig. 1). After winning the Battle of Austerlitz against an alliance of the Austrian and Russian Empires in 1805, Napoleon Bonaparte of France organized the German lands into the Confederation of the Rhine. This led to the dissolution of the Holy Roman Empire in 1806. A coalition of European powers defeated France in 1814 and convened the Congress of Vienna to negotiate new political borders. The German states agreed to unite as part of this process, and the resulting German Confederation was formally recognized in the Congress's Final Act in 1815 (fig. 2). Although some had hoped Germany would become a democracy, the new coalition preserved the power of individual aristocrats and monarchs. During this tumultuous period, debates about national character assumed increased urgency. For the majority of artists discussed in this catalogue, personal and national identities were tightly interwoven, and their attempts to define "Germanness" emerge as an important sub-narrative. For the purposes of this project, "German" refers to shared linguistic and cultural affiliation rather than specific geography; however, the selected works were made by artists who were born or spent most of their lives within the territory of the German Confederation.

LANDSCAPE, RELIGION, AND TRAVEL

This catalogue is organized around three main themes. Two reflect primary subjects that German Romantic artists pursued in their work: landscapes and religious scenes. The third section, dedicated to journeys, reinforces the fluidity among the themes by showing that travel offered a means of gaining insight into both nature and spirit.

FINDING SCIENCE, SELF, AND SPIRIT IN NATURE

At the turn of the nineteenth century, German Romantic landscape artists shifted from creating idealized classical scenes to representing local sites. Informed by scientific ideas about direct observation, they often sketched outdoors. This method allowed artists to experience embodiment in the landscape and explore how they related to the natural world. Georg von Dillis (plate 1) and Carl Wilhelm Kolbe (fig. 3), for example, visited newly opened public parks in Munich and Wörlitz and etched the gardens there, which included areas cultivated to appear wild. Depicting such regional locations helped artists develop a sense of national unity. As the borders of the German lands shifted and territories changed possession, many people believed the landscape symbolized shared German identity. Some artists,

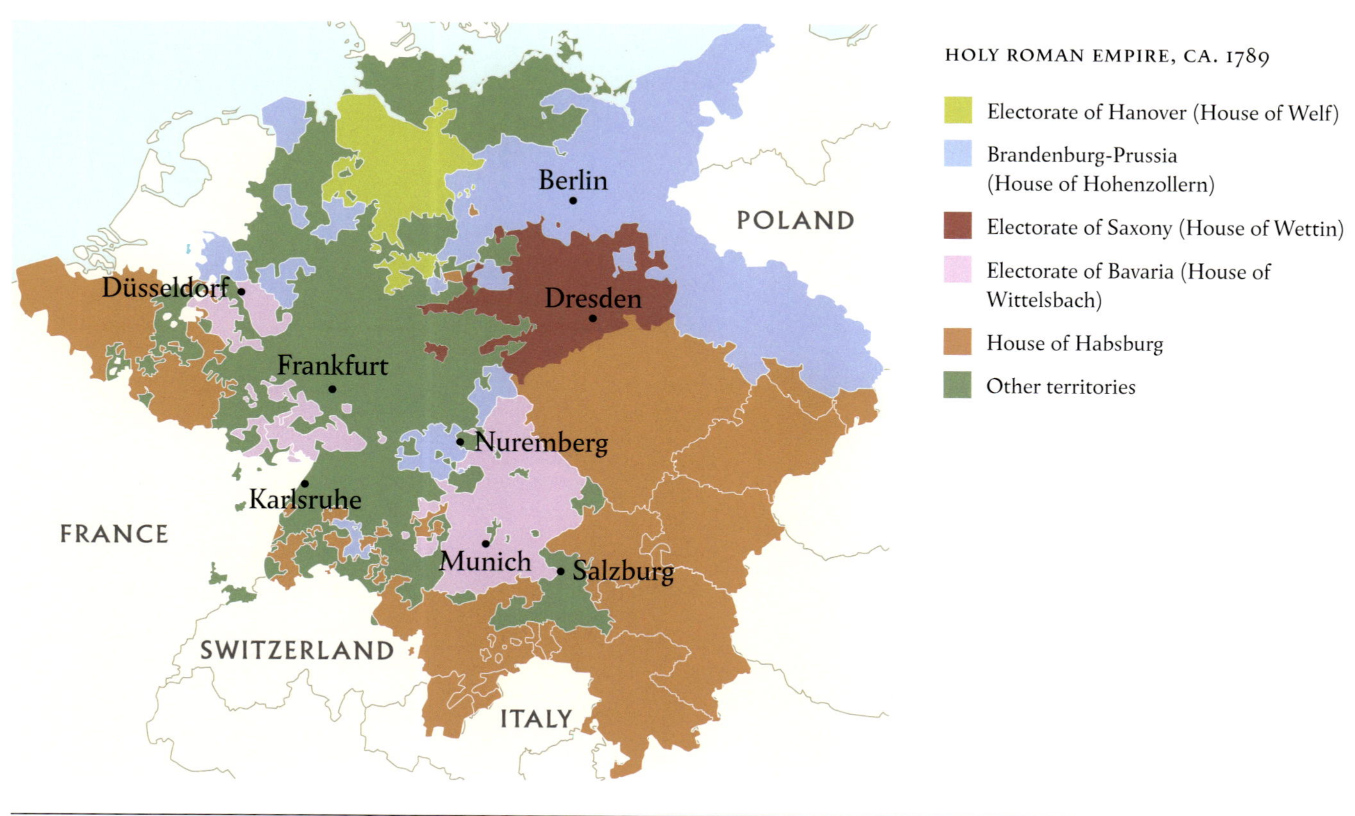

HOLY ROMAN EMPIRE, CA. 1789
Electorate of Hanover (House of Welf)
Brandenburg-Prussia (House of Hohenzollern)
Electorate of Saxony (House of Wettin)
Electorate of Bavaria (House of Wittelsbach)
House of Habsburg
Other territories
POLAND
Berlin
Dresden
Düsseldorf
Frankfurt
Nuremberg
Karlsruhe
FRANCE
Munich
Salzburg
SWITZERLAND
ITALY

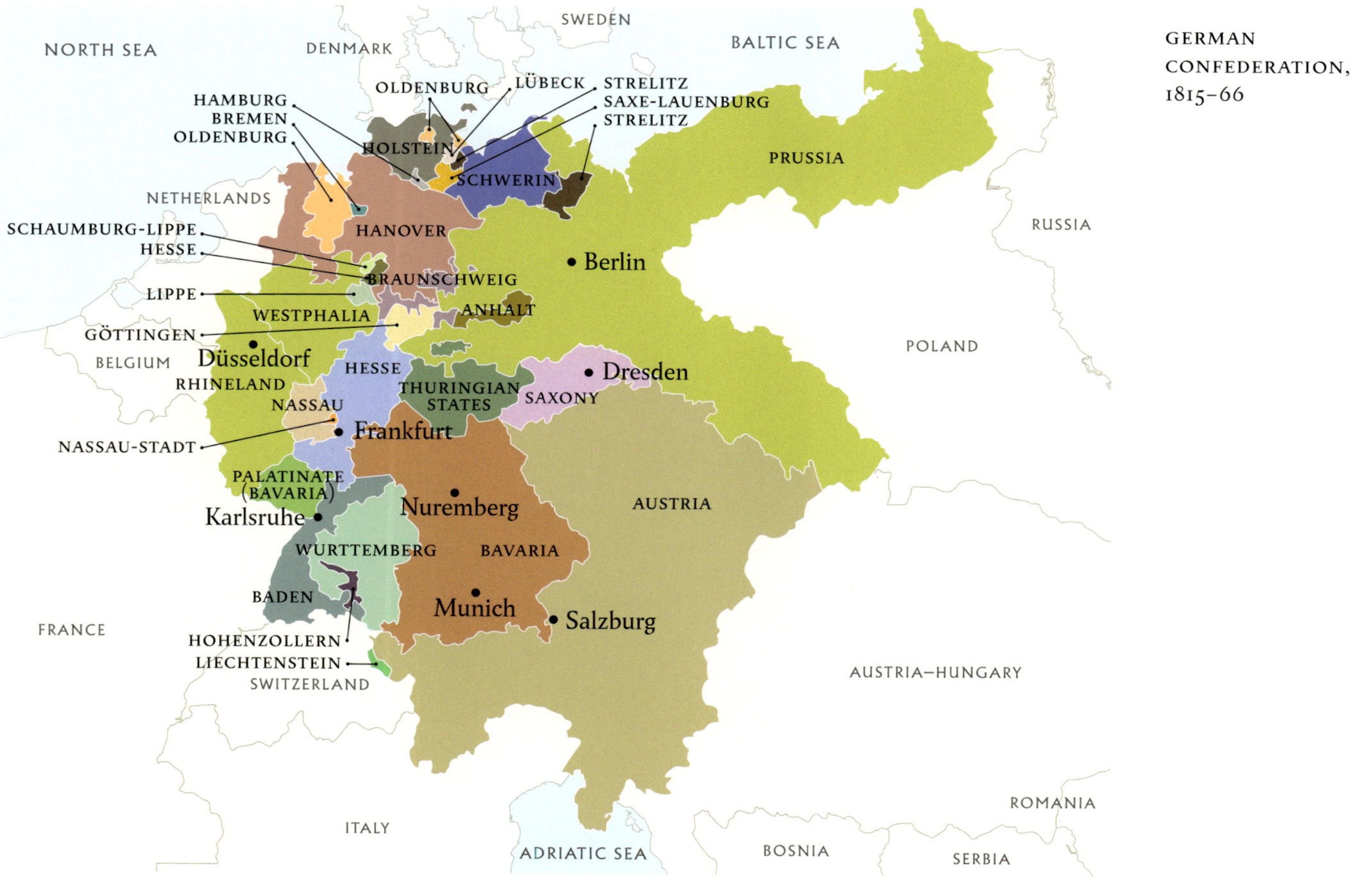

GERMAN CONFEDERATION, 1815–66
NORTH SEA
SWEDEN
DENMARK
BALTIC SEA
HAMBURG
BREMEN
OLDENBURG
OLDENBURG
LÜBECK
STRELITZ
SAXE-LAUENBURG
STRELITZ
HOLSTEIN
SCHWERIN
PRUSSIA
NETHERLANDS
RUSSIA
SCHAUMBURG-LIPPE
HESSE
HANOVER
LIPPE
BRAUNSCHWEIG
ANHALT
Berlin
GÖTTINGEN
WESTPHALIA
BELGIUM
Düsseldorf
HESSE
POLAND
RHINELAND
NASSAU
THURINGIAN STATES
SAXONY
Dresden
NASSAU-STADT
Frankfurt
PALATINATE (BAVARIA)
Karlsruhe
Nuremberg
AUSTRIA
WURTTEMBERG
BAVARIA
BADEN
Munich
Salzburg
HOHENZOLLERN
LIECHTENSTEIN
SWITZERLAND
FRANCE
AUSTRIA–HUNGARY
ITALY
ROMANIA
ADRIATIC SEA
BOSNIA
SERBIA

FIG. 3

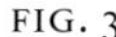

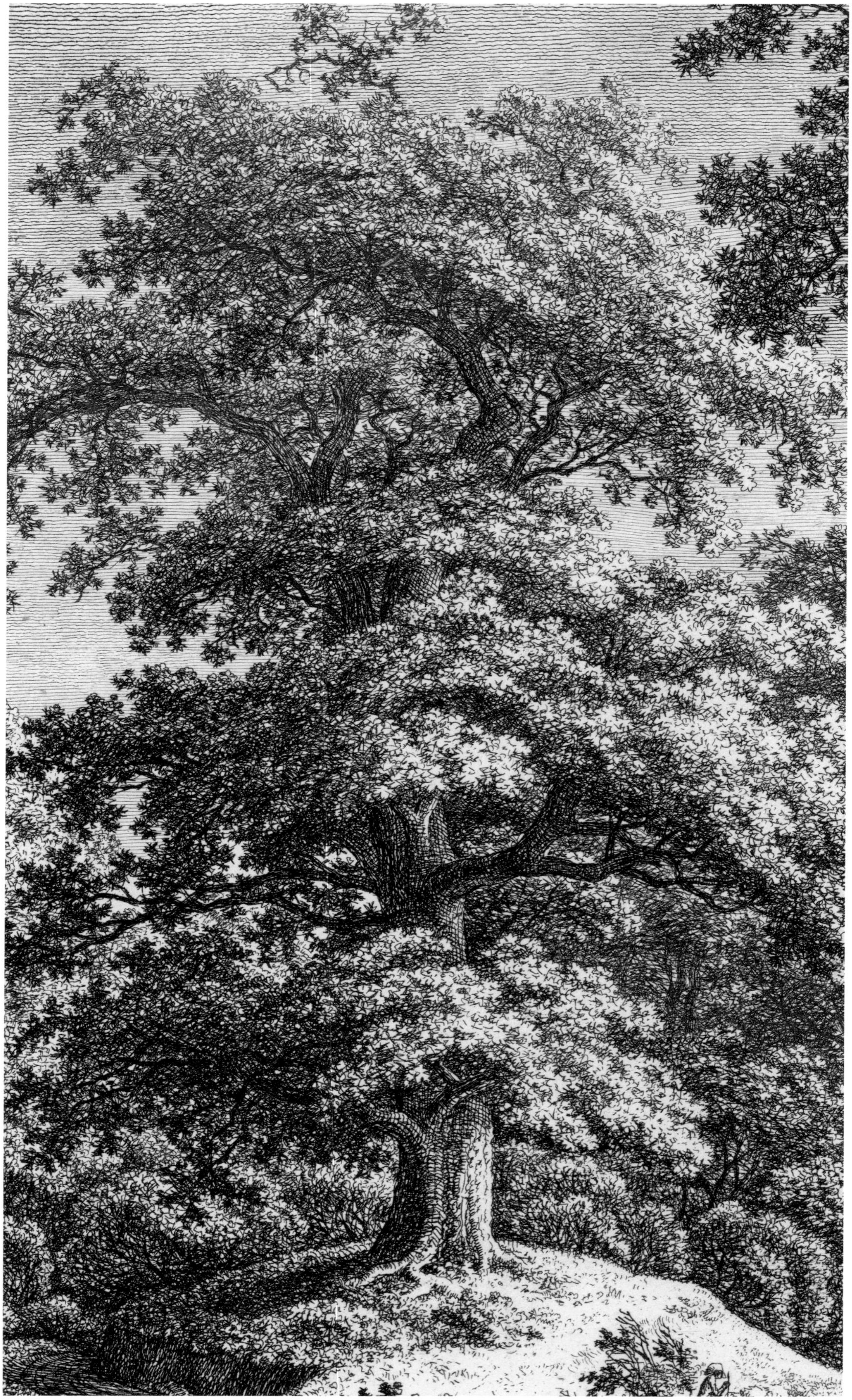

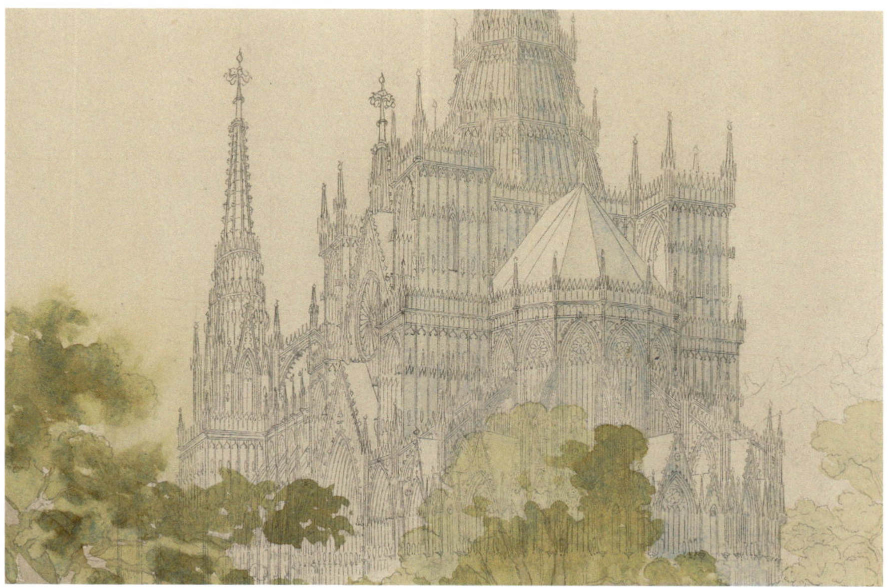

such as Caspar David Friedrich (plate 8) and Karl Friedrich Schinkel (fig. 4), searched for the divine in their surroundings. They represented God's presence by capturing nature's sublime aspects or depicting Gothic cathedrals rising above stands of trees. In her essay, Stephanie O'Rourke examines how emerging forest management policies both complicated and contributed to Romantic artists' understanding of the landscape as a spiritual, specifically German site.

CREATING COMMUNION: THE NAZARENES AND RELIGION

The catalogue's second theme explores how German Romantics sought to transform modern German art by reinvigorating the past and invoking shared religious beliefs. The circle of artists known as the Brotherhood of St. Luke (Lukasbund) developed a set of artistic and religious principles that had a strong influence on the German art world. Six students disillusioned with the education they were receiving at the Vienna Academy formed the brotherhood in 1809, and four members moved to Rome in 1810. Led by Johann Friedrich Overbeck and Franz Pforr, they considered making art to be a form of worship, and they often depicted stories from the Bible. They adopted the lifestyle of monks, living together in a monastery so they could dedicate themselves to developing their work and deepening their devotion. They also worked on group commissions, such as frescoes depicting the Old Testament story of Joseph for Prussian Consul General Jakob Ludwig Salomon Bartholdy's residence in Rome (see plates 34 and 35). Finding the artistic movements of their time to be theatrical and decadent, members of the brotherhood looked to the

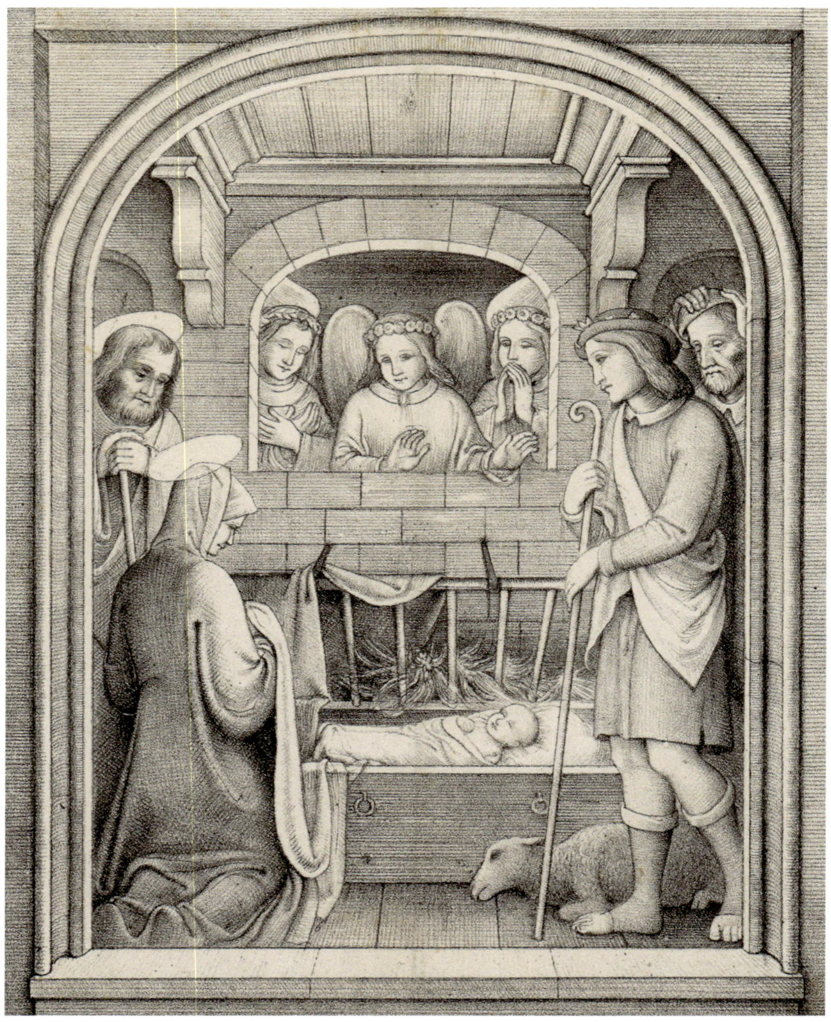

Middle Ages and the Renaissance for approaches they believed were more truthful. They especially admired the emotional sincerity and style of artists such as Albrecht Dürer and Raphael. Ferdinand Olivier's *House Altar* strongly reflects Dürer's influence in its composition and precise contours (figs. 5 and 6). This section further reflects the Lukasbund's impact on a wider group of German artists known as the Nazarenes. Those affiliated with this group also made art with Christian themes and often worked across different media. Heinrich Karl Anton Mücke, for example, created several copies—in etching, oil, and watercolor—of *Angels Carrying the Body of St. Catherine to Mount Sinai*, the painting he made for the 1836 Berlin Art Academy exhibition. Through this repetition (figs. 7 and 8), he produced an iconic image. Cordula Grewe's contribution to the catalogue argues that making multiple versions of their compositions and working

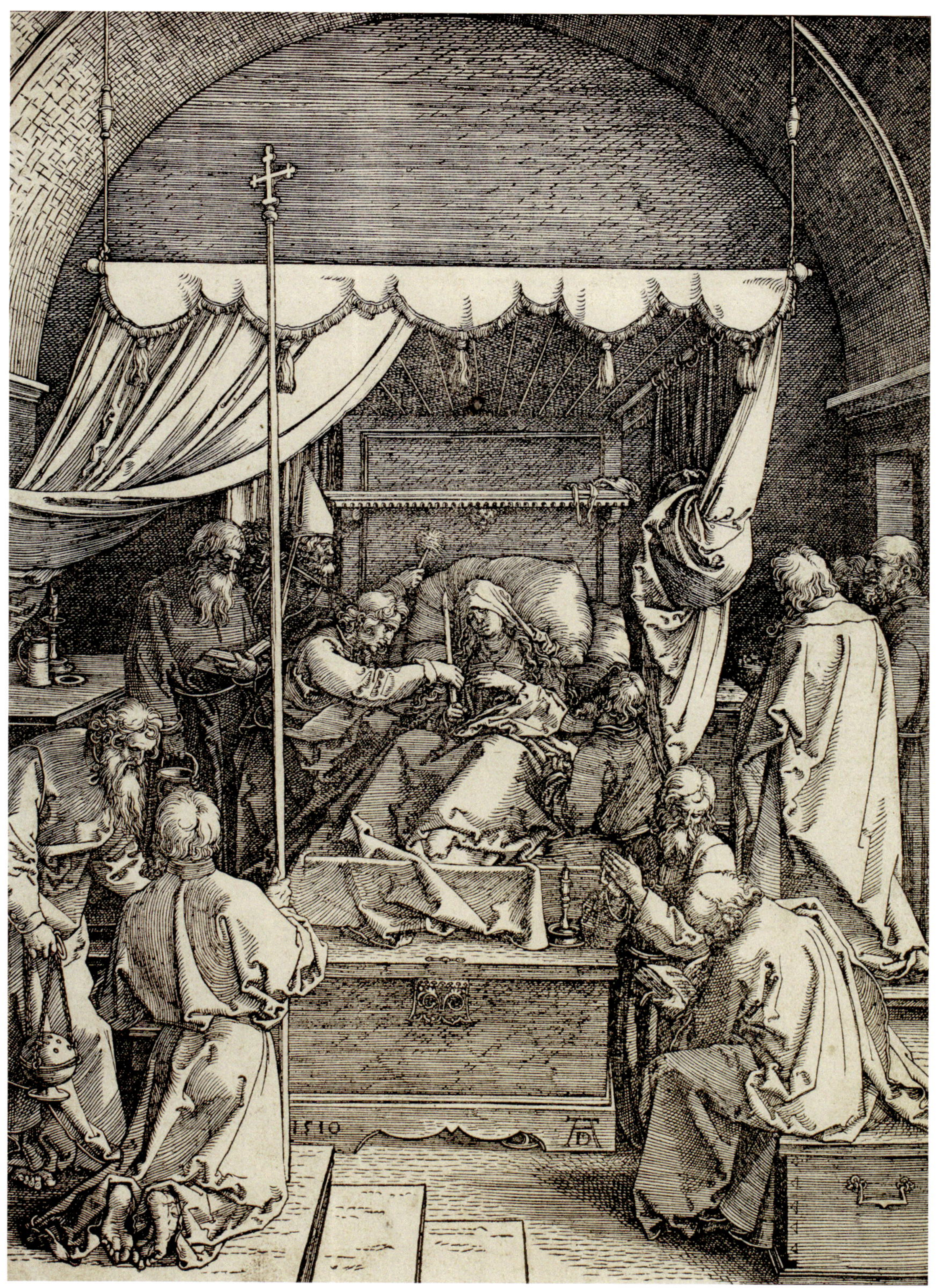

FIG. 6

FIG. 7   Heinrich Karl Anton Mücke, *The Body of Saint Catherine of Alexandria Carried to Heaven by Angels (Der Leichnam der heiligen Katharina von Alexandrien, von Engeln zum Himmel getragen)*, 1836. Oil on canvas. 38³⁄₁₆ × 57³⁄₈ in. (97 × 147.5 cm). Staatliche Museen zu Berlin, Nationalgalerie

FIG. 8   Heinrich Karl Anton Mücke, *The Body of Saint Catherine of Alexandria Carried to Heaven by Angels*, ca. 1836 (cat. p. 160)

at different scales, from monumental fresco paintings to portable prints, played a crucial role in helping the Nazarenes advance their vision of a new German art.

JOURNEYS

Finally, the third theme details the importance of travel within German Romantic art. Although the styles and subjects adopted by landscape artists and the Nazarenes lack the cohesion of a unified movement, artists in both groups recognized that visiting new places allowed them to learn about themselves, their peers, and the broader world. The works in this section document specific locations or depict travelers, like those in Johann Adam Klein's *The Artists on Their Journey* or Johann Wilhelm Schirmer's wanderers (plate 66 and fig. 9). Most could fit within one or both of the other two themes equally well, demonstrating that shared beliefs and priorities link different tendencies within German Romanticism. *Seven Places in Salzburg and Berchtesgaden*, Ferdinand Olivier's series depicting the Alpine landscape, for example, is also a key work of the Nazarene movement (plates 56–64). My own essay addresses how travel within the German and Italian lands opened a liminal space where artists could experience a state of continuous becoming; these trips often strengthened their identities as Germans.

Through these three themes, *Seeking Revelation* examines artists' responses to challenges and important questions posed by modern life. They attempted to ameliorate the ruptures they experienced by creating art that explored belief, identity, and a sense of place as these concepts evolved amid the turmoil seizing early nineteenth-century Germany.

THE *SEEKING REVELATION* CATALOGUE AND EXHIBITION came to fruition only through the collaborative efforts of many people. At the Milwaukee Art Museum, former director Marcelle Polednik and Liz Siegel, chief of curatorial affairs, championed the project from its inception. Kim Sajet, Donna and Donald Baumgartner Director, offered enthusiastic support during its later stages. They all, along with Margaret Andera in her capacity as interim chief curator, also advocated for new acquisitions of German Romantic works on paper. I extend my sincerest thanks to Rebekah Morin, former collections manager for works on paper, for housing and cataloguing these new acquisitions and facilitating the selection, photography, and conservation of works in the exhibition. Liz Flaig, manager of exhibitions and installations, offered essential guidance

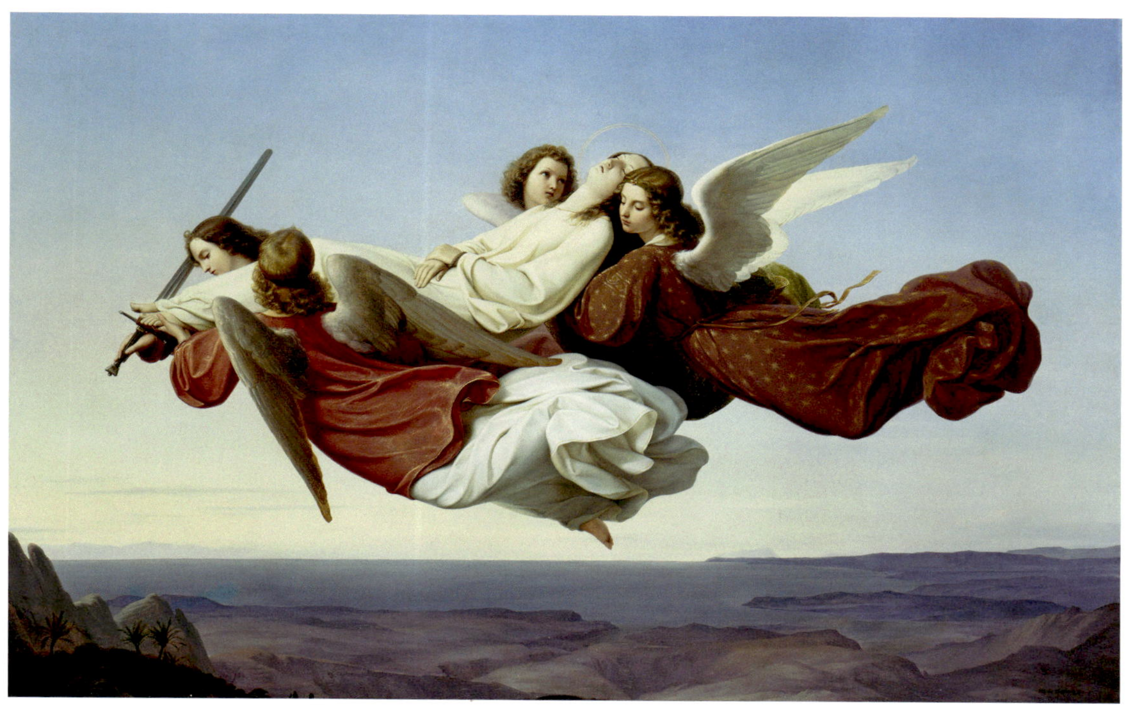

FIG. 7

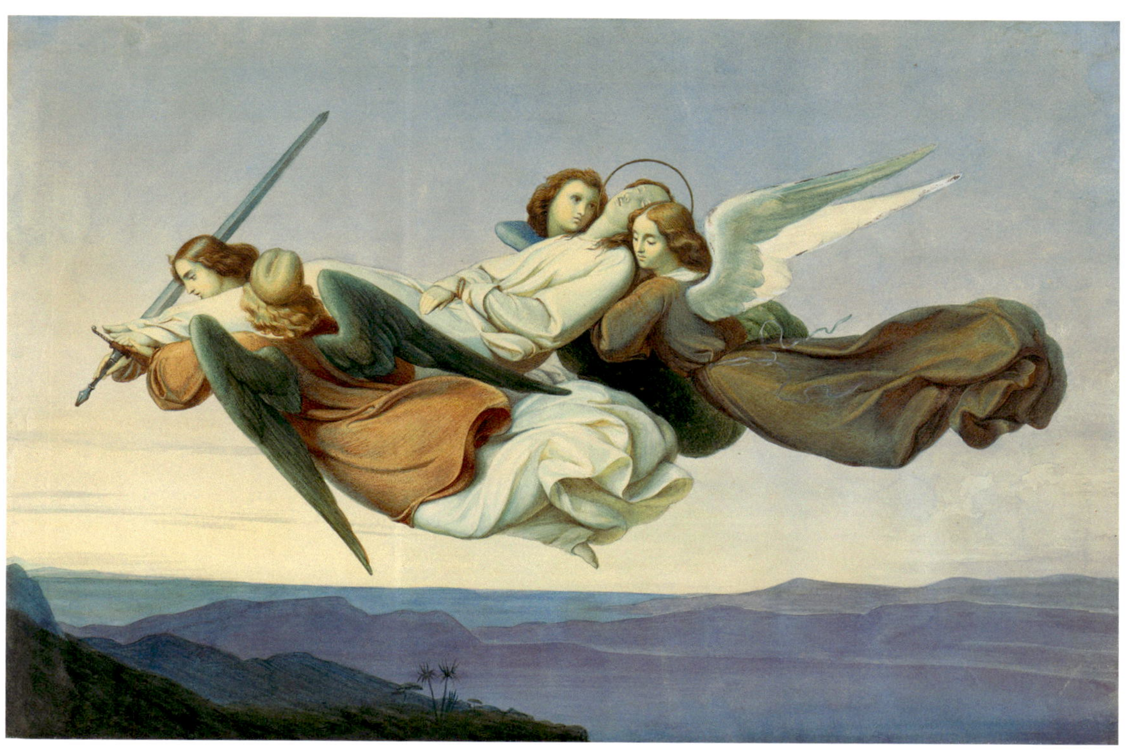

FIG. 8

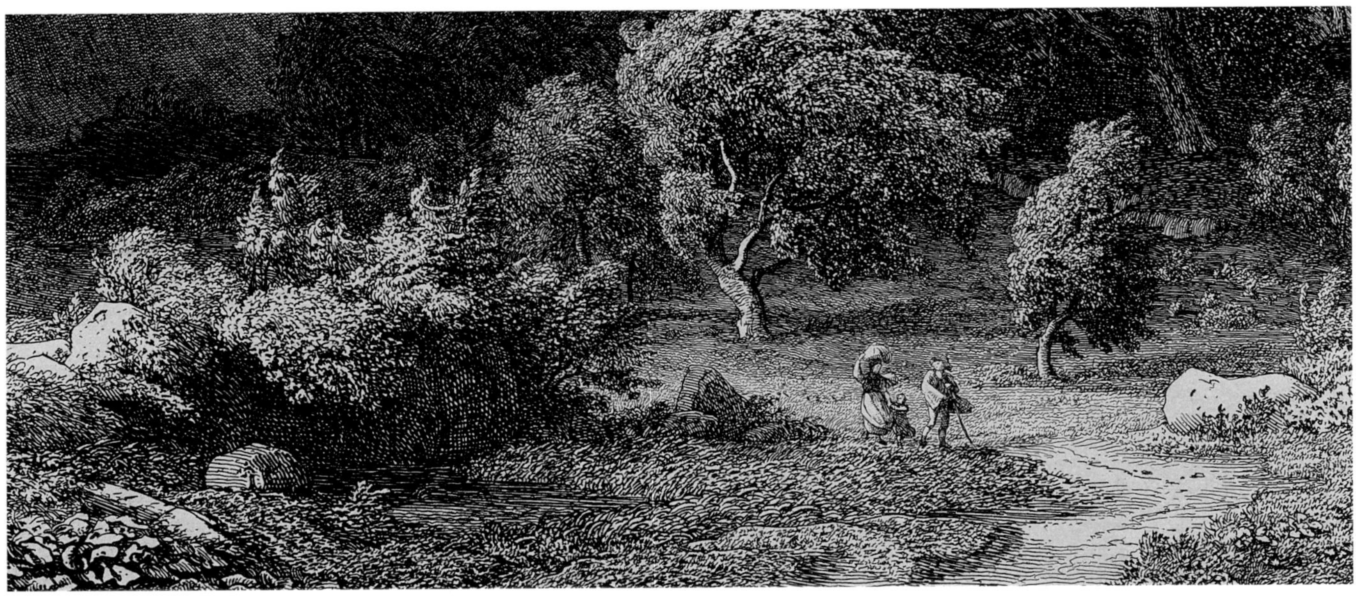

FIG. 9   Johann Wilhelm Schirmer, *Ruined Castle near Meiringen* (detail), ca. 1843 (cat. p. 163)

for the project, managing budgets, schedules, and shifting timelines. Chris Niver and Nicholas Krings made the works look their best with exceptional matting and framing. Emma Fulce, director of registration, arranged logistics and ensured the safety of works from the Museum's collection and loans. Arthur Mohagen and the team of preparators provided their expertise and eye for detail in installing the exhibition. David Russick created the stunning exhibition design. Kraig Przybylski contributed to the effect with impactful lighting. Ted Brusubardis developed a soundscape that immersed visitors in the music of the time. Amy Kirschke, Kantara Souffrant, Candace Tyrrell, and Xoe Fiss activated the exhibition by planning an engaging slate of programs for all ages. Cortney Heimerl and Haven Falk developed welcoming on-site graphics and messaging. André Allaire, Pam Coleman, Kim Theno, Sarah Kolar, Anne Temple, Alma Kneisel, and Madeline Schultz made the project possible by securing support for the exhibition, catalogue, and programs.

I am deeply grateful to Cordula Grewe and Stephanie O'Rourke for the scholarship they contributed to the catalogue. Their thorough research and evocative writing, both here and elsewhere, expanded my understanding of Romanticism, and I have appreciated their enthusiasm throughout this project. I am indebted to Christina Dittrich for her meticulous and thoughtful editing. Cleber Bonato shot the beautiful photography for the majority of works from the Milwaukee Art Museum's collection, which appears on most pages of this catalogue. The Museum's Beret Balestrieri Kohn and Heather Winter, together with Steve Sullivan at Smart Rights, provided essential support in processing image files and managing rights and reproductions. Special thanks go to Armin Kunz at C. G. Boerner, who suggested a wealth of helpful resources during the research process. The project team at Marquand Books—Gina Broze, Kestrel Rundle, Melissa Duffes, Ryan Polich, and Leah Finger—directed the production of this publication and created its beautiful design. Their support made the endeavor seem nearly effortless. I am honored to show prints and drawings lent to the exhibition by the Art Institute of Chicago and by Stephen and Elizabeth Crawford. The works they provided addressed missing elements in the narrative and were crucial to the presentation.

All these individual endeavors contributed to an exhibition that celebrates the Museum's German Romantic collection and examines the creative potential of seeking. It is my hope that Museum visitors and the readers of this catalogue will look closely at the details in the selected works, relating them to our own uncertain time and taking pleasure in all that may be revealed.

Nikki Otten
ASSOCIATE CURATOR OF PRINTS AND DRAWINGS
MILWAUKEE ART MUSEUM

NOTES

1. Scholars of Romanticism have cited critic Arthur Lovejoy's desire to eliminate the term "Romantic," which stemmed from this lack of precision. In general, they do not find this solution satisfactory. See Frederick C. Beiser, *The Romantic Imperative: The Concept of Early German Romanticism* (Cambridge, MA: Harvard University Press, 2003), 6, and Michael Löwy and Robert Sayre, *Romanticism Against the Tide of Modernity*, trans. Catherine Porter (Durham, NC: Duke University Press, 2001), 1–2.

2. This definition is adapted from Michael Löwy and Robert Sayre, who propose that Romanticism can be understood as an expansive worldview with four key parts: "A rejection of contemporary society, an experience of loss, a melancholic nostalgia, and a quest for the lost object: such are the chief components of the Romantic vision." Löwy and Sayre, *Romanticism Against the Tide*, 17, 24.

3. Quoted in Dalia Nassar, *The Romantic Absolute: Being and Knowing in Early German Romantic Philosophy, 1795–1804* (Chicago: University of Chicago Press, 2013), 67.

4. Beiser, *The Romantic Imperative*, 41.

5. Löwy and Sayre, *Romanticism Against the Tide*, 24–25; Beiser, *The Romantic Imperative*, 39. Beiser argues that the Sturm und Drang (Storm and Stress) literary movement of the late eighteenth century had asserted the right to feeling in opposition to the Enlightenment's emphasis on reason, and he suggests that Romantics strove to bring reason and sensibility into balance. Beiser, 28–29.

6. Friedrich Schlegel, *Philosophical Fragments*, trans. Peter Firchow (Minneapolis: University of Minnesota Press, 1991), 32.

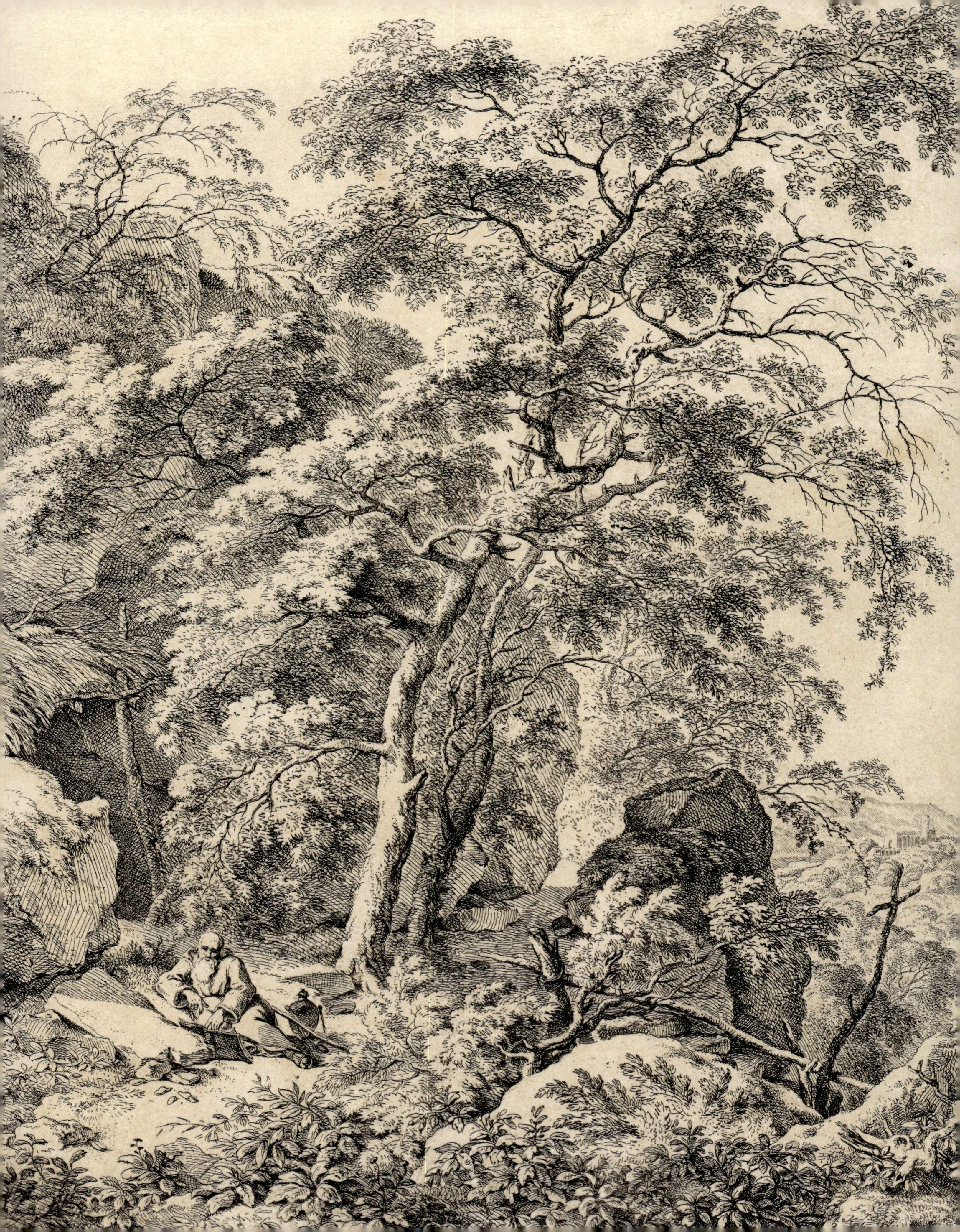

MANY FAIRY TALES published by the Brothers Grimm in 1812 take place in the Black Forest of southwest Germany. Snow White, Sleeping Beauty, and Hansel and Gretel are among the famous characters who encounter the mystery, magic, and danger of the woods. In this sense, the Brothers Grimm participated in the Romantic movement's interest in the natural world, especially in trees and woodlands. Dense and ancient forests—not unlike the fairy tale genre—were regarded as a realm apart from everyday life, places to escape from the ordinary. For artists working in the late eighteenth and early nineteenth centuries, the forest was therefore also an important subject for experimenting with the conventions of art.

At the same time that German Romantic artists were celebrating the mystical and spiritual characteristics of woodlands, modern economic imperatives were radically redefining that natural environment. Enlightenment Germany pioneered a new science of forest management in the late eighteenth century that sought to optimize timber production. In the 1820s and 1830s, German scientific forestry would be adopted in Britain, France, and beyond. When Romantic artists represented the forest, they were, in fact, portraying a contested and rapidly changing space. The spiritual properties that Romantic artists and writers attributed to ancient woodlands served as a bold rejection of both the rationalizing scientific principles of timber harvesting and the Enlightenment ideals out of which they grew.

Romantic representations of the forest had their roots in the art of Albrecht Altdorfer, whose *St. George and the Dragon* (fig. 1) from the early 1500s was the first significant German painting to lavish attention on the rich texture of trees. The image depicts the Christian legend in which Saint George slays a dragon. As his white horse rears up, George confidently leans forward, brandishing his lance. The dramatic encounter between George and the dragon typically took center stage in paintings, prints, and drawings. In Altdorfer's painting, by contrast, the figures occupy a relatively small portion of the composition. The dragon itself is difficult to see. Its feathery wings blend in with the grass. Instead, the vast majority of the painting is devoted to portraying a dense tapestry of varied foliage. Thick deciduous plumes are punctuated by compact sprays of conifer needles. An ancient oak on the left spreads its leaves above the crowded undergrowth. This is a painting, in other words, in which the forest as a physical setting seems more important than the Christian allegory. It reverses the artistic hierarchies of the period, in which biblical narrative was considered more significant than the setting.

In the late eighteenth century, the forest was increasingly central to the idea of a Germanic identity rooted in the natural scenery of Northern Europe. This coincided with a new artistic interest in moving away from

The Romantic Forest and the Industrial Forest

STEPHANIE O'ROURKE
Senior Lecturer in Art History
University of St. Andrews, Scotland

OPPOSITE   Ferdinand Kobell, *Philosopher's Path near Heidelberg*, 1780 (cat. p. 160)

FIG. 1   Albrecht Altdorfer (Regensburg ca. 1480–1538 Regensburg), *St. George and the Dragon (Drachenkampf des hl. Georg)*, ca. 1510. Oil on parchment laid down on linden-wood. 11⅛ × 8⅞ in. (28.2 × 22.5 cm). Bavarian State Painting Collections–Alte Pinakothek Munich

FIG. 2   Jacob Philipp Hackert (Prenzlau 1737–1807 San Piero di Careggio), *View of Villa Albani in Rome (Blick auf die Villa Albani in Rom)*, 1779. Oil on canvas. 25⅘ × 35 in. (65.5 × 89 cm). Anhaltische Gemäldegalerie Dessau

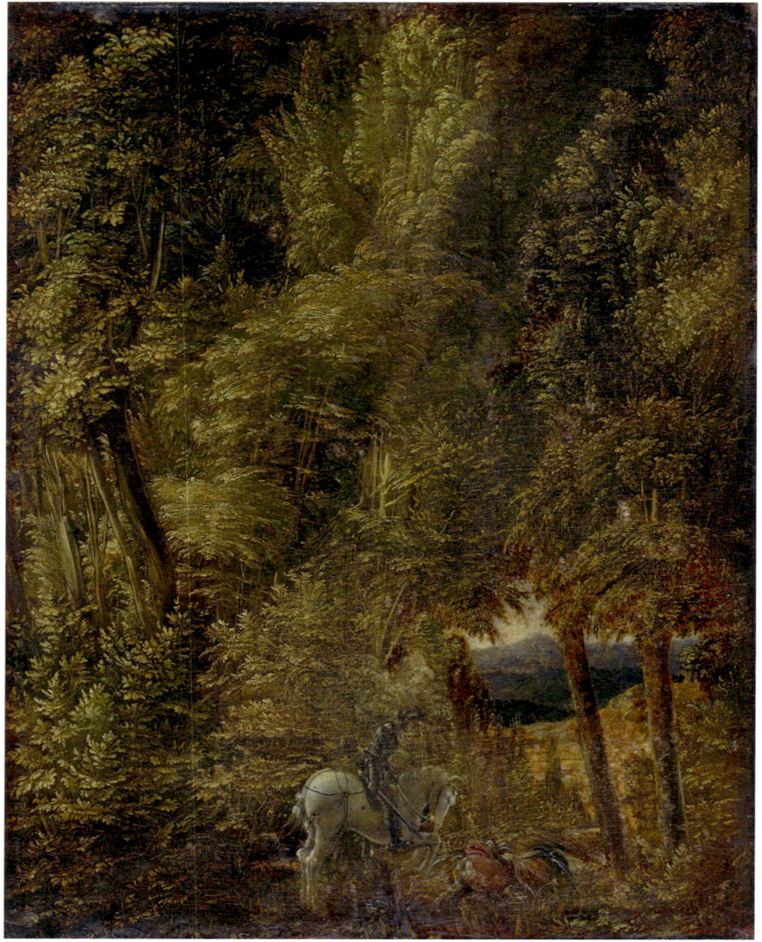

the Italian style of landscape, which had dominated for several centuries. As seen in Jacob Philipp Hackert's 1779 painting of Rome (fig. 2), Italian-style landscapes often placed human figures in the foreground, rolling meadows in the middle ground, and mountains in the distance. Lush greenery and bright illumination created a sense of abundance and harmony, balancing humans and natural elements. The viewer could often see far into the depths of such landscapes, taking in a broad and clear view. Italianate landscapes also typically included human narratives drawn from the Bible or Greco-Roman antiquity. These narratives gave moral weight and greater artistic significance to the landscape genre, traditionally considered less elite than portraiture and history painting.

German artists were eager to explore the idea that Northern Europe's landscape had fostered unique artistic traditions. During this period, for example, the principles of Gothic architecture—understood as an intrinsically northern style, in contrast to the southern European

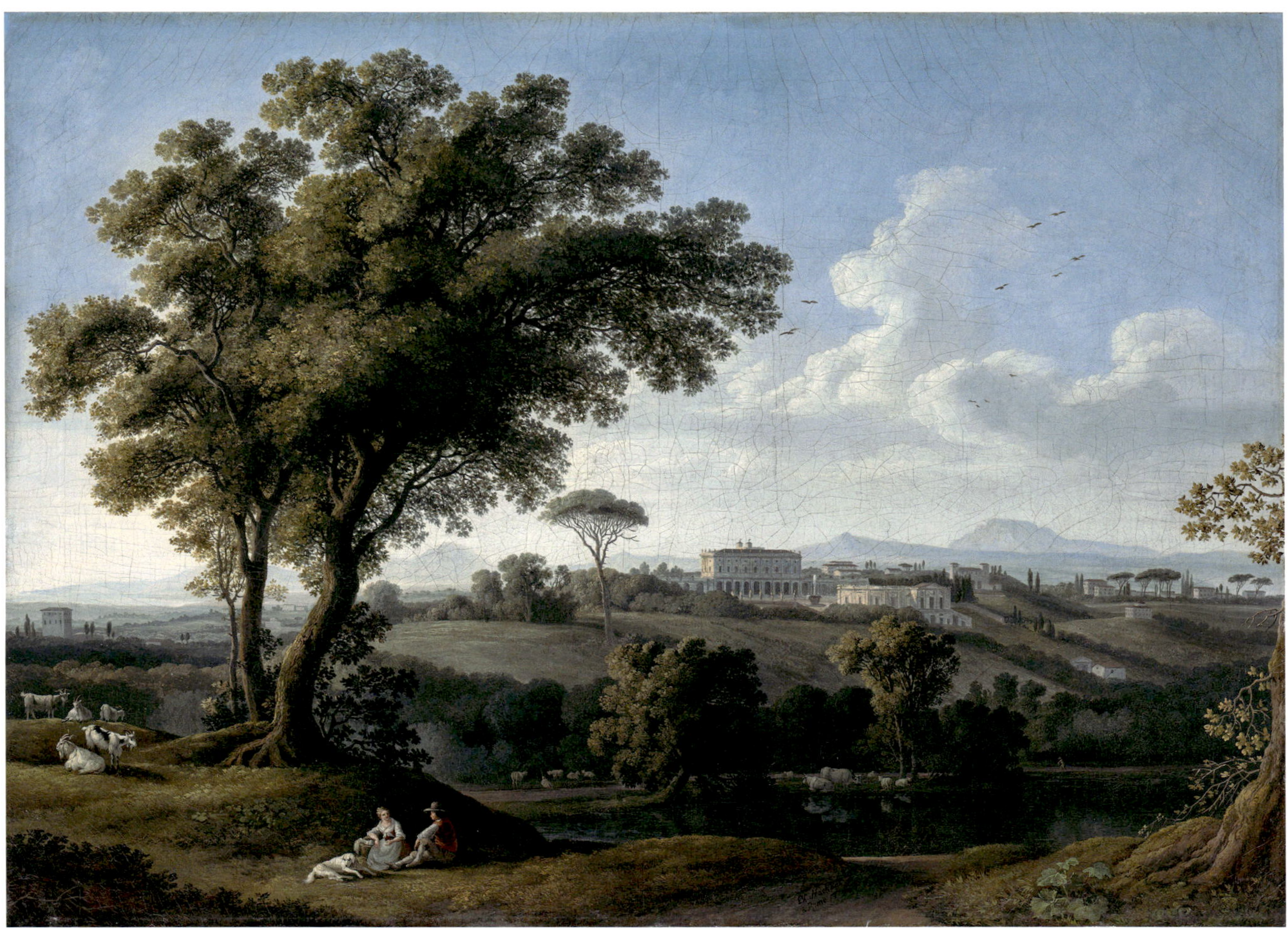

Renaissance—were associated with the woods of Northern Europe. The interlacing branches of high-growth trees allegedly inspired the tall, pointed arches that characterized Gothic churches. According to this theory, "Gothic was an authentic, Teutonic style, gradually tamed and civilized by pious German Christians," as historian Robin Fleming has shown.[1] Although there was no conclusive evidence that trees influenced Gothic architecture, the forest came to symbolize Northern Europe's artistic distinctiveness. Early modern Dutch landscapes provided another important northern alternative to the stylistic tradition of Southern Europe. Carl Wilhelm Kolbe the Elder and Georg von Dillis were among the many German artists who emulated the detail-rich naturalism, dramatic tonal contrasts, and compositional asymmetry made famous by the masters of the Northern Renaissance.

Romantic artists were also paying closer attention to the defining characteristics of different kinds of trees, including their trunk and branch

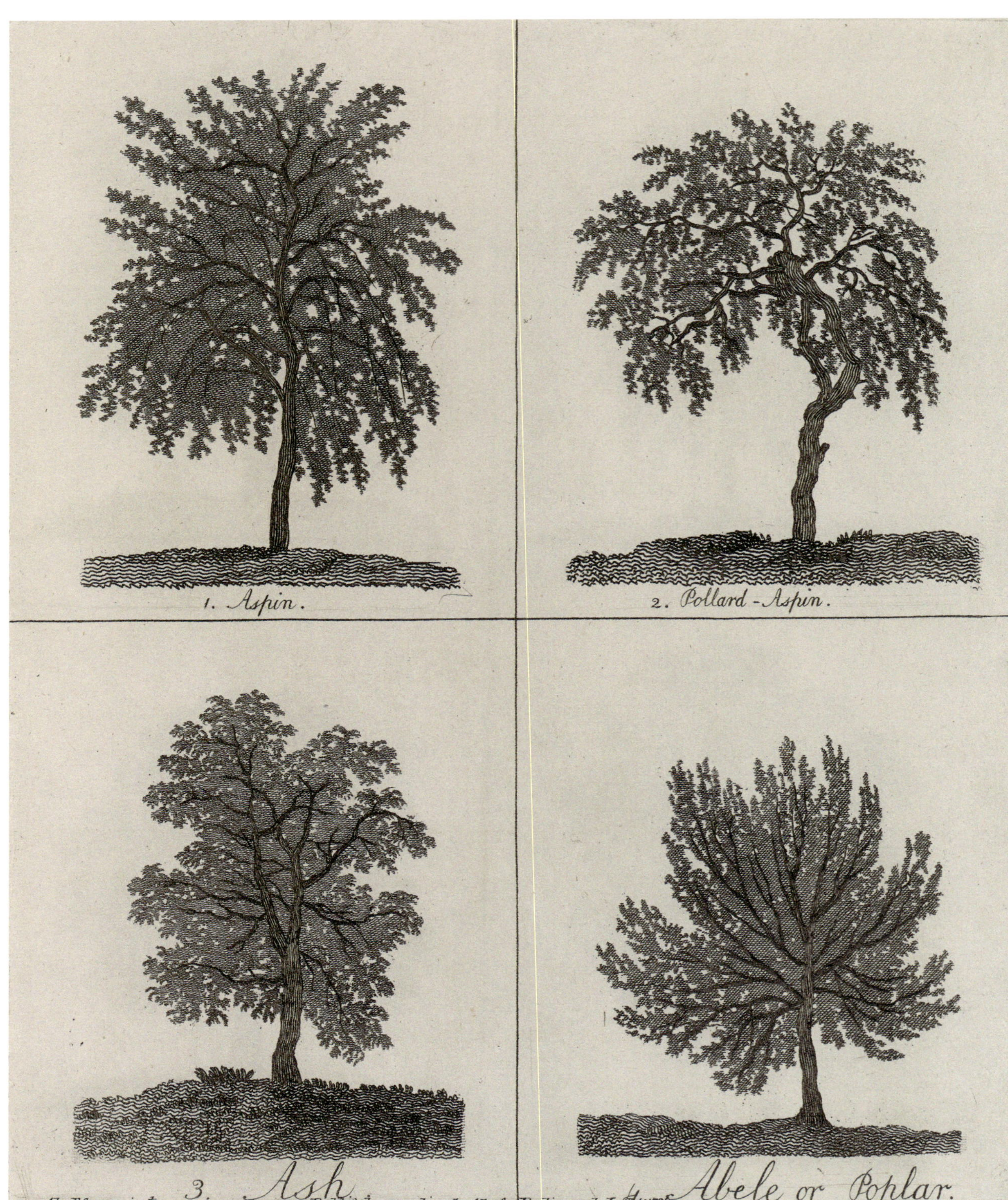

1. Aspin.
2. Pollard-Aspin.
3. Ash
Abele or Poplar.
Alex.r Curzon inv.t
Publish'd according to Act of Parliament July 1. 1786.

structures, foliage patterns, and silhouettes. Printed illustrations demonstrating how to draw important varieties were circulating among artists and elite amateurs. The British artist Alexander Cozens, for example, published an influential collection of plates titled *The Shape, Skeleton and Foliage of Thirty-Two Species of Trees* in 1786 (fig. 3). Artists began studying prints by Cozens and others to represent more accurately the beech and oak species that populated historical German woodlands, as well as the pine and spruce trees that later spread throughout the region. By painting readily identifiable trees, they could satisfy the growing appetite for landscapes that looked unmistakably German.

Ferdinand Kobell's *Philosopher's Path near Heidelberg* from 1780, which opens this essay, exemplifies these efforts by artists to distinguish German Romantic art from the Italian tradition. Instead of rolling meadows that recede into distant mountains, two old trees impose their vertical presence. The intensely varied texture of the foliage suggests the artist's debt to Altdorfer's earlier painting. On the far right, a separate branch takes the form of a cross, alluding to a natural German piety whose origins lie in the trees. On the left, a philosopher reclines beneath a tree's canopy and consults a book. Behind him, tree branches and ground cover form a rustic dwelling space, as if the landscape has felicitously provided him with shelter. Both the asymmetry of the composition and the vertical format put it at odds with the Italian landscape tradition. But Kobell still strove to create a sense of harmony among the many natural elements of the scene.

Kobell's etching captures a broader Romantic interest in wooded, rocky terrain as a space for serious intellectual and spiritual contemplation. The philosopher's immersion in the natural environment gives visual expression to German *Naturphilosophie*, the philosophy of nature. The forest embodied one of the core principles of *Naturphilosophie*, which is the interdependence of individual parts and a larger whole. While woodlands may appear heterogeneous—containing myriad kinds of plants and animals—they belong to a fundamental organic unity. Similarly, Romantic writers and philosophers in this period believed in the inherent oneness of humans and the natural world. As art historian Nina Amstutz has shown, they saw profound analogies between the interlacing branches of a tree and the interconnected arteries of the human body.[2] Romantic thinkers believed the oneness of nature encompassed the divine, too. Immersion in the natural world doubled, for them, as a form of spiritual worship. This was yet another way they rejected Enlightenment science, which they perceived as overly rational, mechanistic, and utilitarian. From this vantage point, Kobell's print invites viewers to open themselves up, like the Romantic philosopher, to the natural world for intellectual and spiritual inquiry and enrichment.

The German forest's variety, shadowy recesses, and lush undergrowth are celebrated in Kobell's print. Yet these are the very features that would come to be criticized with the rise of scientific forest management in the late eighteenth and early nineteenth centuries. The use of Germany's forests was a major source of social conflict following the Thirty Years' War (1618–48). Energy-intensive industries such as glassworks, charcoal production, and ore smelting required significant quantities of firewood. It was feared that as the region's industries grew, the woodlands upon which they depended would dwindle. In addition to being the primary source of energy for Germany until the middle of the nineteenth century, timber was the dominant material for construction, domestic heating, and shipbuilding. Rural communities were also accustomed to using woodlands to graze their animals and as a shared resource for materials such as firewood, building supplies, and bark for tanning. The right of rural populations to draw upon the woodlands was historically protected by tradition and law.

Carl Wilhelm Kolbe the Elder's *Landscape with Clumps of Tall Oak Trees* (fig. 4) commemorates the assorted uses and communities served by Germany's traditional woods. Towering over the scene, old-growth oak trees spread their foliage. The oak was an especially important tree for German artists and writers, who regularly leveraged its symbolic associations with Germanic fortitude and national unity. Oak leaves featured on

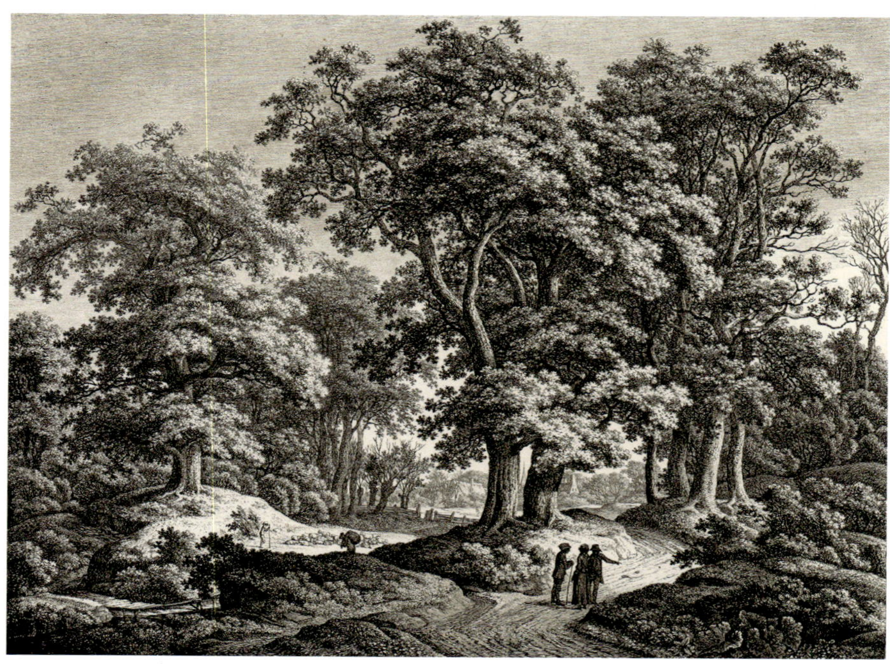

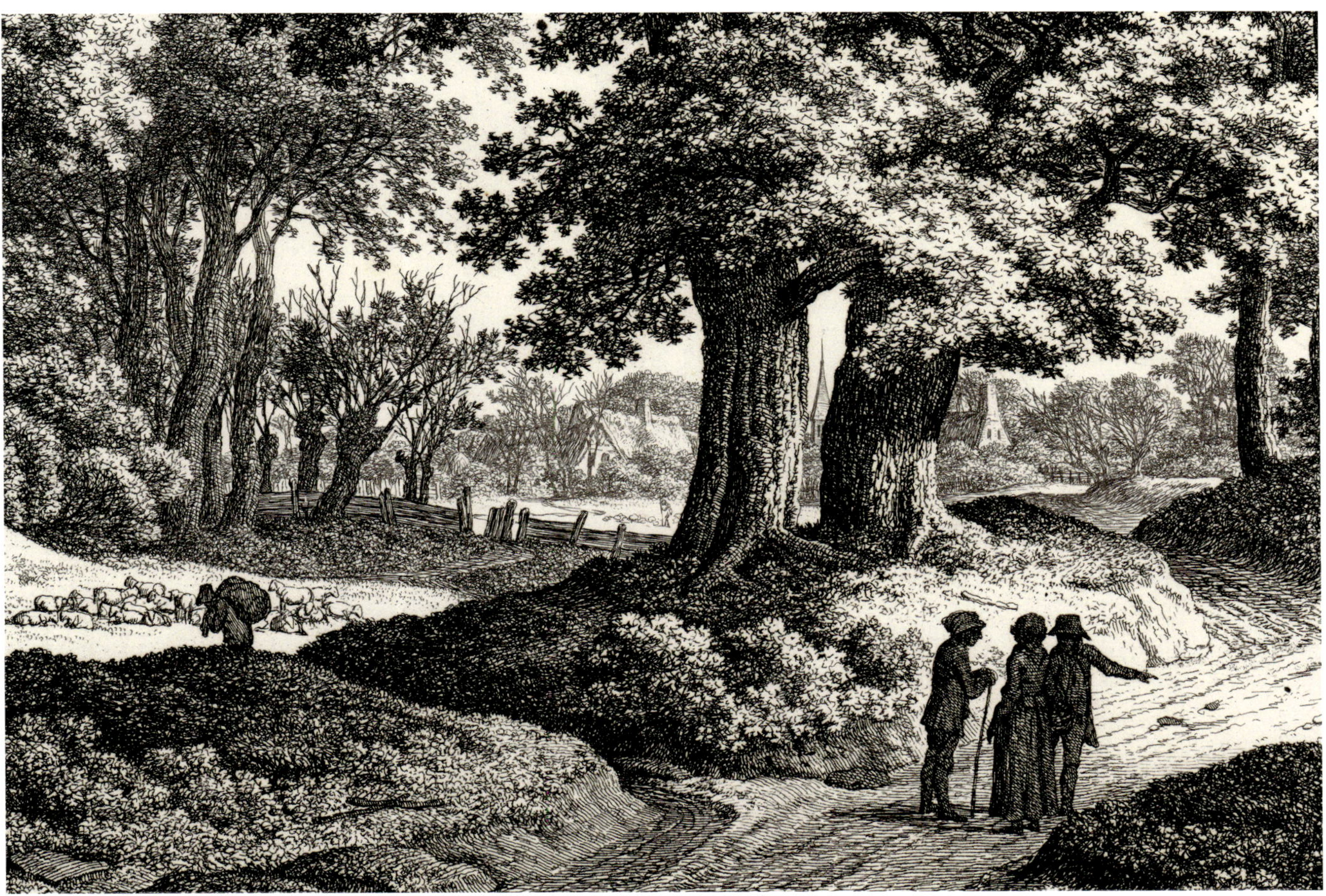

German state coins and insignias throughout the nineteenth century. Viewers would have recognized the trees in this print as old-growth or "ancient" oaks due to their size and the structural complexity of their trunks, indicating they had been growing for a century or longer. In the middle ground, three people are paused in conversation on a dirt road that leads toward a distant town (fig. 5). To the left, a solitary figure carrying a large sack prepares to cross a modest wooden bridge, and a shepherd tends to a flock in a brightly lit natural clearing. A rustic wooden fence, more animals, and some houses can be glimpsed in the depths of the print.

Kolbe's etching pictures the harmonious coexistence of foraging animals, historical woodlands, rural laborers, and built infrastructure all in close proximity to a village. A spire between the trunks of the two central oaks implies the presence of a church and a larger local community. Although this landscape has been "improved" by human intervention in the form of roads, bridges, and fences, the trees in the foreground have been allowed to grow naturally and have clustered into a copse, or small group. The trees near the distant fence have been pollarded, or trimmed down to their trunks, to regulate their growth. Pollarded trees produce clusters of thin upright branches, which were used for fencing, kindling, and basketry. The merits of the practice were intensely debated among German foresters at the time. Even more controversial at the turn of the nineteenth century was the practice of grazing animals in woodlands, which Kolbe portrayed in a positive light.

State administrators and elite landowners were increasingly convinced that the agricultural and pastoral practices of rural populations had become harmful to German forests.[3] (In reality, there was little evidence of actual wood shortages or, indeed, that communal use rights posed a threat to forests.) Efforts to strip rural communities of these centuries-old rights were motivated by a desire for social reform as much as by an aim to regulate timber supplies.[4] Allowing peasants to graze their livestock in woodlands was regarded by many as a vestige of a feudal social system that was antithetical to modern German society. Reformers sought to enforce the separation of grazing pasturage from woodlands, restrict traditional communal access, privatize and consolidate land for timber and agriculture, and "rationalize" the forest. In other words, the scene portrayed by Kolbe's print was coming under threat.

The science of forest management that was developed in what is now Germany emerged under the auspices of cameralism.[5] This term names a broader effort to maximize the economic prosperity of a centralized state through careful management of its natural resources and population. In this regard, the "improvement" of nature through standardization, systematization, and quantification was a deeply Enlightenment pursuit. Forest management was one of many large-scale cameralist initiatives to modify the natural environment to better serve the needs of an economically modernizing state. Other projects included draining marshlands in the name of "land reclamation," straightening the course of the Rhine River, planting pines to stabilize sand dunes, and building new roadways.[6]

Georg von Dillis's *The Rotting Trunk* (fig. 6) portrays the disorder and decay found in the region's historical forests that reformers abhorred. An evocative motif, the large rotting tree trunk dominating the composition suggests a past era of glory and growth that has degenerated. Clustered passages of ink across the trunk give way to the blank paper underneath as if to replicate the material disintegration of the wood as it rots. Through the eyes of reformers, the etching demonstrates a lack of rational forest management. The free-form, sketch-like lines of the foliage reaffirm the impression that these woods are being permitted to grow in a chaotic and compressed manner. To make matters worse, the dead trunk is taking up valuable space where new trees could otherwise grow. In place of the

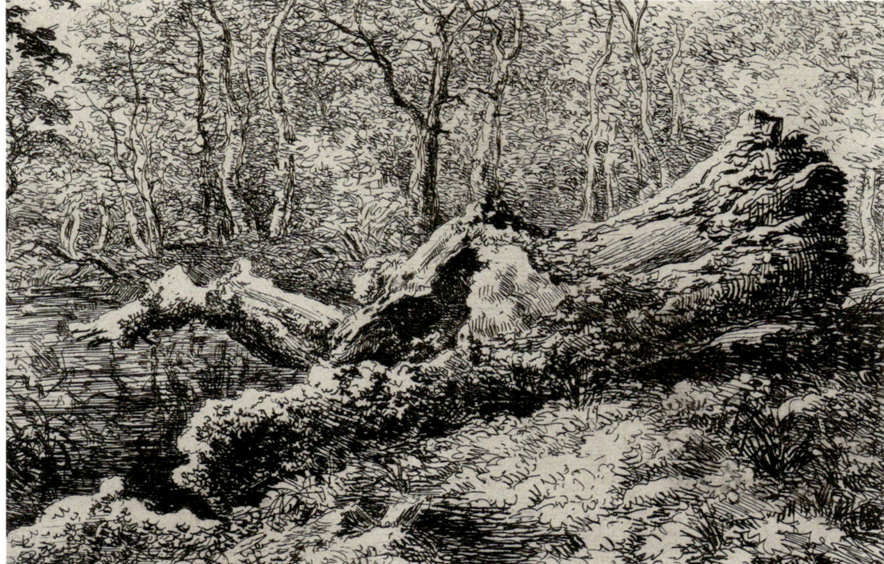

mighty oaks thought to be synonymous with Germanic greatness, these trees look scrawny, messy, and insubstantial. Influenced by the Dutch tradition of using dead trees to symbolize the passage of time, Dillis likely did not intend for this print to bolster the views of forest reformers. *The Rotting Trunk* instead depicts the beauty of an environment that has not been optimized according to the Enlightenment science of forest management.

In the second half of the eighteenth century, administrators and scientists proposed novel systems for evaluating and managing German forests. The aim was to achieve annual timber yields that were roughly equal and not over-harvest the forest. This entailed redefining the forest as a quantity of timber, to the exclusion of all the other plants and animals that thrived there. Their narrow definition of utility further failed to recognize the social and economic value communities derived from secondary uses of woodland, from pasturage to medicinal plants and materials for tanning, fencing, and roofing.[7] Initially, forests were divided into "cutting areas" of equal size. Based on how long the dominant type of tree needed to grow to produce a certain quantity of timber, cutters would return to an area only after the proper number of years had elapsed.

It was in the financial interest of the state to plant forests with just one type of tree so they would grow at the same rate and produce timber of the same density. (Timber with a consistent density and moisture content burns in the same way, which was desirable for forges.) Thick vegetal undergrowth was cleared, trees were planted at regular intervals, and grazing was often forbidden. Foresters increasingly planted pine and spruce, fast-growing trees with reliably straight trunks that did well

FIG. 7 Johann Wilhelm Schirmer, *The Mill near a Forest* (detail), ca. 1845 (cat. p. 163)

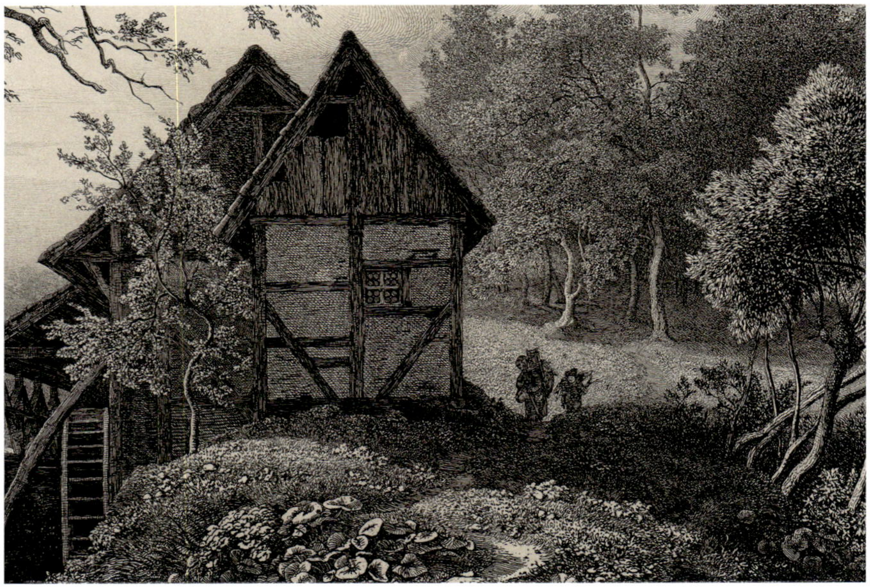

in German growing conditions. Their wood was also lightweight and therefore easy to transport. These forests were antithetical to the scenes portrayed by Romantic artists such as Dillis and Kolbe, who commemorated the organic environments under threat from economic and scientific modernization.

Yet not all Romantics rejected this modernization. Several of the most prominent writers, including Johann Wolfgang von Goethe and Novalis (Georg Philipp Friedrich Freiherr von Hardenberg), were employed as directors at ore mines, another major form of cameralist state resource management.[8] In *The Mill near a Forest* (fig. 7), Johann Wilhelm Schirmer integrated the growing presence of industry in the landscape with Romantic notions about the forest. In the center of the composition, a wooden building sits atop a wooden waterwheel, a vivid reminder that timber remained the primary material for construction and energy until the middle of the nineteenth century. The mill is an orderly, geometric structure that aligns with the mathematical principles of state-regulated industrial growth and is shown alongside both old and young trees. On the left, a large and irregular ancient trunk frames the scene. On the far right, pollarded trees send up slender sprays of new growth. The forest of the print's title appears in the distance, substantial and dense. It is, however, also "managed": Note the regular spacing between the trunks and the lack of significant undergrowth on the forest floor. The two laborers who approach the mill in shadow appear to be exiting the woods with sticks and other materials they may have cleared. In Schirmer's etching, Romantic aspects of the forest—the organic irregularities, the presence of ancient trees, the sense of texture and abundance—are in balance with the indus-triousness of human activity.

One of the most important legacies of German scientific forest management is the concept of sustainability. The German mining adminis-trator Hans Carl von Carlowitz introduced the idea when he published the first comprehensive treatise on forest management, *Sylvicultura oeconomica,* in 1713. Carlowitz argued that foresters should strive for a sustainable timber yield—that is, they should remove only the maximum quantity of timber from a forest that can be continuously regrown. In the decades that followed, forest management became the epicenter for discussions about sustainability, termed *Nachhaltigkeit* in German.[9] By the end of the eigh-teenth century, foresters were taught to calculate and plan forest growth more than a century into the future.[10]

Botanist Friedrich August Ludwig von Burgsdorf detailed the benefits of regularly spaced, mature, tall-growth forests in his book from 1783. The image on its title page, printed with the words "for posterity," foregrounds the importance of sustainable yields (fig. 8). Foresters can be seen staking trees at mathematically determined intervals. This enabled the timber yields to be accurately measured and predicted in future decades, and ensured a uniform quantity and quality of timber when the area was ready to be cut. The young coniferous tree in the left foreground is likely pine or spruce, indicative of the trend to plant foreign species rather than the slower-growing beeches and oaks indigenous to the region. Illustrations in forest management texts from the period portray woods as legible, uniform, and quantifiable. Abundant foliage, biodiversity, and irregular clustering of growth were expunged from such imagery.

As the Schirmer print demonstrated, Romantic artists were not uniformly opposed to the principles of scientific forest management. They shared in the period's anxieties about the decline of German woodlands (even if unfounded). Also, the ascendant practices of the timber industry remained compatible with some of the spiritual and nationalistic meanings they associated with the forest. This is acutely reflected in the work of Caspar David Friedrich, the most famous of the German Romantic artists. Friedrich's *Times of Day: Evening* (fig. 9) is the final painting in his four-part series portraying a landscape at different moments in the day. Each of the paintings prominently features high stands (*Hochwald*) of equal age—precisely the kind of woodlands imposed on the landscape by forest administrators. In *Evening,* two figures wander amid the trees in contem-plation. Unlike the philosopher in Kobell's earlier print, they encounter a decidedly managed version of the natural world. The scene shows no undergrowth or grazing animals, and the trees are all evenly spaced and of the same species.

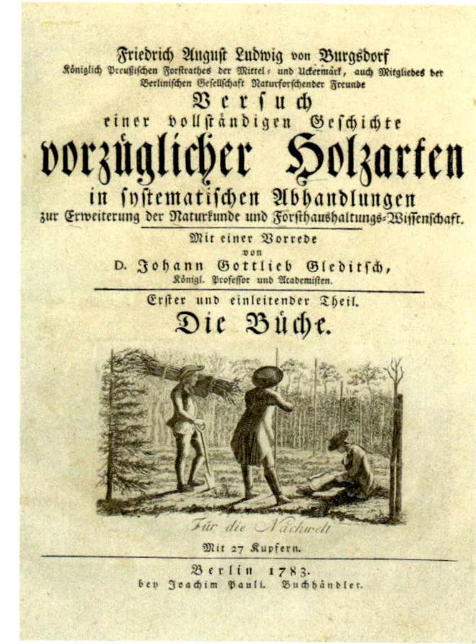

FIG. 8   Friedrich August Ludwig von Burgs-dorf (Leipzig 1747–1802 Berlin), Frontis-piece, from *Attempt to Provide a Complete History of Excellent Types of Wood in a System-atic Treatise to Expand Natural History and the Science of Forest Management (Versuch einer vollständigen Geschichte vorzüglicher Holzarten in systematischen Abhandlungen zur Erweiter-ung der Naturkunde und Forsthaushaltungs-Wissenschaft),* 1783

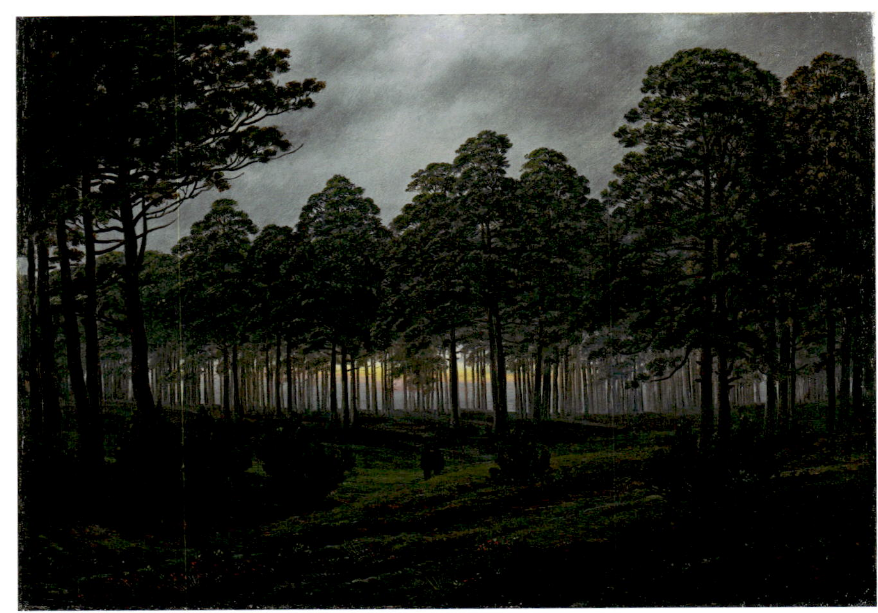

FIG. 9

FIG. 10

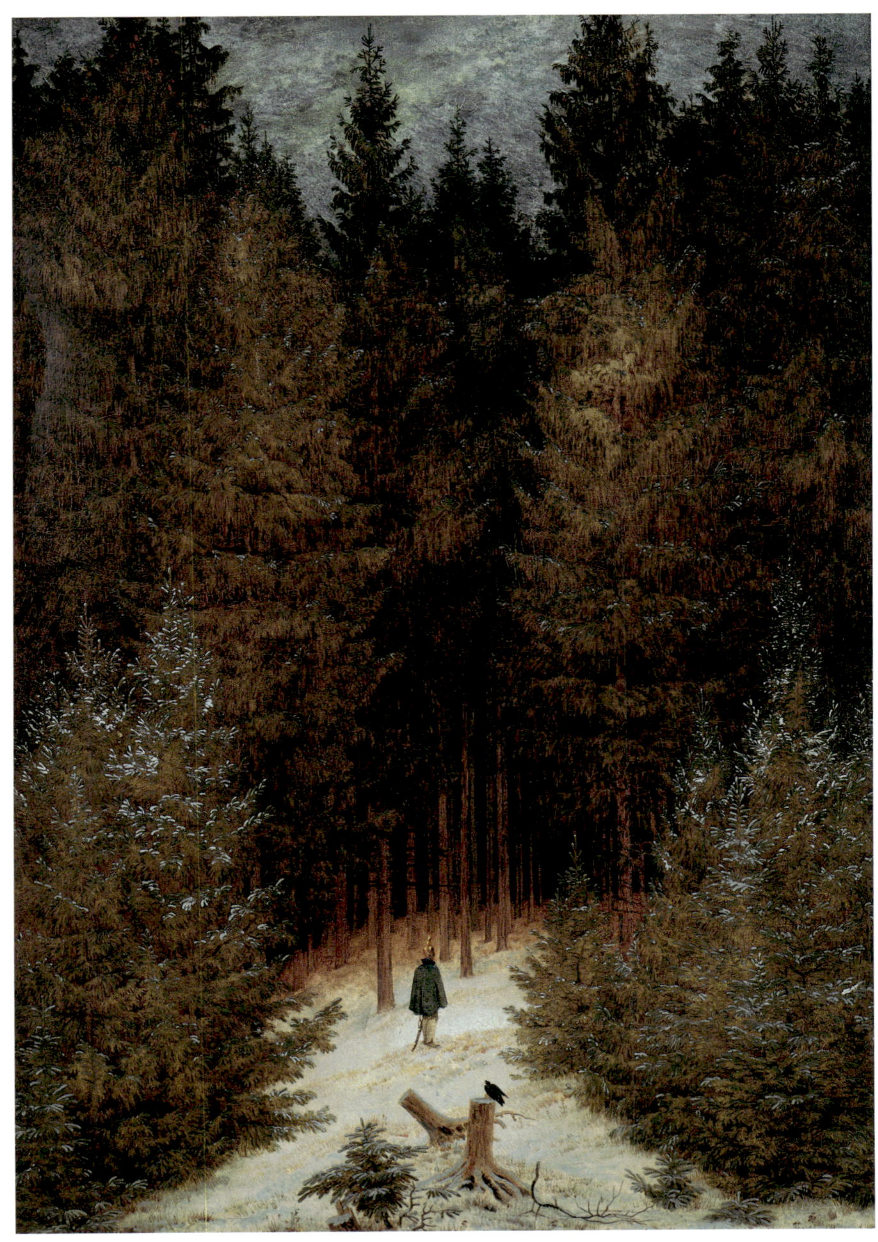

Although we regard this painting today as exemplifying the symbolic importance of nature and especially of forests to Romantic artists, someone viewing this painting circa 1820 would have instantly recognized it as a modern, artificially planted, and highly managed woodland. Friedrich portrayed the beauty of the technocratic values of resource management. An 1820s viewer would have *also* seen important nationalistic values in this forest, harkening back to the Napoleonic Wars (1803–15), which had concluded a few years earlier. Friedrich was known for his intense nationalism, particularly during and after this conflict.[11] French forces occupied German lands on the Rhine starting in 1793 and made major political and military advances into German territories under Napoleon. Many states were compelled to join the Confederation of the Rhine under French control. This occupation spurred a sense of collective national identity among Germanic states.

The uniform expanses of tall straight trees that German forest scientists had been planting since the late eighteenth century offered a sharp contrast in both principle and appearance to French forest management practices. The typical French forest was relatively heterogeneous in species, height, age, and appearance. During Napoleonic occupation, the German woodlands became a symbol of national identity that stood in opposition to France. It was even proposed that German forests could act as a physical barrier against French forces, who would struggle to navigate this unfamiliar and imposing environment.[12]

Like Friedrich's famous painting *The Chasseur in the Forest* (fig. 10), in which a retreating French soldier confronts a dense German conifer forest, *Evening* invokes the woods as a natural fortress protecting German territorial integrity against future French encroachment. The fact that this forest has been rationalized, regulated, and optimized has only enhanced its patriotic associations. Scientific forestry denied rural laborers their customary use rights and legislated against diverse, multispecies environments—yet this seemingly did not disqualify the forest from promoting a unifying sense of national belonging, at least for Friedrich.

As the middle of the nineteenth century approached, artists, writers, and philosophers grew more vocally critical of the uniform, monocultural, utilitarian forest. Schirmer's *The Hunter's Departure from the Forest* (fig. 11) shares with earlier prints an interest in the woods as a place of old and irregular trees accompanied by lush undergrowth. Rather than portraying the forest in harmony with industry, as seen in *The Mill*, he pictured the forest from the perspective of the animals who inhabit it. Viewers are located beneath the dark canopy of an old tree. We join the animals in the foreground, who watch as distant hunters depart at the end of the day's hunt. We are invited to share their vantage point, in which the presence of

FIG. 9   Caspar David Friedrich, *Times of Day: Evening (Vier Tageszeiten: Der Abend)*, ca. 1820. Oil on canvas. 8¾ × 12³⁄₁₆ in. (22.3 × 31 cm). Landesmuseum, Hannover

FIG. 10   Caspar David Friedrich, *The Chasseur in the Forest (Der Chasseur im Walde)*, 1814. Oil on canvas. 26 × 18½ in. (66 × 47 cm). Private collection

humans in the woods is a threat. (Hunters had long been an important voice advocating against scientific forest management because they wanted to preserve historic woodlands for their sport.)[13] Late Romantic artists resisted the notion that the forest should be standardized and that trees could be treated as interchangeable units of timber mass. Although it was not until the second half of the nineteenth century that German scientists developed the term "ecology," we can see in the Schirmer print and others the stirrings of an alternative science of the forest that embraced interdependence, biodiversity, and shared use. Throughout the remainder of the nineteenth century, the forest would be both a symbolically important and a contested space for German artists and scientists alike.

NOTES

1. Robin Fleming, "Picturesque History and the Medieval in Nineteenth-Century America," *American Historical Review* 100, no. 4 (1995), 1063.

2. Nina Amstutz, "Friedrich and the Anatomy of Nature," *Art History* 37, no. 2 (2014): 454–481.

3. Richard Hölzl, "Historicizing Sustainability: German Scientific Forestry in the Eighteenth and Nineteenth Centuries," *Science as Culture* 19, no. 4 (2010): 437.

4. Paul Warde, *The Invention of Sustainability: Nature and Destiny, c. 1500–1870* (Cambridge: Cambridge University Press, 2018).

5. Bernd-Stefan Grewe, "Forestry in Germany, c. 1550–2000," in *Managing Northern Europe's Forests: Histories from the Age of Improvement to the Age of Ecology*, ed. Jan K. Oosthoek and Richard Hölzl (Oxford: Berghahn Books, 2018), 15–65. Henry E. Lowood, "The Calculating Forester: Quantification, Cameral Science, and the Emergence of Scientific Forestry Management in Germany," in *The Quantifying Spirit in the Eighteenth Century*, ed. Tore Frängsmyr et al. (Berkeley: University of California Press, 1990), 315–343.

6. David Blackbourn, *The Conquest of Nature: Water, Landscape, and the Making of Modern Germany* (New York: W. W. Norton, 2006).

7. Robert Pogue Harrison, *Forests: The Shadow of Civilization* (Chicago: University of Chicago Press, 1992), 122.

8. Theodore Ziolkowski, *German Romanticism and Its Institutions* (Princeton, NJ: Princeton University Press, 1990).

9. Warde, *The Invention of Sustainability*.

10. Grewe, "Forestry in Germany," 25.

11. William Vaughan, "Correcting Friedrich: Nature and Society in Post-Napoleonic Germany," in *Art in Bourgeois Society, 1790–1850*, ed. A. Hemingway and W. Vaughan (New York: Cambridge University Press, 1998), 208–228.

12. Hansjörg Küster, "Forests Against France: An Important Impetus for German Forest Plantations in the 19th Century," in *Revue de géographie historique* 5 (2014), https://doi.org/10.4000/geohist.4344.

13. Joachim Radkau, "Wood and Forestry in German History: In Quest of an Environmental Approach," *Environment and History* 2, no. 1 (1996): 63–76.

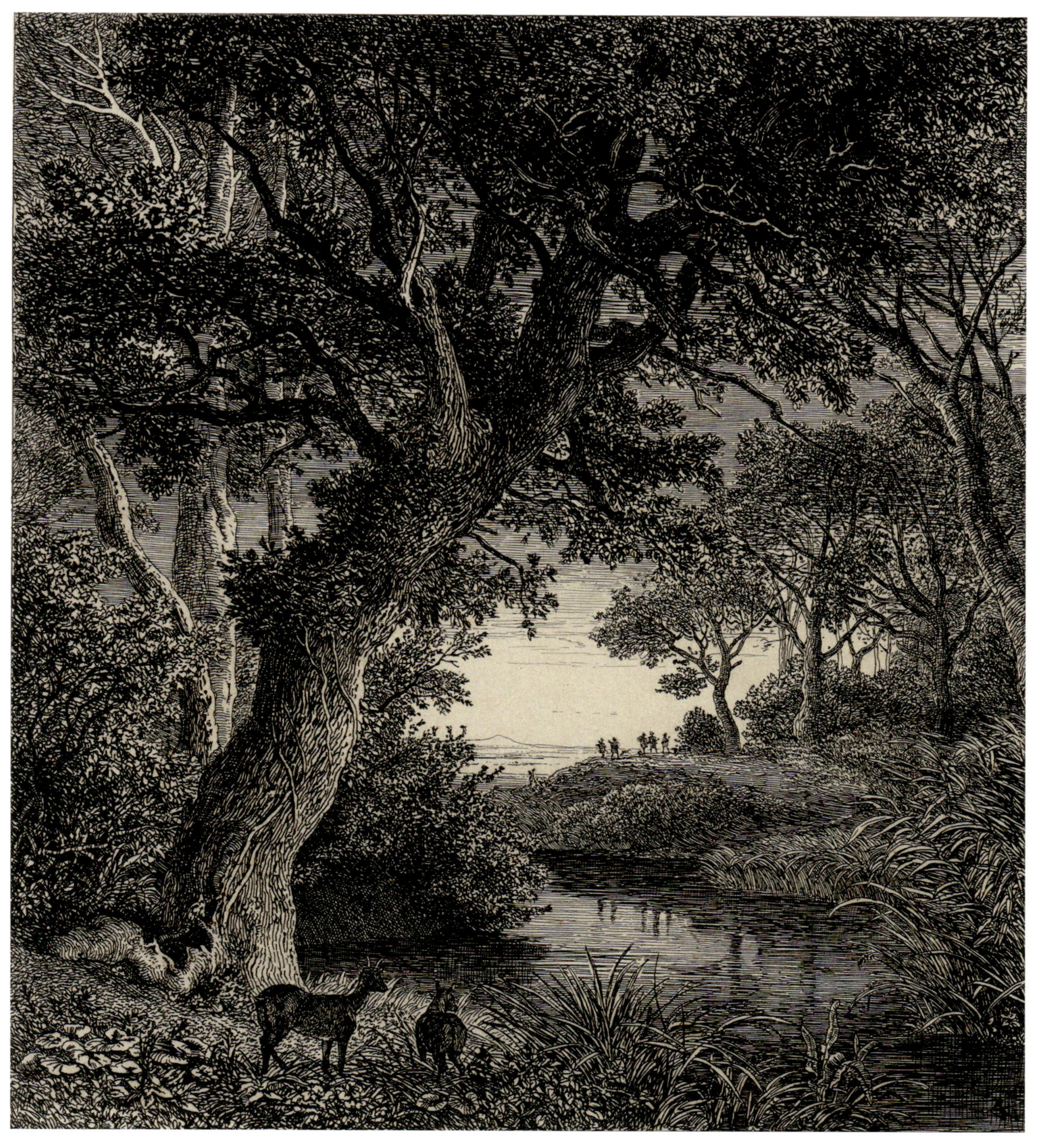

FIG. 11

Finding Science, Self, and Spirit in Nature

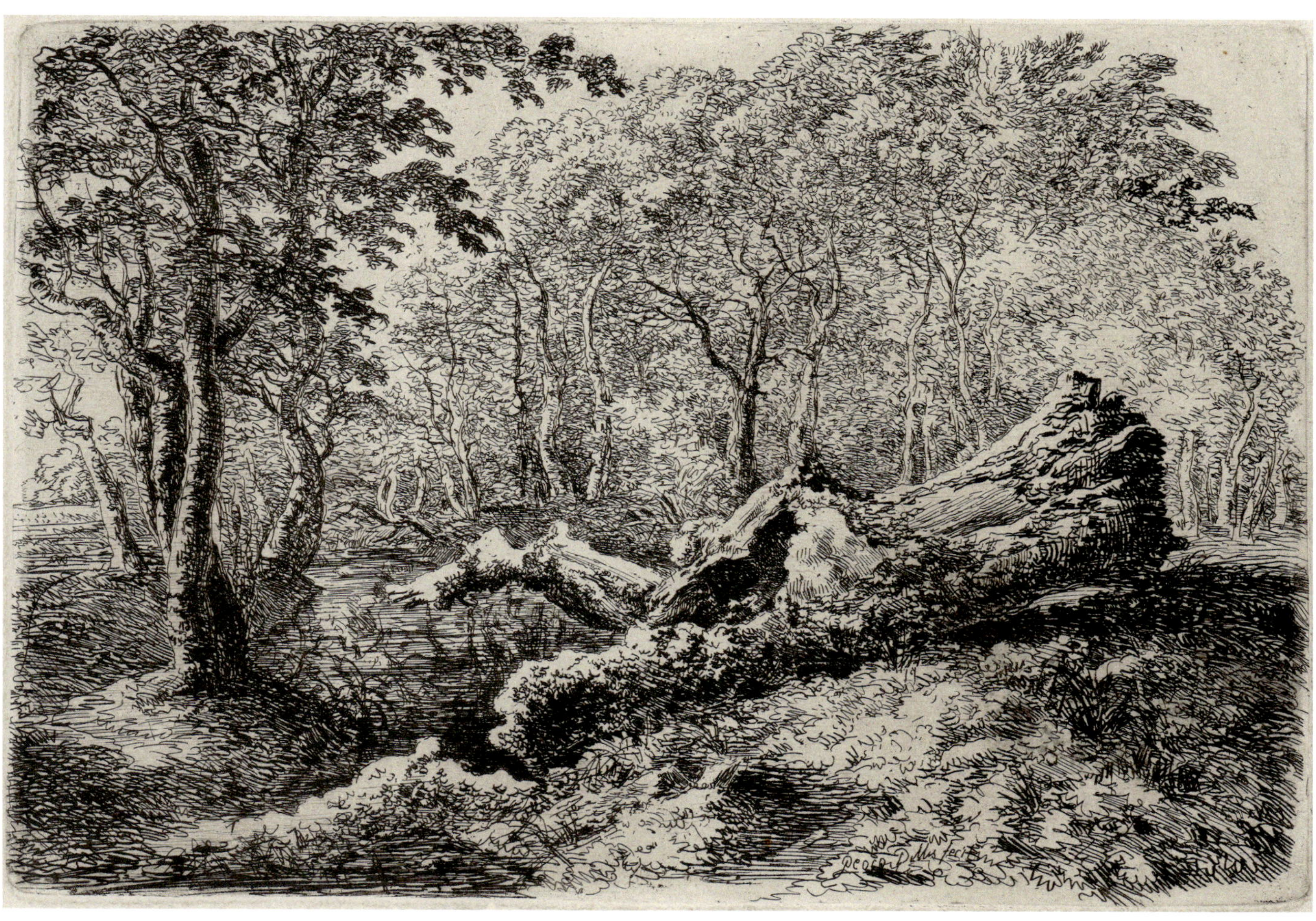

1.

Georg von Dillis

GRÜNGIEBING 1759–1841 MUNICH

The Rotting Trunk (Der modernde Baumstamm), 1793

Etching

Early in the German Romantic movement, landscape artists such as Georg von Dillis began to depict nature as they observed it rather than shaping it into imposing classical scenes. Dillis often worked in the newly opened English Garden in Munich. Designed to appear wild, it contrasted the formal and symmetrical French-style gardens that were popular across Europe. The move away from geometrical arrangements reflected an emerging understanding that nature was not guided by reason. Gardens became spaces for individual emotional responses to the landscape, an important aspect of Romanticism.

Influenced by the portrayal of life's brevity through fallen trees in seventeenth-century Dutch prints, Dillis included a decaying trunk in this image. He drew directly on a prepared etching plate, resulting in a sketch-like quality that appealed to an interest in spontaneity among eighteenth-century collectors. Dillis became a professor of landscape painting at the Munich Art Academy in 1808, allowing him to impart his ideas about the genre to generations of students.

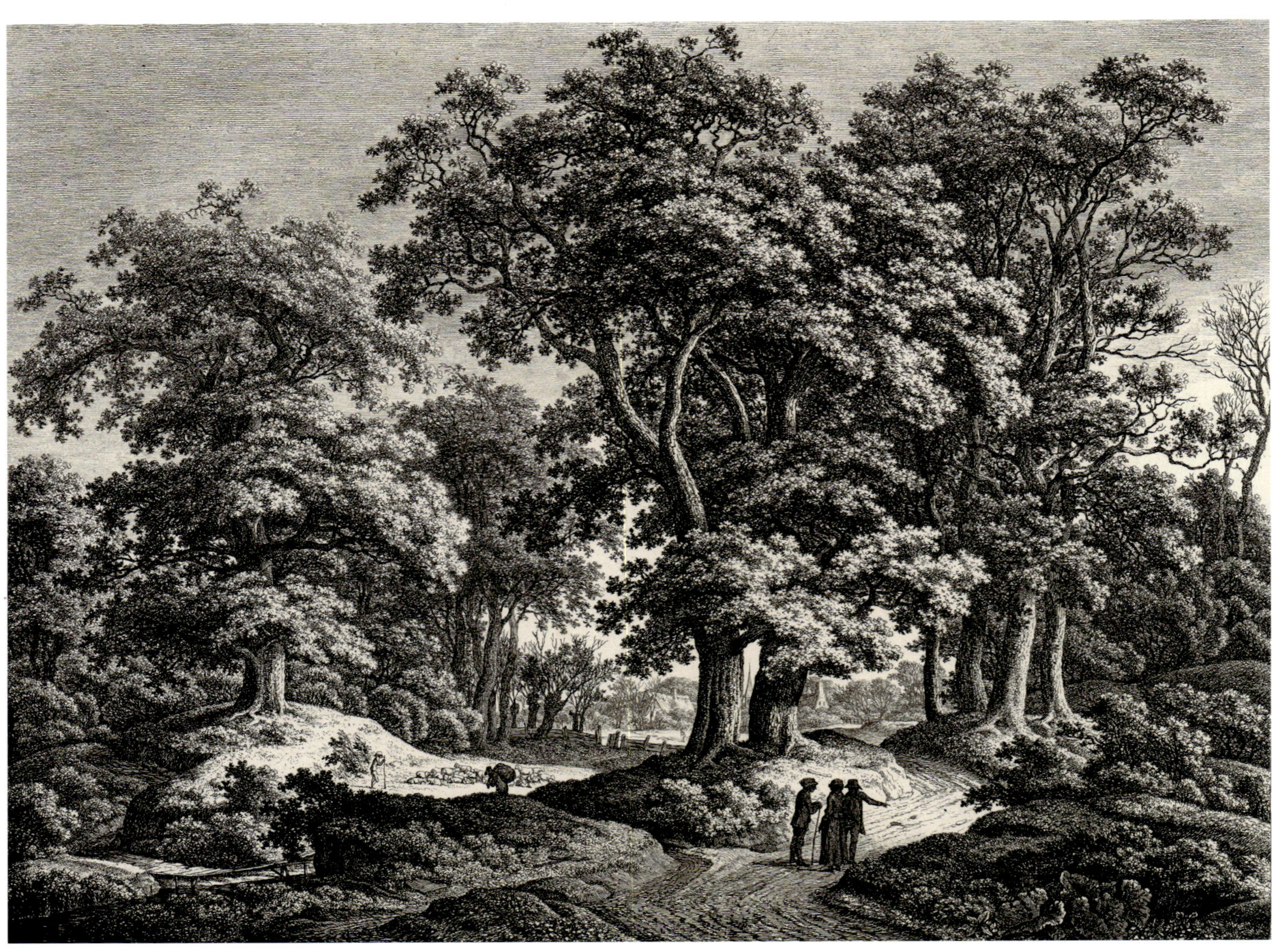

Carl Wilhelm Kolbe the Elder

Landscape with Clumps of Tall Oak Trees (Landschaft mit Gruppen hoher Eichen), ca. 1802

Etching

This print represents Wörlitz Park near Dessau, where Carl Wilhelm Kolbe taught drawing and French and served as court engraver. As the first English-style park in the German lands, it included both wild forest and cultivated gardens. Kolbe was especially interested in the park's oak trees, which symbolized strength and resilience and became increasingly associated with German identity during the nineteenth century. He claimed, "Trees have turned me into an artist," and his contemporaries nicknamed him Oak-Kolbe (*Eichen-Kolbe*) for his many landscapes featuring this national emblem.[1]

The immense oaks in this etching tower over the figures, reflecting the forest's majesty. Yet Kolbe feared his art would never capture the transcendent power he observed in person: "Nature has so much that is alive and spiritual that it will be impossible for even the most practiced pen to express it faithfully and purely on paper."[2]

1. Anna Schultz, "'Trees Have Turned Me into an Artist': The Graphic Work of Carl Wilhelm Kolbe (1759–1835)," in *German Romantic Prints and Drawings from an English Private Collection*, ed. Giulia Bartrum (London: Contemporary Editions Ltd., 2011), 175–176.

2. Carl Wilhelm Kolbe, *Mein Lebenslauf und mein Wirken im Fache der Sprache und der Kunst* (Berlin: Reimer, 1825), 9.

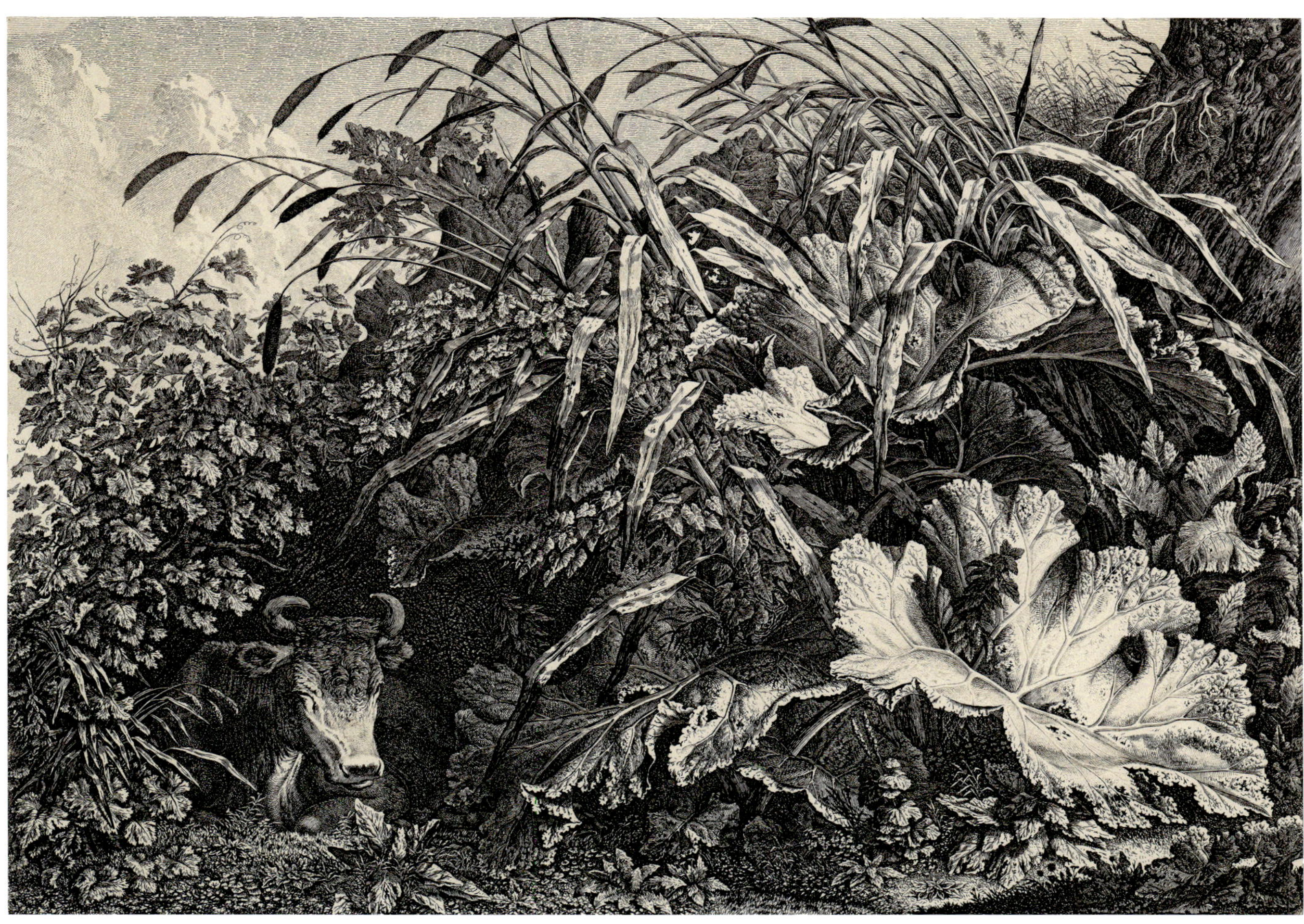

Carl Wilhelm Kolbe the Elder

Cow in the Reeds (Die Kuh im Schilfe),
ca. 1800/03

Etching

Cow in the Reeds exemplifies Carl Wilhelm Kolbe's *Kräuterblätter* (foliage prints), or fanciful etchings of massive vegetation. He admired the truthfully rendered flora in seventeenth-century Dutch prints but exaggerated the scale of the plants he depicted to convey their grandeur and significance. The cow in this print rests beside the nearly equally sized leaves of a burdock bush.

Kolbe generally preferred to etch from memory after sketching essential outlines and proportions outdoors, and he wrote in his autobiography that he invented the *Kräuterblätter* "from my own head." He added that he regretted taking this approach: "I readily admit that I was wrong, and very wrong," he conceded, explaining that his aesthetically pleasing forms "cannot withstand the scrutinizing gaze of the nature observer."[3]

3. *Mein Lebenslauf,* 12.

4.
Ferdinand Kobell
MANNHEIM 1740–1799 MUNICH

*Philosopher's Path near Heidelberg
(Philosophenweg bei Heidelberg)*, 1780

Etching

In a forest clearing, a bearded figure wears the cowl and sandals of a monk. The branch supporting a thatched roof behind him indicates that he is living among the trees. As a religious figure in the woods, the man symbolizes the divine in nature, which Ferdinand Kobell further reinforced by including a cross made from branches at the right. The figure's isolation in this print, as well as the solitude associated with monastic life, suggests that nature can provide a space removed from worldly concerns for enriching one's mind and spirit.

Kobell's colleagues recognized him as an exemplary landscape artist. Max Josef Wagenbauer's book of landscape models (plate 6), for example, advises students to copy his works, along with those of a few select Dutch artists, before they begin to draw outdoors.

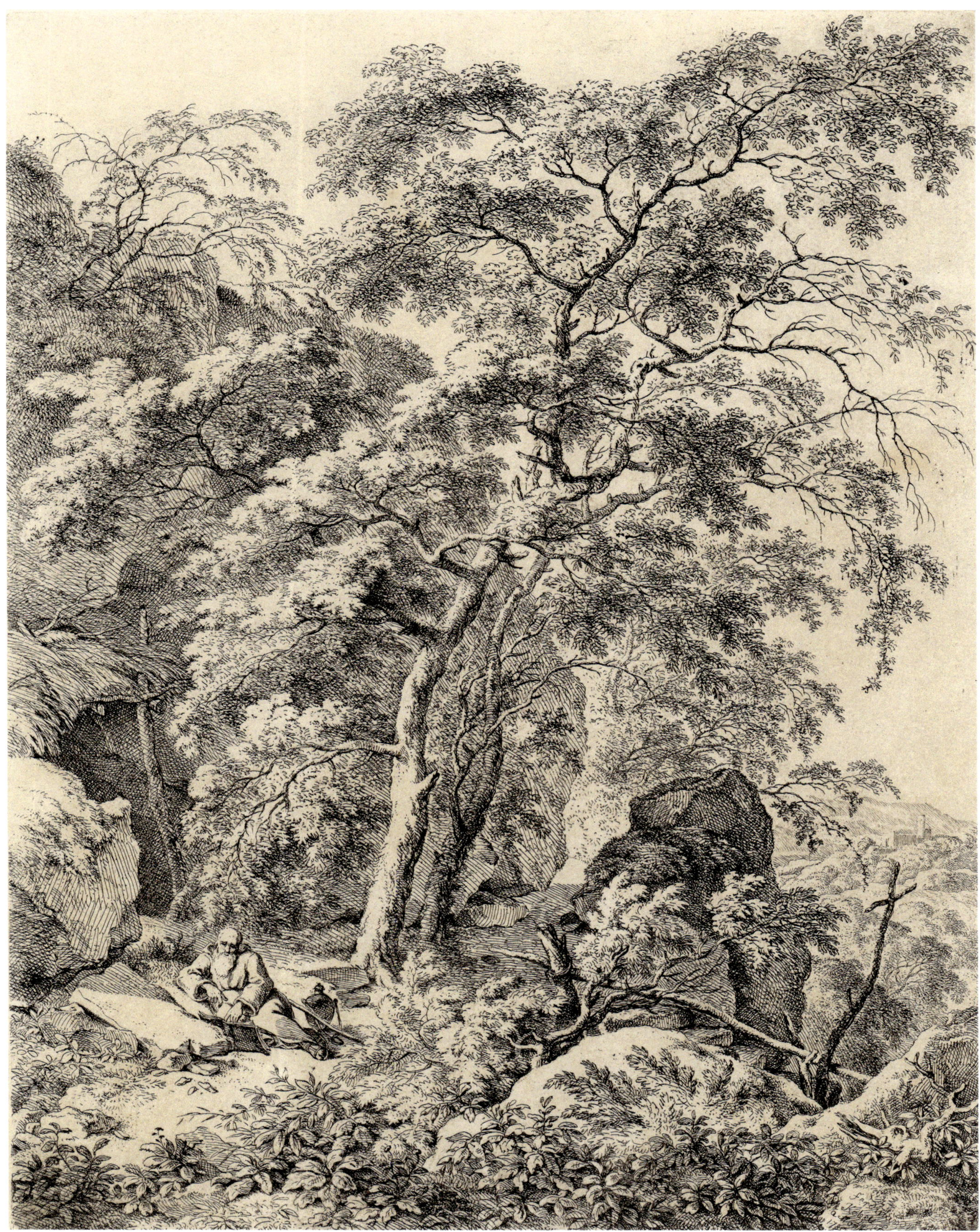

5.

Adrian Zingg

ST. GALLEN 1734–1816 LEIPZIG

Blooming Thistle (Große Distel or *Blühende Distelpflanze),* ca. 1810

Pen and ink and wash over graphite on paper

Adrian Zingg moved to Dresden in 1766, after spending nine years working in Bern and Paris. He had learned the importance of sketching from nature while in France, and when he began teaching engraving at the Dresden Academy of Fine Arts, he encouraged his students to draw outdoors. His work was based on close observation of local sites, and he was especially well known for sepia drawings like this one.

The plant featured here is a marsh thistle, found in Dresden's wetlands. Zingg captured its distinctive spiny stalk, broad leaves, and thin-petaled flowers in great detail. Around the thistle, Zingg rendered gently curving grasses. The damaged leaf in the lower center, which appears to have been eaten by insects, may have been present in the plant Zingg used as a model, or he may have added it to serve as a reminder of life's brevity.

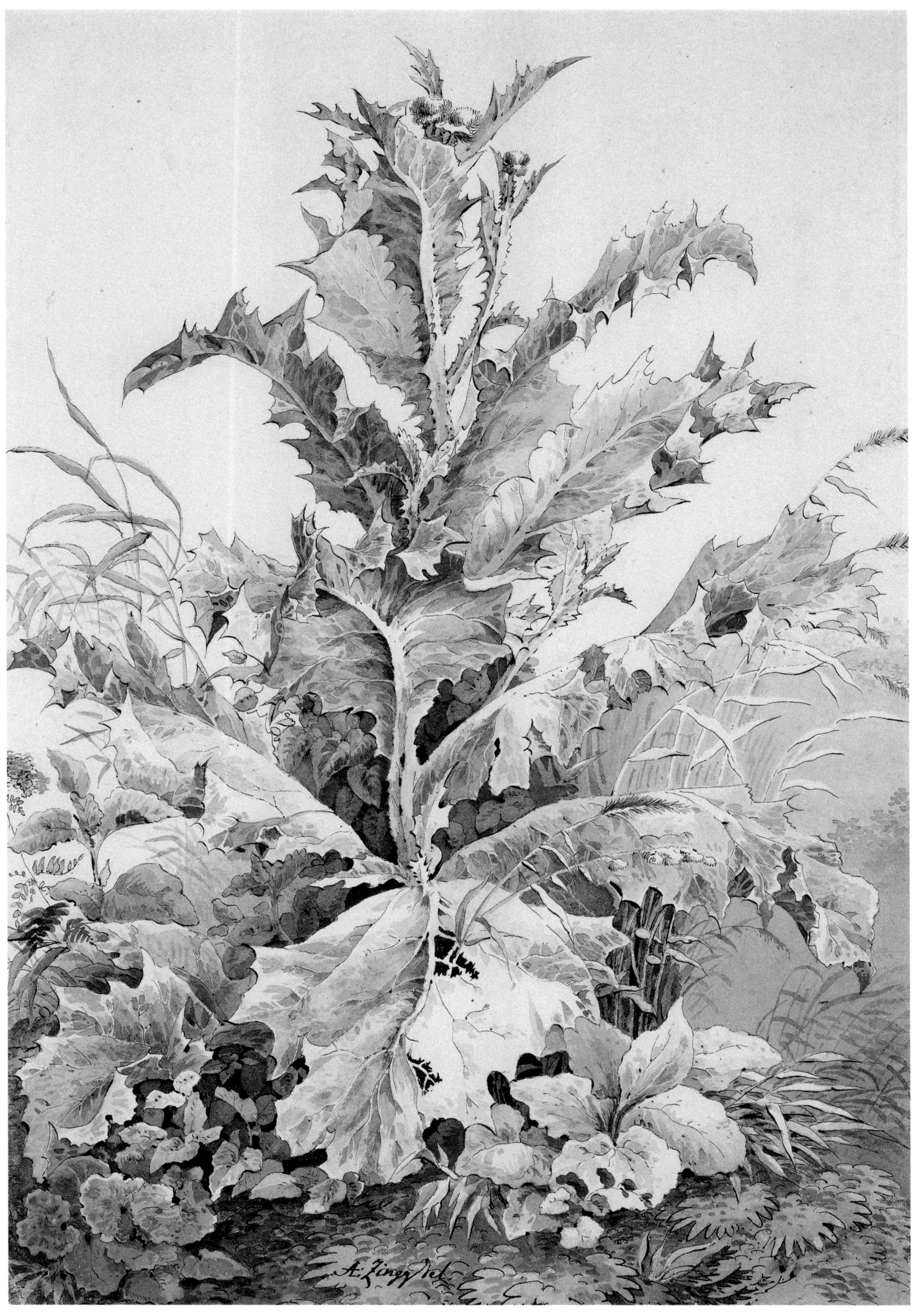

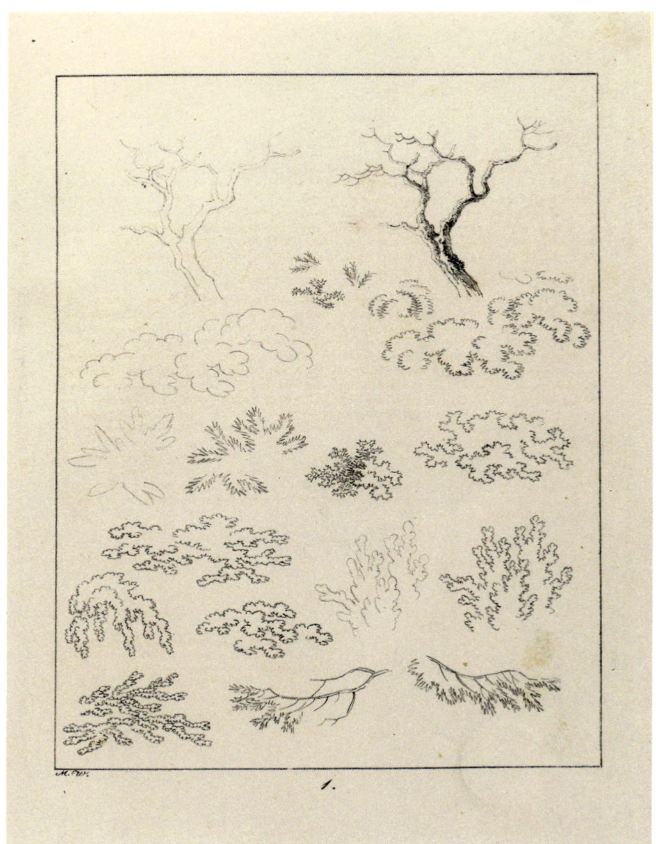 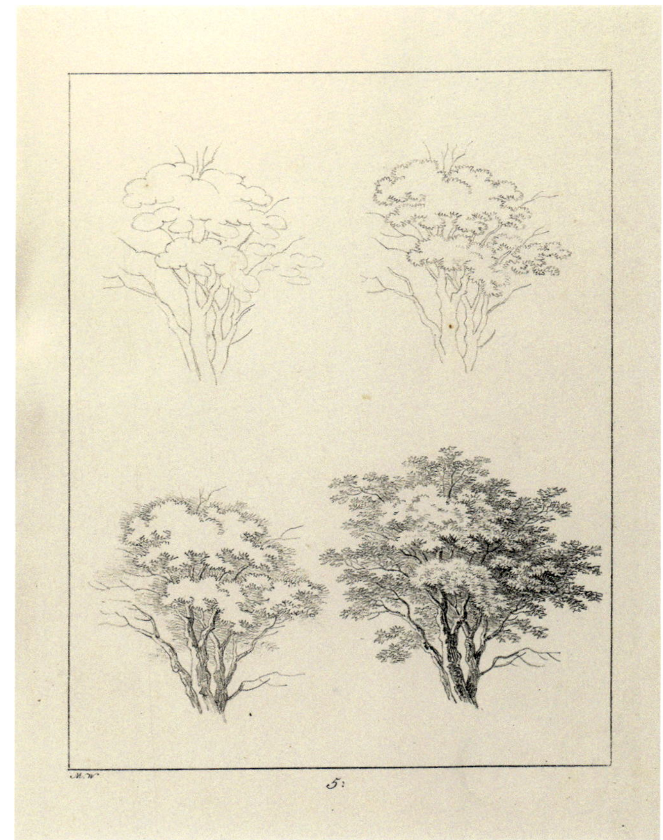

6.

Max Josef Wagenbauer
ÖXING 1775–1829 MUNICH

Model Sheets for Landscape Draftsmen (Vorlagen für Landschaft-Zeichner), 1805, published 1823

Lithographs; bound volume

Draftsman to the Bavarian court, Max Josef Wagenbauer produced this manual to teach landscape composition in southern German drawing schools. Wagenbauer's preface explains that students should begin by first copying the included models, then works by Dutch and German artists, such as Ferdinand Kobell (plate 4) and Anthonie Waterloo. Those who successfully completed this training could progress to sketching from nature. The manual's lithographed illustrations, provided by Wagenbauer, include parts of trees, landscape details, and full scenes.

The Museum's copy of the book is part of the fourth edition. A handwritten inscription on the flyleaf notes that it was given to the student awarded first prize in history drawing at the Munich Gymnasium in 1823. Graphite sketches opposite some of the illustrations indicate the manual was used, perhaps by the winner. Such additions provide insight into how landscape drawing was taught during the early nineteenth century.

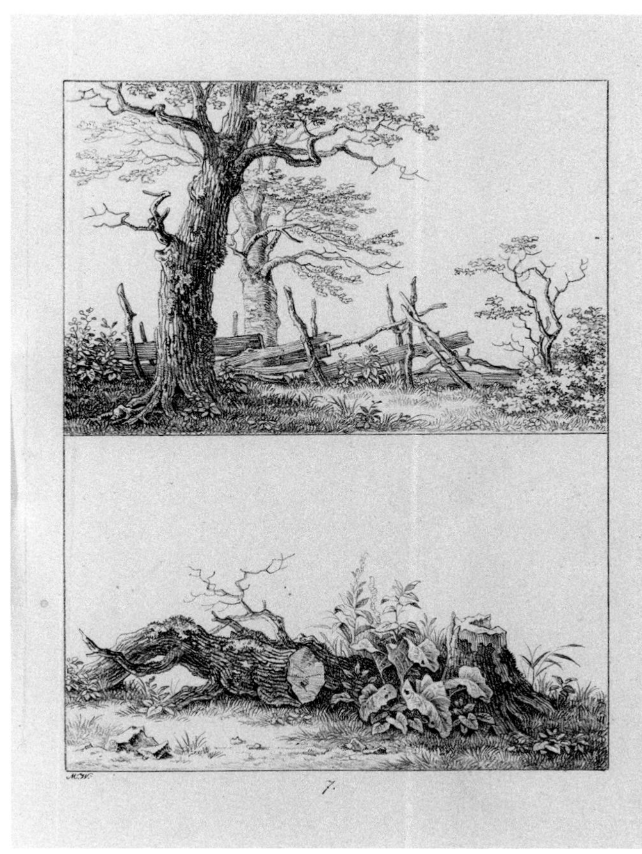

7.

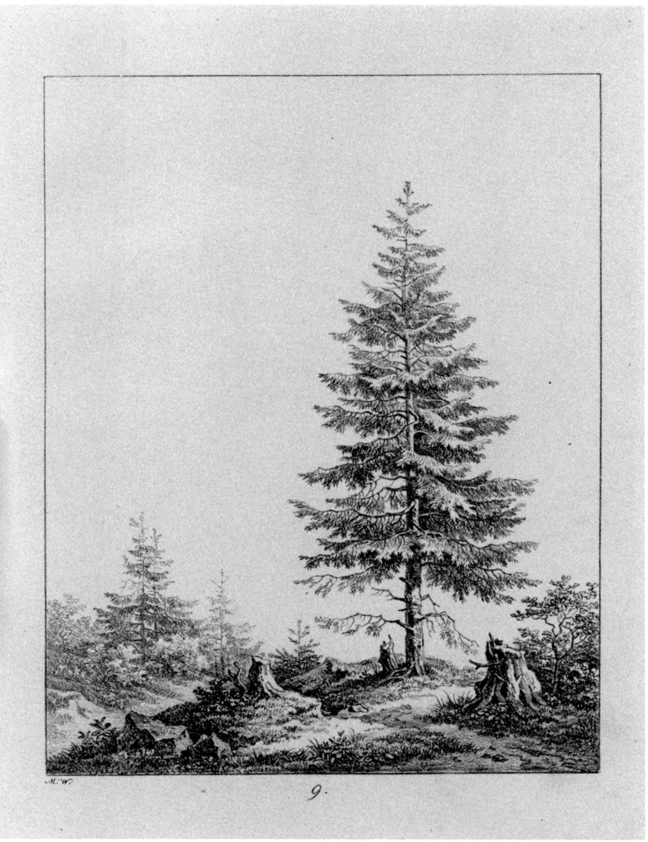

9.

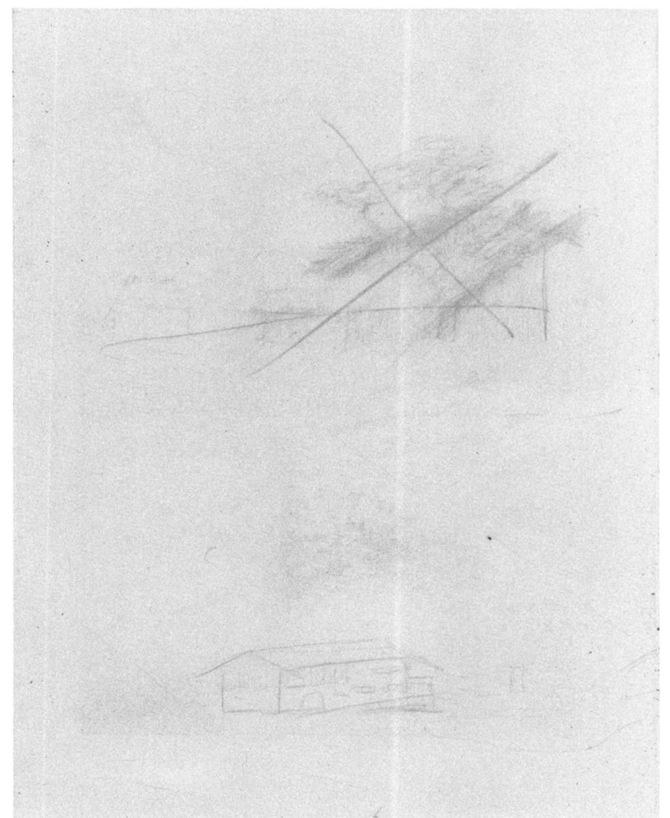

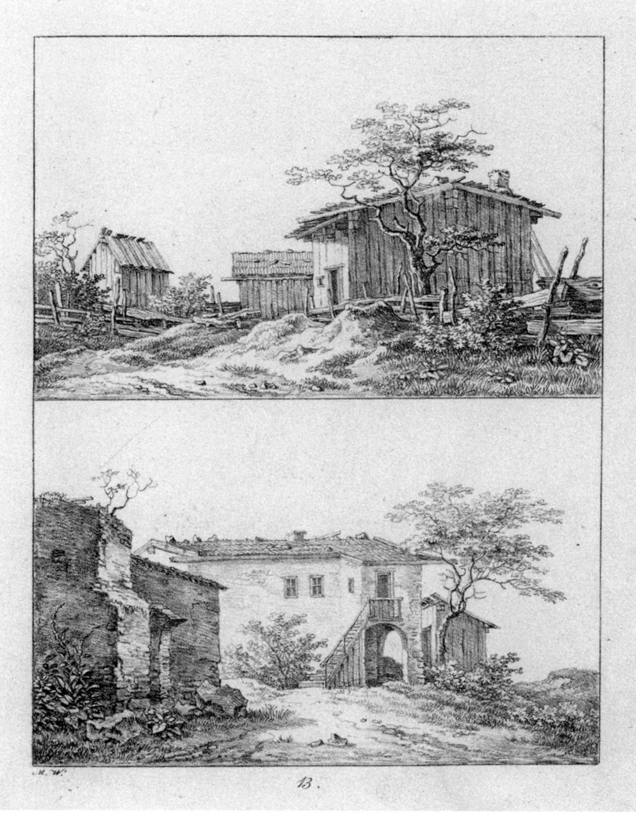

13.

Angelica Kauffman

CHUR 1741–1807 ROME

Published by John Boydell
LONDON 1719–1804 LONDON

Seated Contemplative Girl (Sitzendes nachdenkendes Mädchen), 1766, published 1780

Etching and aquatint

The figure deep in thought in Angelica Kauffman's etching embodies a melancholy strain within Romanticism. Melancholy opposed idealism, another topic of interest for the Romantics. Finding balance between such contradictions was central to the movement. Kauffman's career spanned Neoclassicism and Romanticism, and this print contains aspects of both. The figure's dress and the setting emulate classical antiquity; her expression, pose, and solitude suggest Romantic emotion and subjectivity.

Kauffman etched and printed this image in Venice in 1766, just before relocating to London. She sold her plates in anticipation of her 1781 move to Rome, and publisher John Boydell purchased many of them. He added aquatint before reprinting this work, enhancing its drama by darkening the shadows throughout the composition.

Born in Switzerland, Kauffman traveled widely and spent most of her life in London and Rome. She gained renown as a portrait painter among British nobles, and those on the Grand Tour visited her Italian studio to sit for her.

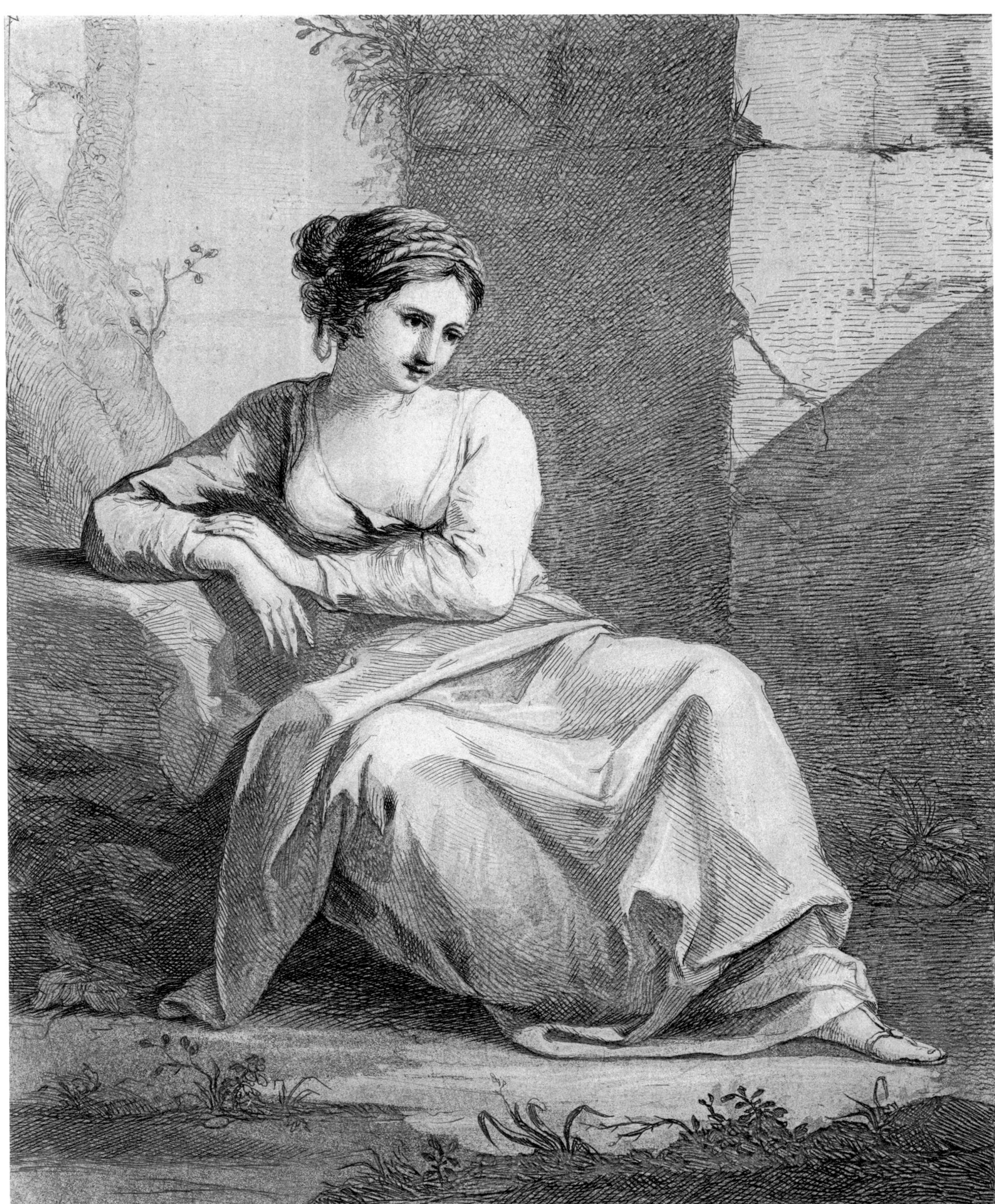

8.

Caspar David Friedrich
GREIFSWALD 1774–1840 DRESDEN

Block carved by Christian Friedrich
GREIFSWALD 1779–1843 GREIFSWALD

*Woman with a Raven at the Abyss (Die Frau mit
dem Raben am Abgrund)*, 1803

Woodcut

Woman with a Raven at the Abyss encapsulates the feelings of isolation and preoccupation with death that permeated Romanticism. The woman in Caspar David Friedrich's woodcut steadies herself, alone at the edge of a steep mountainside. Two ravens, along with fallen trees and a writhing snake near the figure's feet, symbolize death or disaster. The vast mountains in the distance emphasize the sublime power of nature, a theme Friedrich often returned to in his work. He also represented the divine in the environment by including crosses and churches in his landscapes; here, the figure's likely fall may portend her demise, while the young tree behind her suggests resurrection.

Friedrich's brother Christian carved this image into a woodblock, following Caspar David's design. Scholars have suggested that this print, along with three others made around 1803, may have been illustrations for a poem.

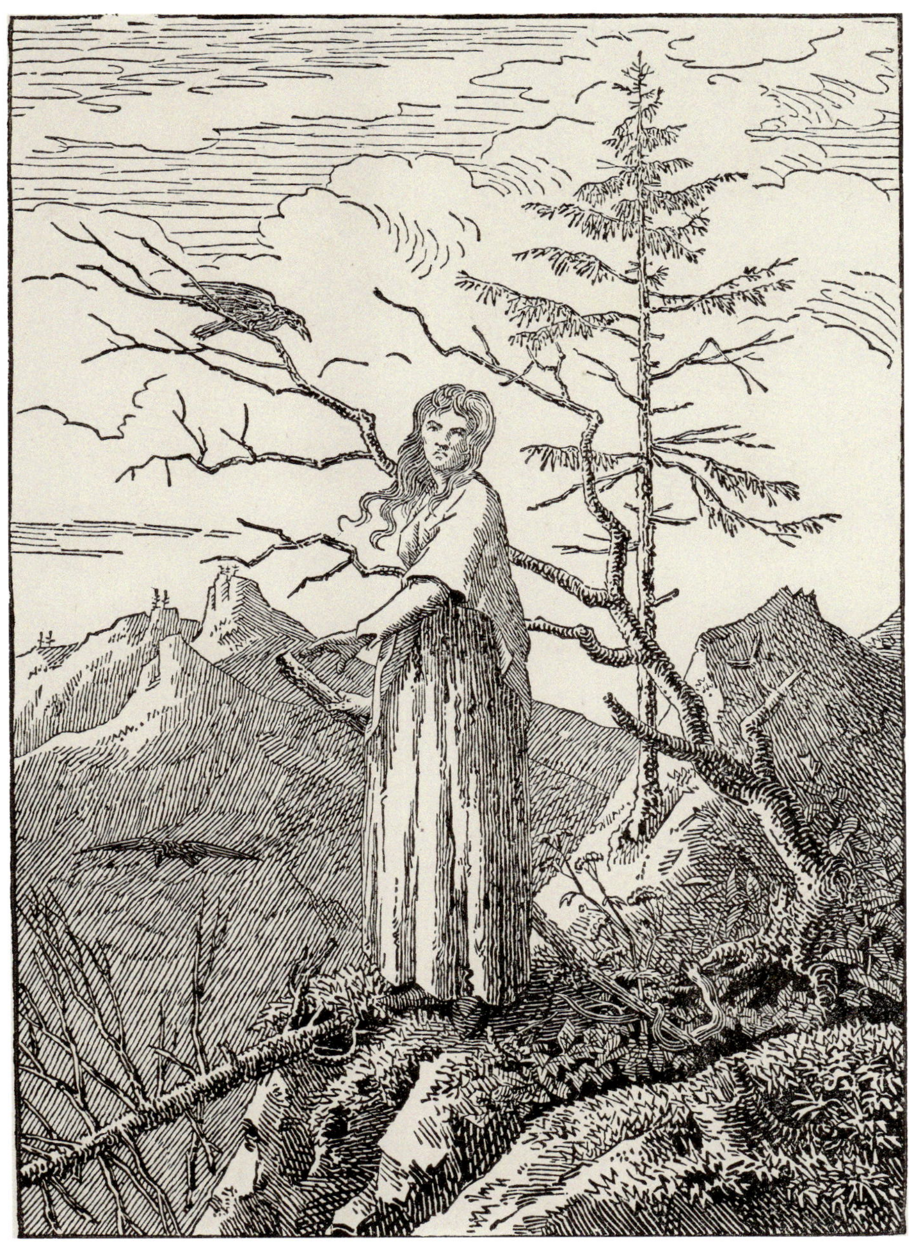

Franz Kobell

MANNHEIM 1749–1822 MUNICH

Nocturnal Landscape with Two Figures, ca. 1807

Pen and brown ink and wash over graphite
on paper

Like his older brother Ferdinand (see plate 4), Franz Kobell specialized in landscape. Here, Kobell represented nature's power by depicting the cascade of an immense waterfall. The two figures below are overwhelmed by their surroundings, minuscule and vulnerable compared to the sheer rock face to the right and the towering trees to the left. At the same time, the soft light of the moon creates a mysterious atmosphere. Romantic artists favored nocturnal scenes for their ability to elicit reverence and wonder.

Encouraged by Romantic writer Johann Wolfgang von Goethe, whom he met in 1780 during a trip to Italy, Kobell dedicated himself to drawing from nature. He created few paintings throughout his career, preferring the rapidity of pen and ink. As in this drawing, he often used washes to emphasize the effects of light.

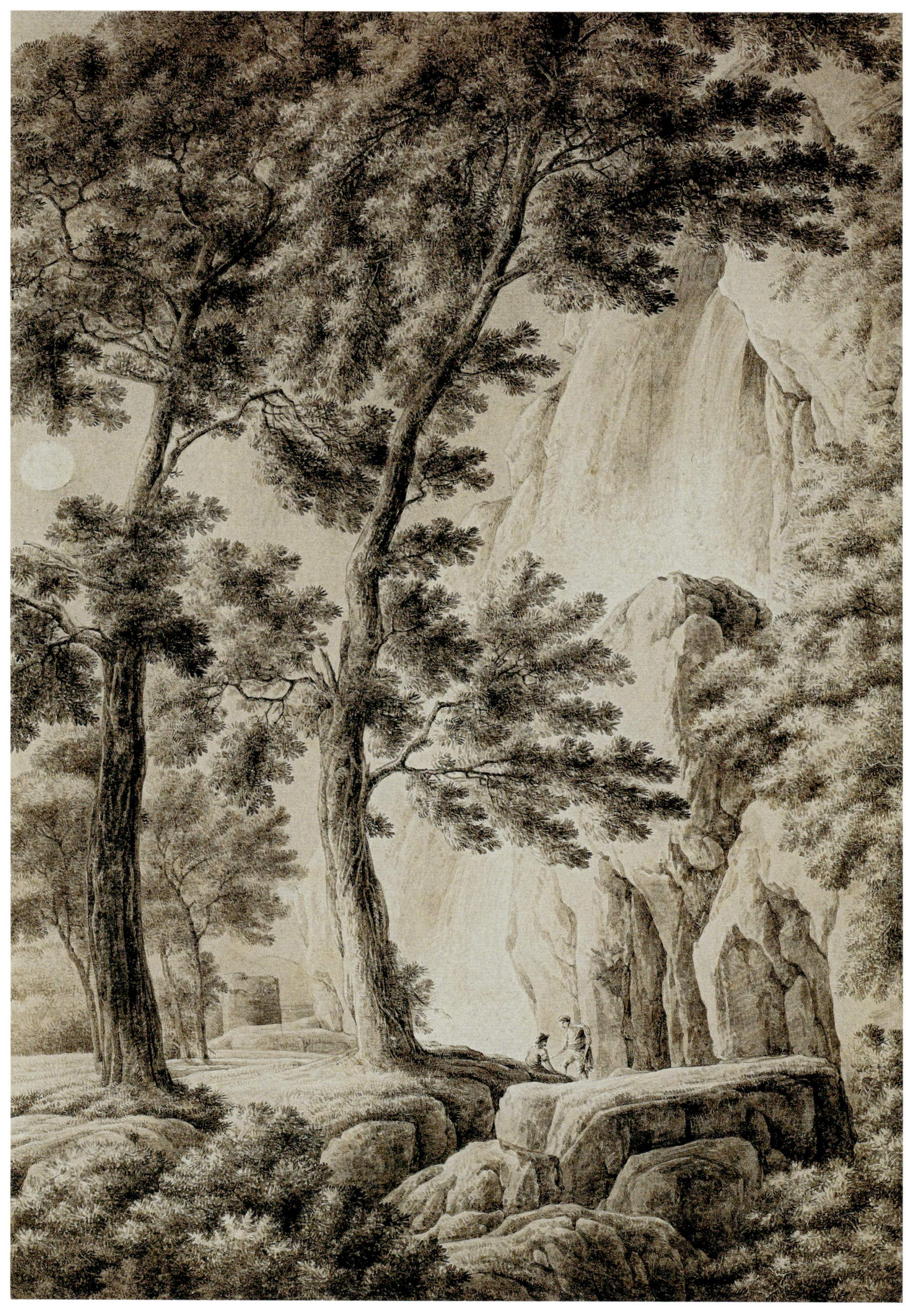

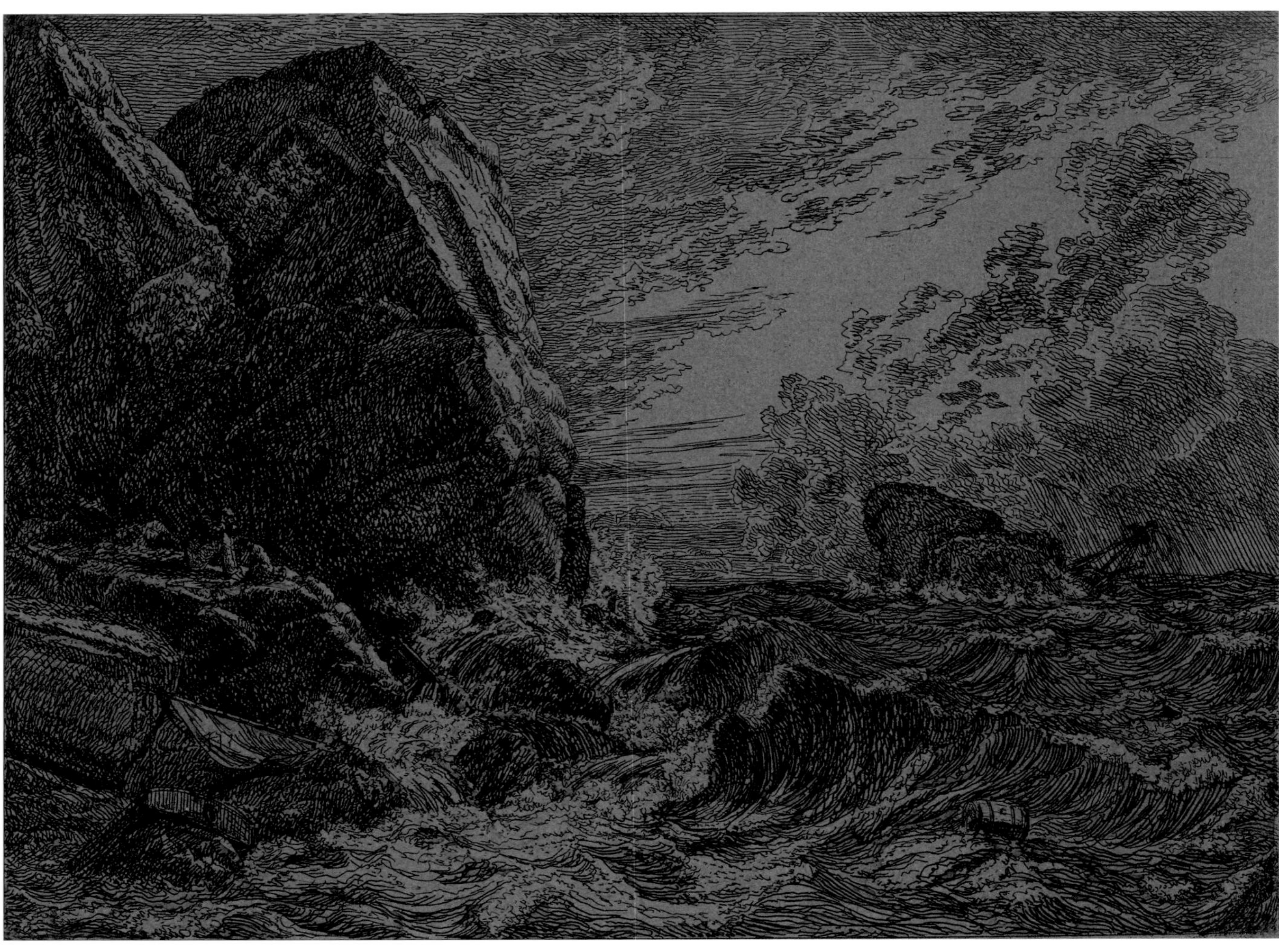

Johann Christian Clausen Dahl
BERGEN 1788–1857 DRESDEN

*Shipwreck on a Rocky Coast (Morning After a
Stormy Night) (Norwegische Seeküste während
eines Sturms)*, 1819

Etching with drypoint on brown-gray paper

This etching is based on one of Johann
Christian Clausen Dahl's earliest paintings of a shipwreck, which he completed that same year. The tragic subject
evoked a sense of awe and terror in the
face of nature that reflected the Romantic idea of the sublime.

In this print, the ship's mast and
prow rise from the water near the boul-
der at the right that presumably caused
the wreck. Dahl's frenetic line work reinforces the swirling motion of the waves,
and the brown-gray paper suggests
cloudy skies and churning water. The
small size of a surviving sailor and his
dog compared to the landscape, as well
as the destructive force of the waves,
emphasizes their helplessness.

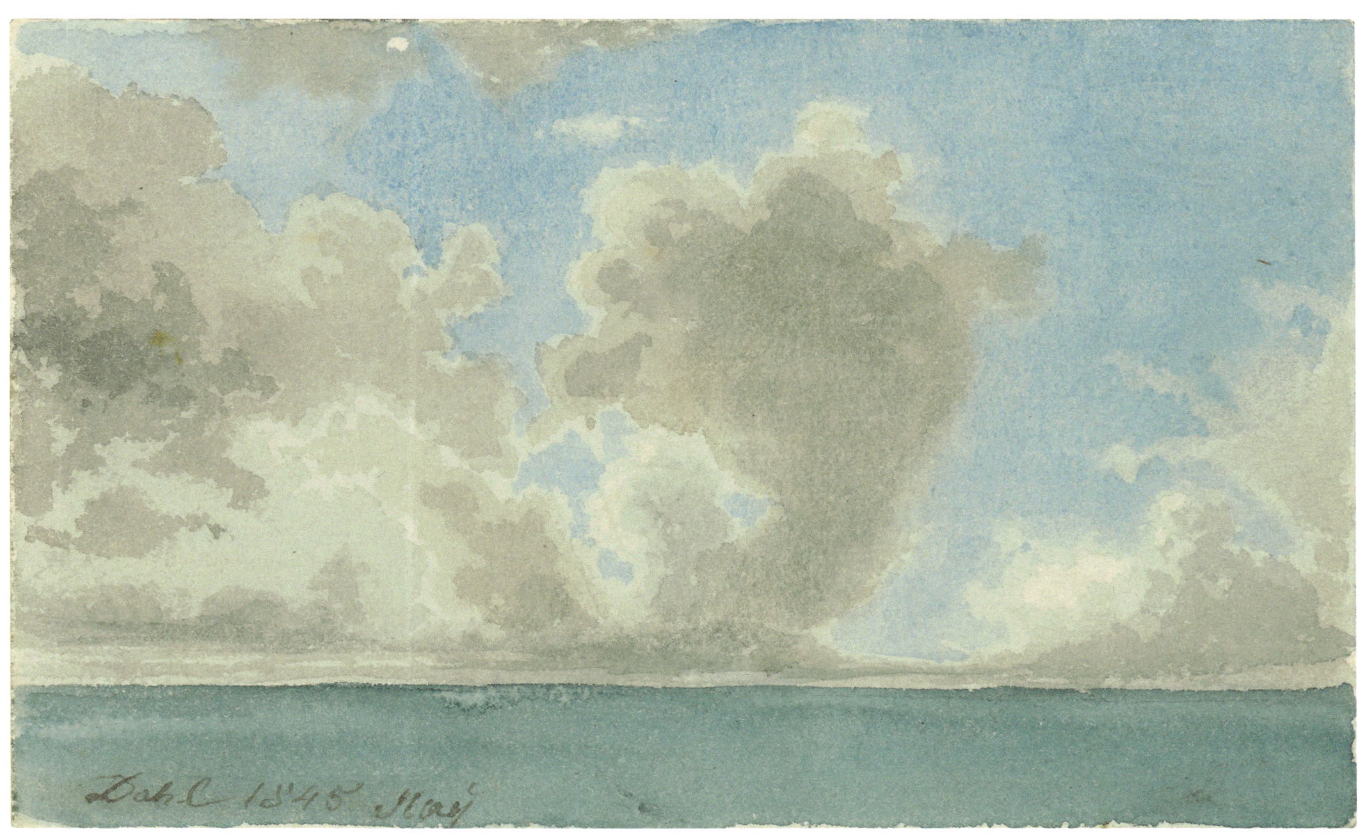

11.

Johann Christian Clausen Dahl
BERGEN 1788–1857 DRESDEN

Cumulus Clouds (Kumuluswolken), 1845

Watercolor on paper

Cloud studies became increasingly common in the late eighteenth century, and fascination surged after amateur meteorologist Luke Howard developed a cloud classification system in the 1820s. Johann Christian Clausen Dahl was among the artists who began to represent clouds as a primary subject rather than as part of a history painting or landscape. In this watercolor, Dahl used different opacities of gray to depict a billowy cumulus formation passing in front of the sun without fully obscuring its light.

Romantic artists appreciated that clouds were impermanent, continuously affected by atmospheric conditions.

Dahl generally painted quickly, which allowed him to capture the sensation of such fleeting moments in time. For some, these transformations offered a metaphor for the soul. Dahl's friend and fellow Dresden artist Carl Gustav Carus wrote, "Like drifting clouds in a constant state of change, so are the inner states of man."[4]

4. Florian Illies, "Endlich Frey!: Die Wolke als Lockerungsübung der Schweizer Malerei der Romantik," in *Im Herzen wild: Die Romantik in der Schweiz*, ed. Jonas Beyer (Munich: Prestel, 2020), 77.

Domenico Quaglio II

MUNICH 1786/7–1837 SCHWANGAU

Court in a Gothic Abbey (Gotischer Klosterhof),
1808

Crayon manner lithograph

Gothic buildings were popular in Germany during the nineteenth century, and like fellow architectural artist Karl Friedrich Schinkel (plate 13), Domenico Quaglio reveled in specific features of the style in this print. Positioning the viewer near a portal allowed him to depict ribbed vaults overhead. Across the sunny courtyard, pointed arches frame additional portals and windows, which are decorated with ornate tracery. Sculptures adorn the columns and roof and top the bell tower.

Quaglio used lithography to capture these intricate details. Invented in Munich in 1796, this printmaking process involves using a greasy crayon to create an image on limestone. Many artists adopted it in the decades following its development since it is similar to drawing on paper. Quaglio's print is a remarkably early example of the technique in practice.

Quaglio belonged to a lineage of Italian artists who specialized in designing and painting theater sets, and contemporaries recognized his talent for depicting architecture.

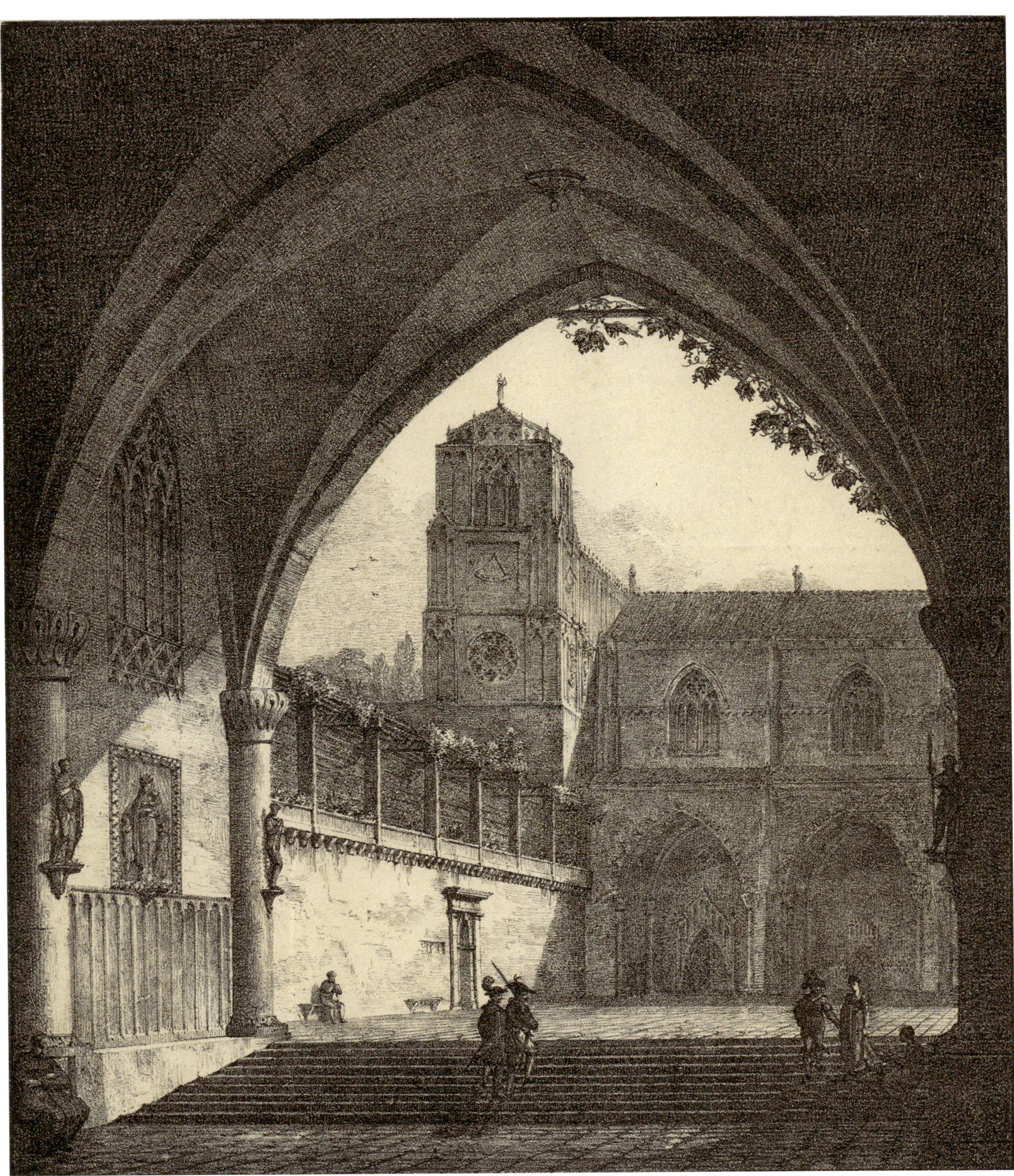

13.
Karl Friedrich Schinkel
NEURUPPIN 1781–1841 BERLIN

*Gothic Courtyard, Classical Landscape with
a Fountain, Landscape Sketch (Gotischer
Hof, Klassische Landschaft mit Brunnen,
Landschaftsskizze)*, 1800

Etching

This early etching by Karl Friedrich
Schinkel offers insight into his training
and provides a glimpse of the Gothic
subject matter he would adopt in his
later work. The three sketch-like images
on the sheet depict the pointed arches of
a Gothic courtyard, the clean symmetry
of a classical fountain and colonnade,
and wild foliage. At the time, Schinkel
was studying with architect Friedrich
Gilly and his father, David, and lived
in their home. Schinkel and Friedrich
became close friends, and Schinkel often
copied the younger Gilly's drawings.

The motifs Schinkel chose were likely
based on or inspired by sketches Gilly
made while traveling across England,
France, and Germany in 1797 and 1798.
Gilly died of tuberculosis at the age of
28 in 1800, the year Schinkel made this
etching, and the artist may have been
thinking about his departed friend and
his teachings.

This print is incredibly rare; the only
other known impression is in the collection of the Herzog Anton Ulrich
Museum in Braunschweig.

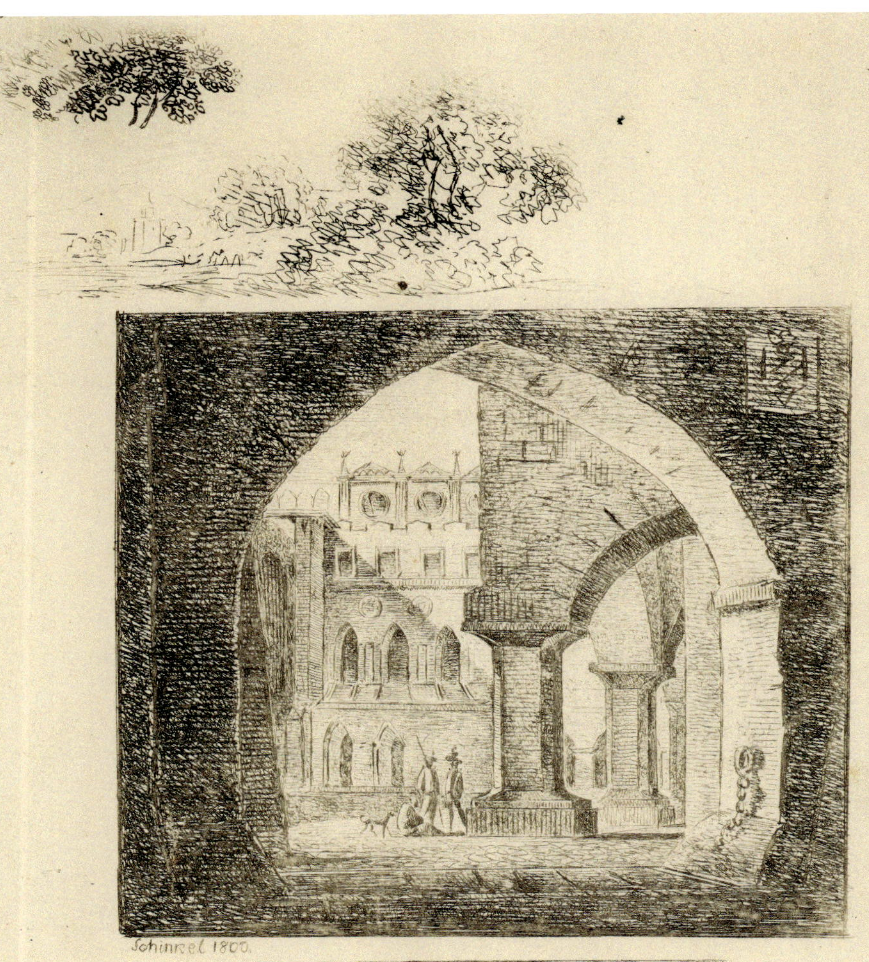

Schinkel 1800.

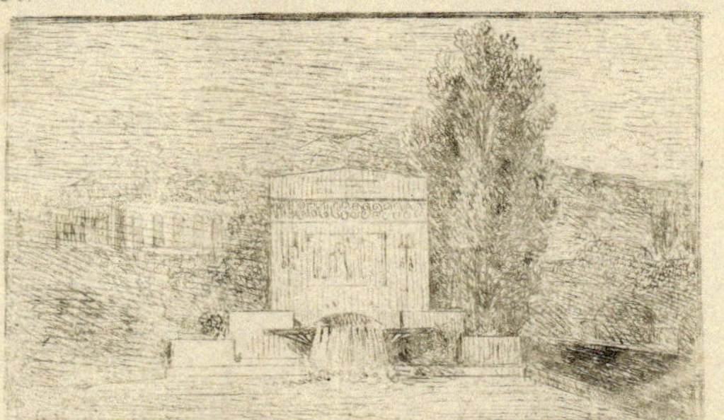

14.

Karl Friedrich Schinkel

NEURUPPIN 1781–1841 BERLIN

A Gothic Cathedral Behind Trees, 1810/15

Pen and gray ink and watercolor over graphite on paper

Architect and artist Karl Friedrich Schinkel represented the divine and his desire for national renewal by depicting cathedrals in the woods. Schinkel served as head of artistic matters and then chief building inspector in Berlin. Unable to work on building commissions during the Napoleonic Wars (1803–15), he began to make drawings, paintings, and prints of imagined Gothic churches. In this drawing, he delineated the structure's arches, buttresses, spires, and windows in immaculate detail. At the time, many Germans adopted medieval architecture as a symbol of their history, and Schinkel believed it represented Germany's liberation from French rule. Contemporaries also noted Schinkel's talent for capturing the spiritual aspects of nature. Here, the loosely rendered trees and stream evoke life coursing through the rustling leaves and rushing water. Through a national style of architecture rooted in the forest, Schinkel's drawing expresses his hope for the future.

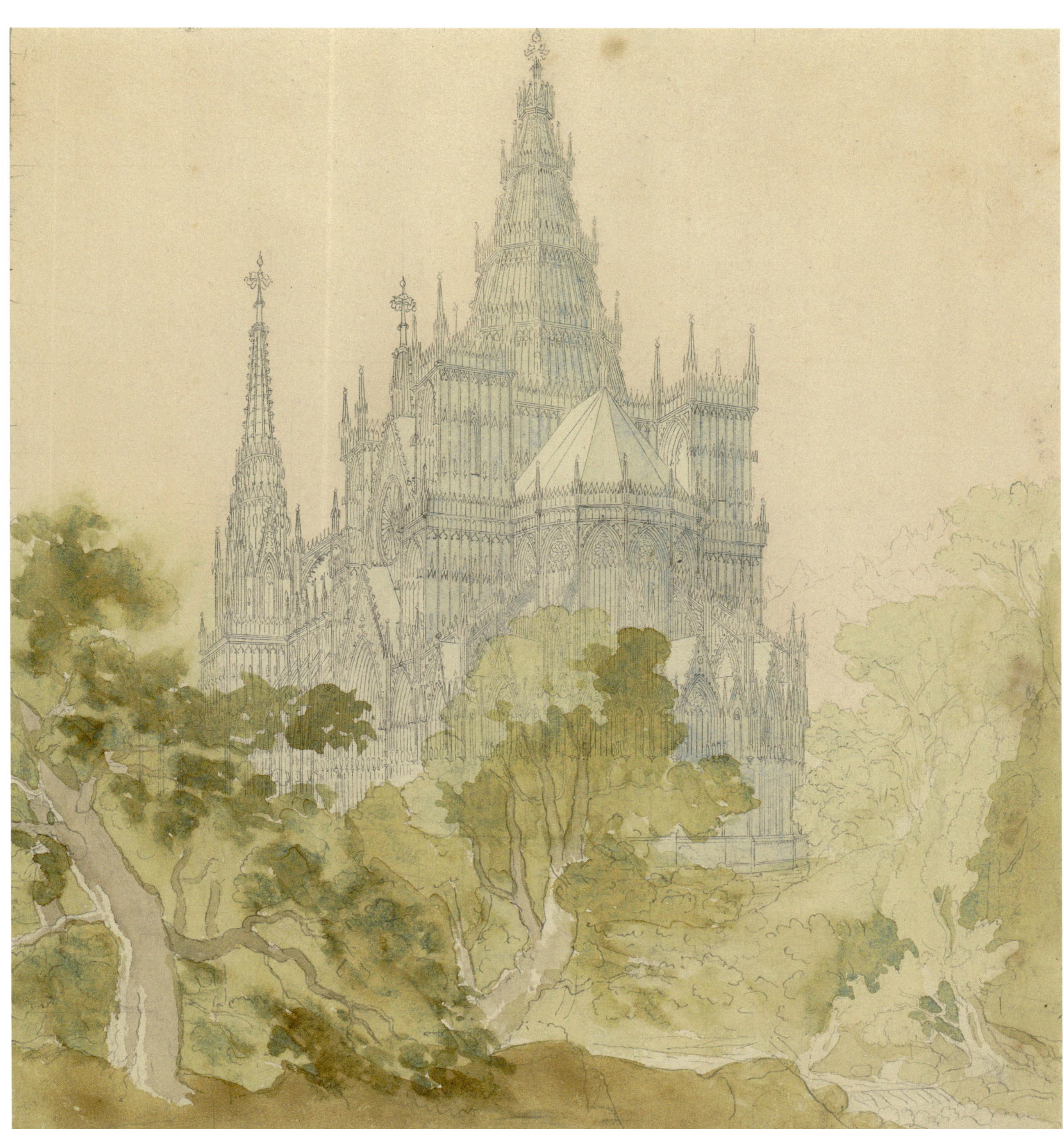

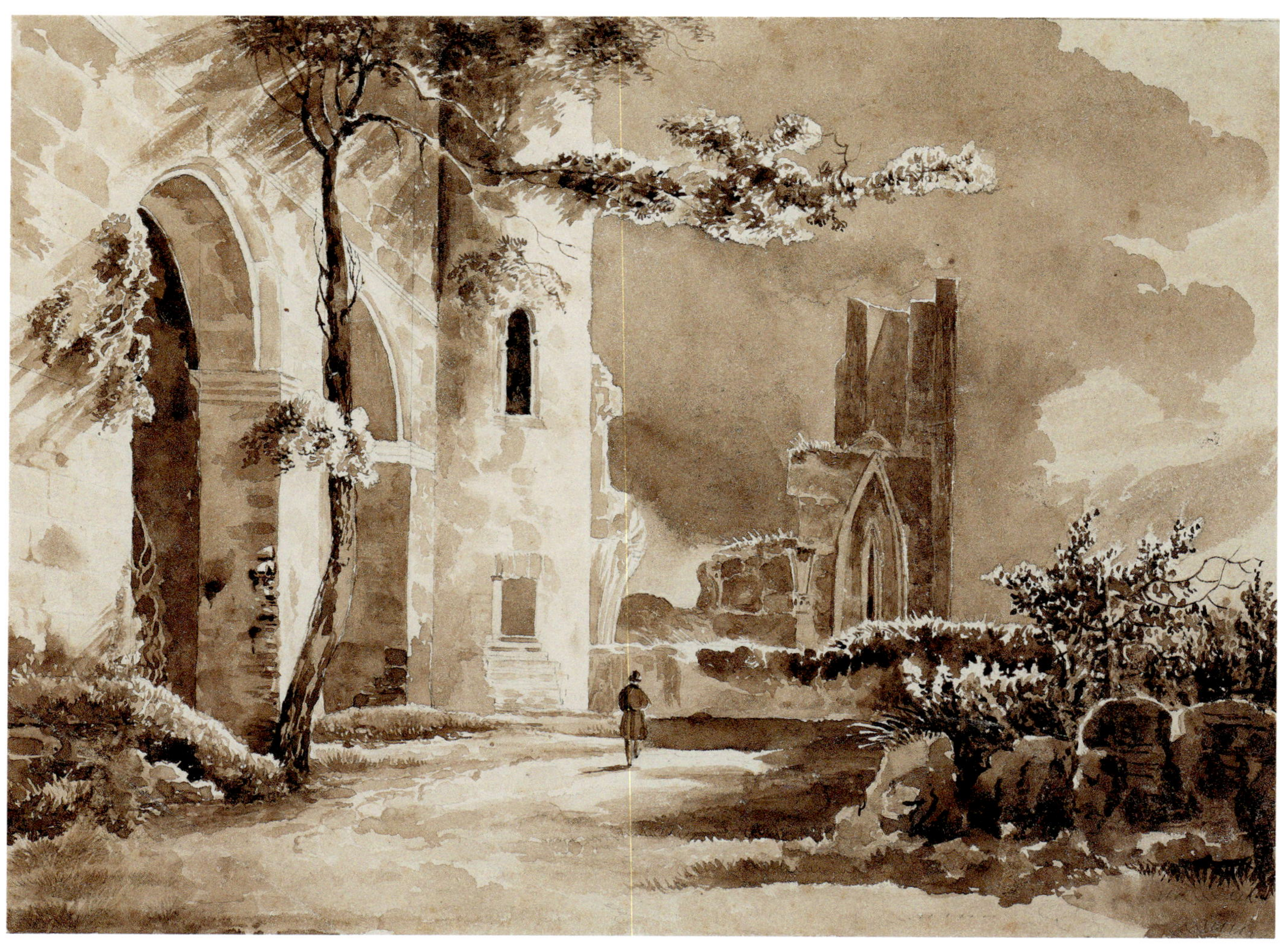

Carl Blechen

*Figure Amidst the Ruins of a Gothic Abbey
(Figur bei gotischer Ruine)*, ca. 1825

Pen and sepia ink and wash over graphite
on paper

A solitary figure in a top hat, perhaps a self-portrait of artist Carl Blechen, walks past the soaring walls of a building toward a ruin. The structure's remaining pointed arch is characteristic of Gothic architecture, which Germans understood to be a symbol of their shared cultural history. Blechen drew this scene early in his artistic career, shortly after staying in Dresden for a few months. There, he met Johann Christian Clausen Dahl and Caspar David Friedrich, both of whom depicted ruins in their work.

Blechen, too, made several paintings of this subject. For these artists, the stone remains of once-magnificent buildings were sites of longing, a prominent quality of Romanticism. They evoked a desire for the fragments to become whole and a yearning to commune with a lost past. By including the figure in contemporary clothing, Blechen further highlighted the contradiction between his present moment and the medieval grounds represented in this drawing.

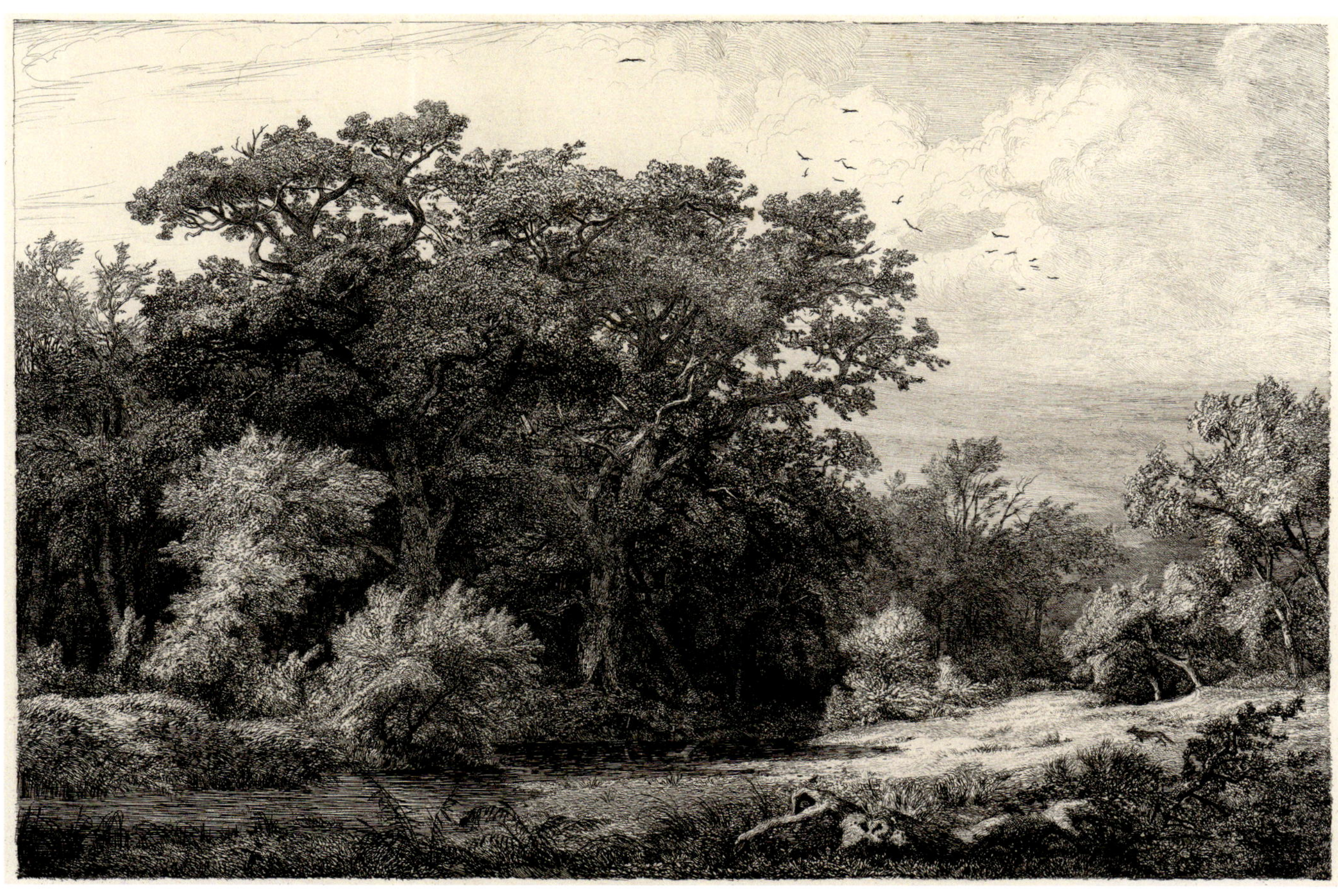

16.

Johann Wilhelm Schirmer
JÜLICH 1807–1863 KARLSRUHE

The Forest with a Prowling Fox (Der Wald mit dem schleichenden Fuchs), ca. 1829

Etching, printed chine collé

In a sweeping forest glade, light plays over the expanse of grass as birds circle near the treetops overhead. Below, a fox slinks toward a pond, perhaps in search of its next meal. Such carefully observed details and realistic effects of light became characteristic of the Düsseldorf school of painting, whose style Johann Wilhelm Schirmer helped establish.

Schirmer entered the Düsseldorf Art Academy in 1825, where he became friends with Carl Friedrich Lessing (see plate 55). Together, they founded the Society of Landscape Painting in 1827. Members of the society critiqued each other's compositions, which were based on direct study of nature. Schirmer went on to teach the inaugural landscape painting class at the academy in 1829, and he helped the school become a respected destination for training in the genre.

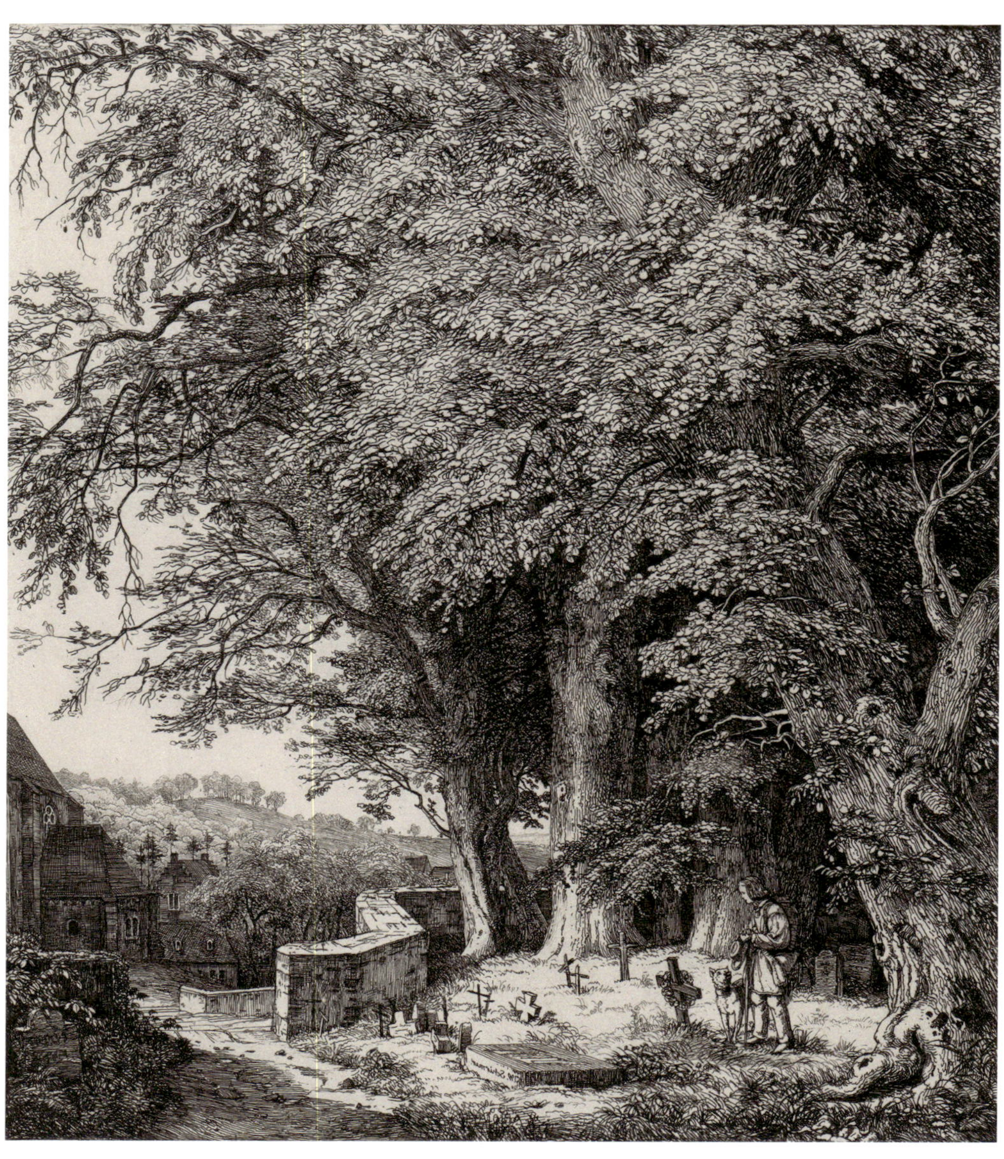

17.

Johann Wilhelm Schirmer
JÜLICH 1807–1863 KARLSRUHE

Churchyard (Der Kirchhof), ca. 1838

Etching, printed chine collé

18.

Johann Wilhelm Schirmer
JÜLICH 1807–1863 KARLSRUHE

The Hunter's Departure from the Forest (Der Jäger Abschied vom Wald), ca. 1843

Etching, printed chine collé

In addition to their activities as teachers and landscape painters, Johann Wilhelm Schirmer and others affiliated with the Düsseldorf Art Academy were involved with literature, music, and theater. Schirmer etched these two prints for books of poems and songs. *Churchyard* illustrates "Under the Dark Linden Trees" (1838) by artist Robert Reinick. The song narrates a young man's return to the linden grove where he used to meet his beloved. He expects to find her waiting there, but instead, he comes upon a graveyard and a marker bearing her name. Schirmer captured the devastation of this unexpected loss, depicting a stricken figure with hat in hand staring down at a cross.

The Hunter's Departure from the Forest is based on Joseph von Eichendorff's poem "The Hunter's Farewell" (1810), which expresses reverence for the beauty and national significance of the woods. In Schirmer's print, two deer look on as a group of hunters vanishes into the distance. In the verses, the hunters praise God for the forest and promise to honor it after they leave.

These etchings are the first state (version) of each print; the titles of the poems were printed below the images when they were published.

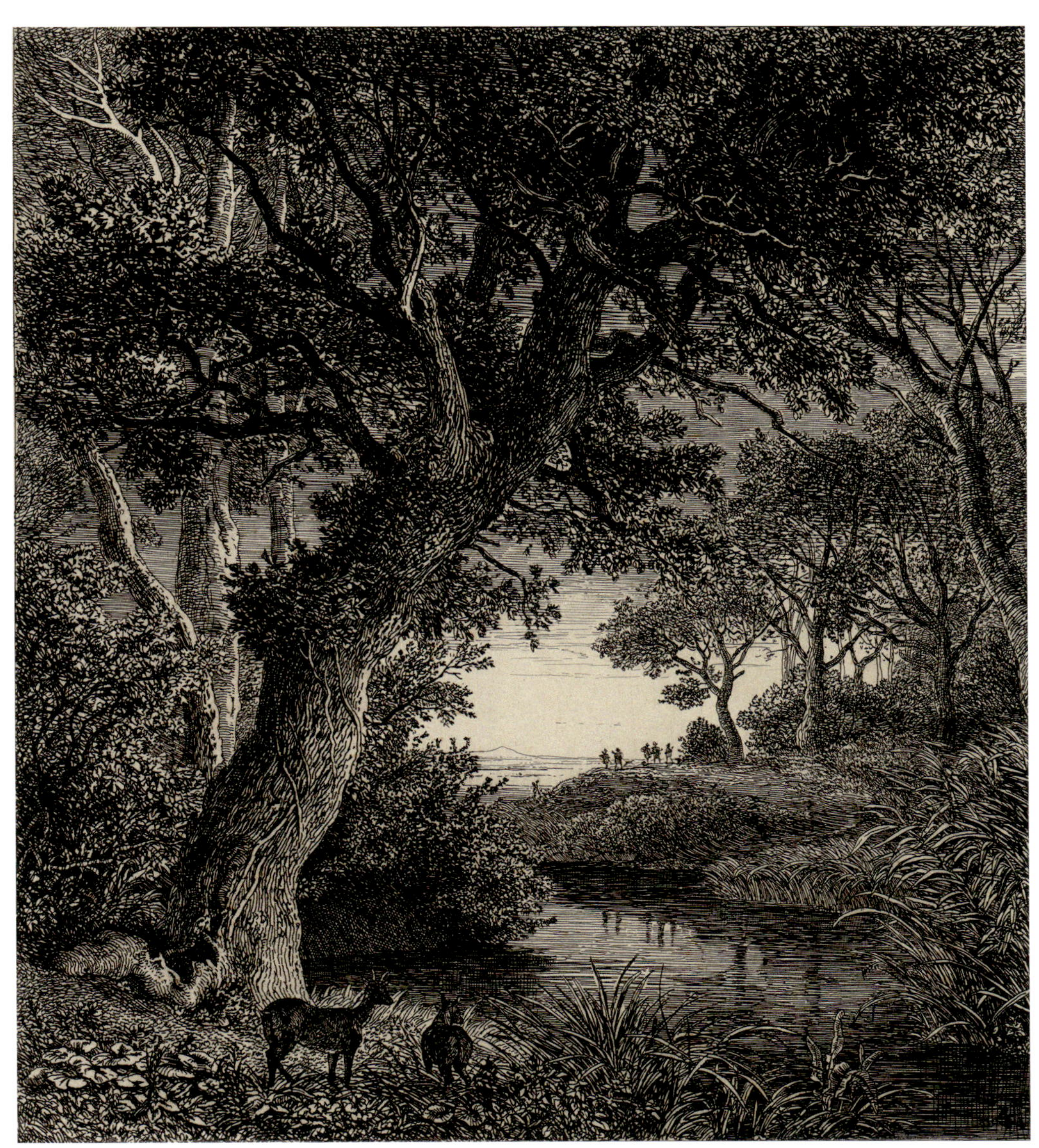

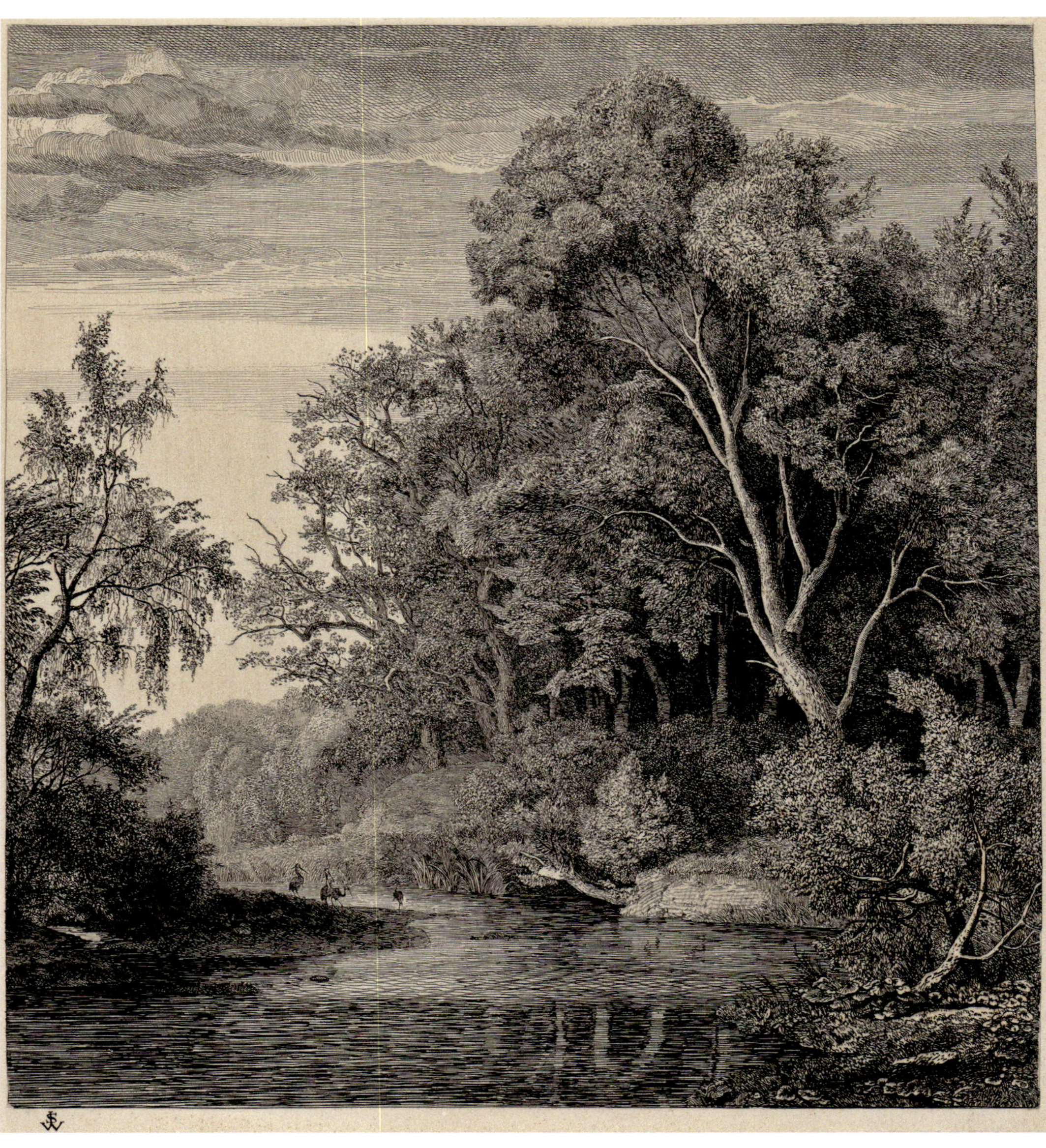

19.

Johann Wilhelm Schirmer
JÜLICH 1807–1863 KARLSRUHE

The Forest Brook with Storks (Der Waldsturm mit den Störchen), 1845

Etching with touches of graphite

20.

Johann Wilhelm Schirmer
JÜLICH 1807–1863 KARLSRUHE

The Forest Brook with Storks (Der Waldsturm mit den Störchen), 1845

Etching, printed chine collé

This pair of etchings depicts a bend in a river where four storks wade in shallow water. A willow grows from the damp soil at the left, and the deep forest at the right suggests impenetrable wilderness. The print on the left is a proof, and pencil marks reveal changes the artist wanted to make before pulling another impression. Johann Wilhelm Schirmer was known for creating rhythm in his work through areas of light and shadow, and he was seemingly correcting parts of the composition that looked too bright. The riverbank at the center, for example, originally had no printed lines, but Schirmer drew them in on the proof. The finished print is darker overall; in addition to adding new marks, he may have left previously etched lines exposed when he submerged the copper printing plate in acid. This would have created deeper grooves that held more ink.

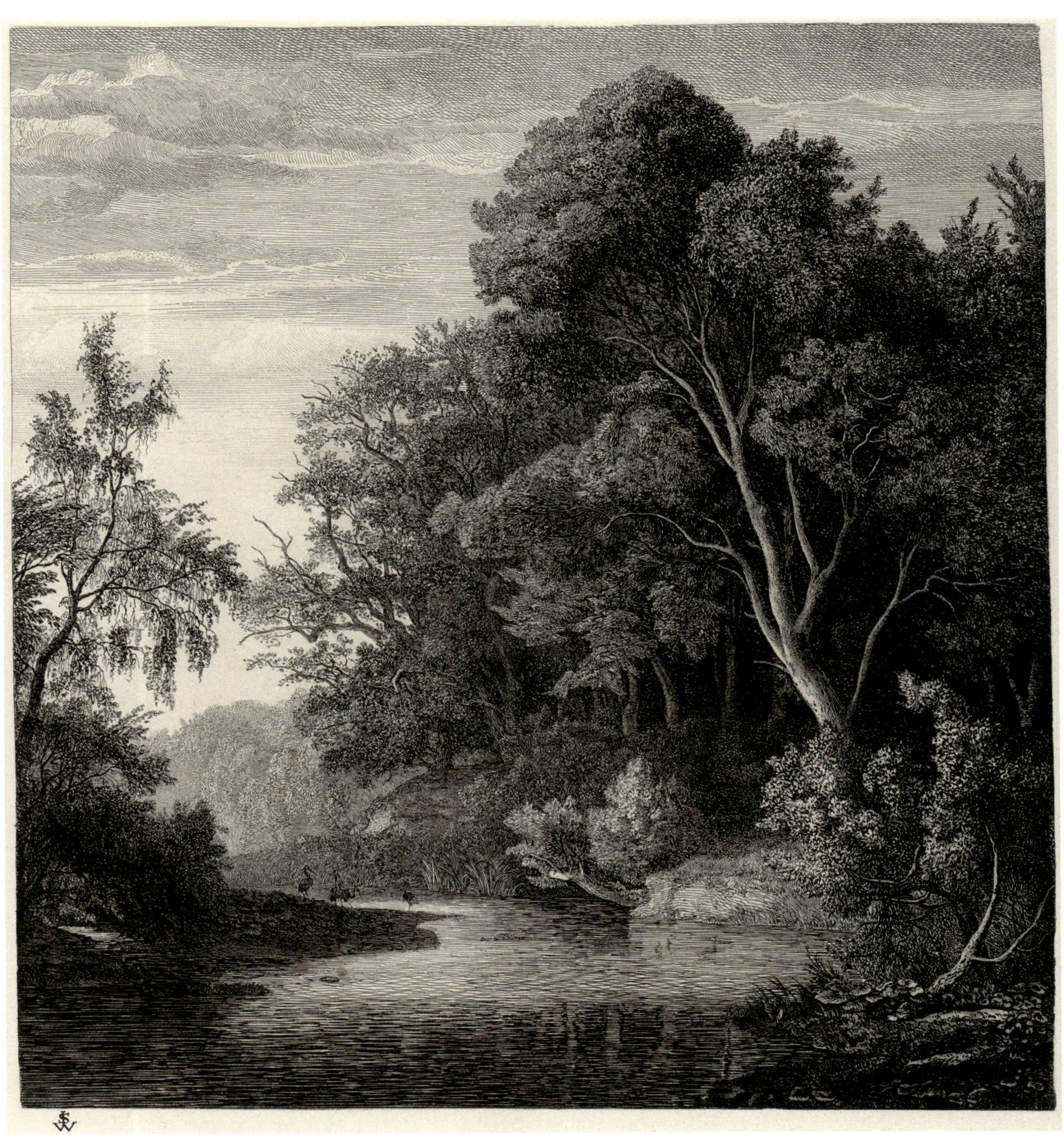

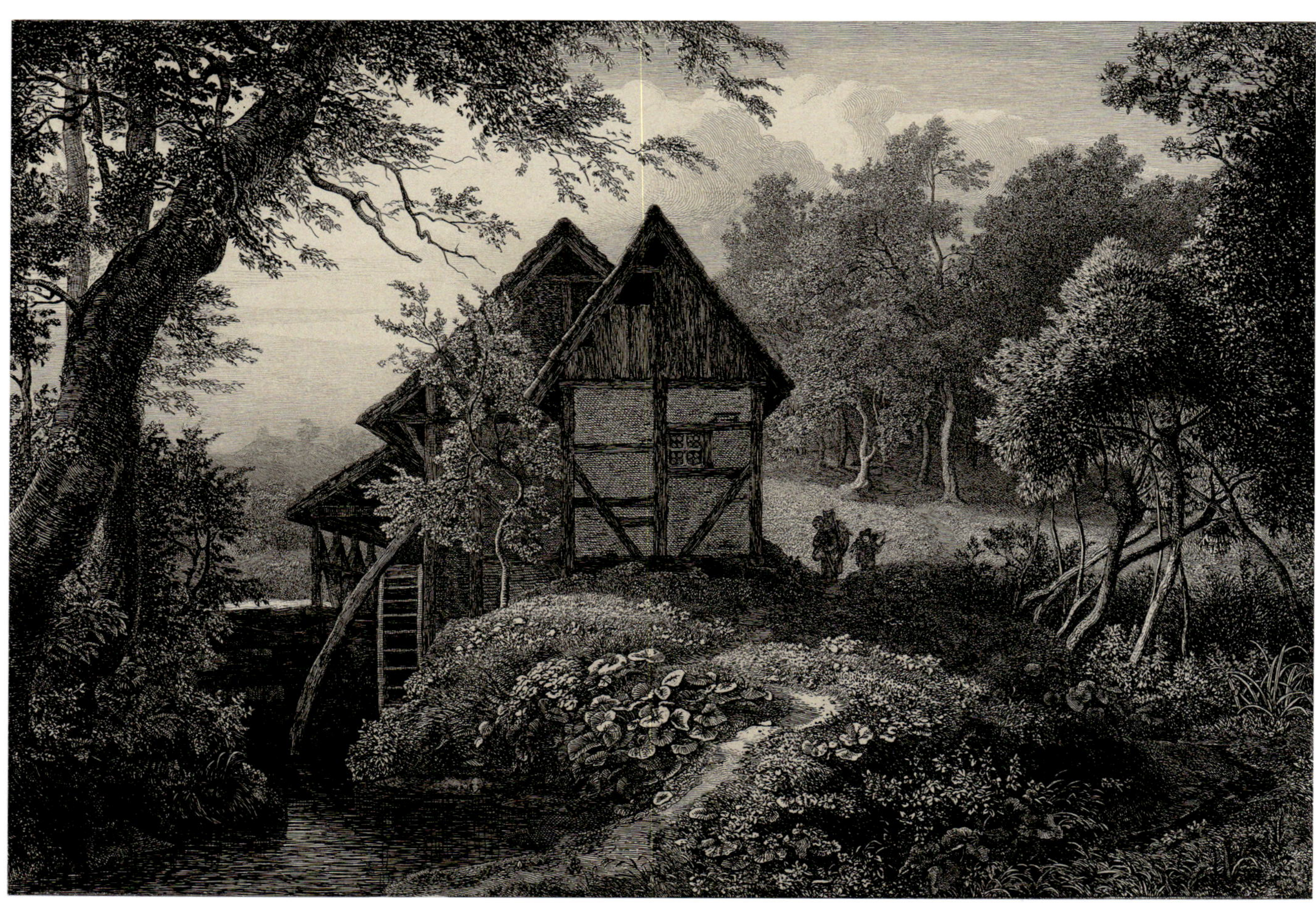

21.

Johann Wilhelm Schirmer
JÜLICH 1807–1863 KARLSRUHE

The Mill near a Forest (Die Mühle am Wald),
ca. 1845

Etching, printed chine collé

The water mill featured at the center of Johann Wilhelm Schirmer's etching suggests that he was familiar with sixteenth- and seventeenth-century Dutch and German printmakers. These artists were among the first to pursue landscape as an independent subject, and they sometimes included water wheels in their depictions of rivers. Here, the wooden structure sits next to a narrow dirt path in a clearing. Two figures approach, carrying branches they have gathered from the forest behind them. Schirmer etched the vegetation and the texture of the mill's wooden slats in meticulous detail, adding a sense of veracity to the scene. By representing a rustic setting and long-standing technology, Schirmer celebrated the past and rural ways of life.

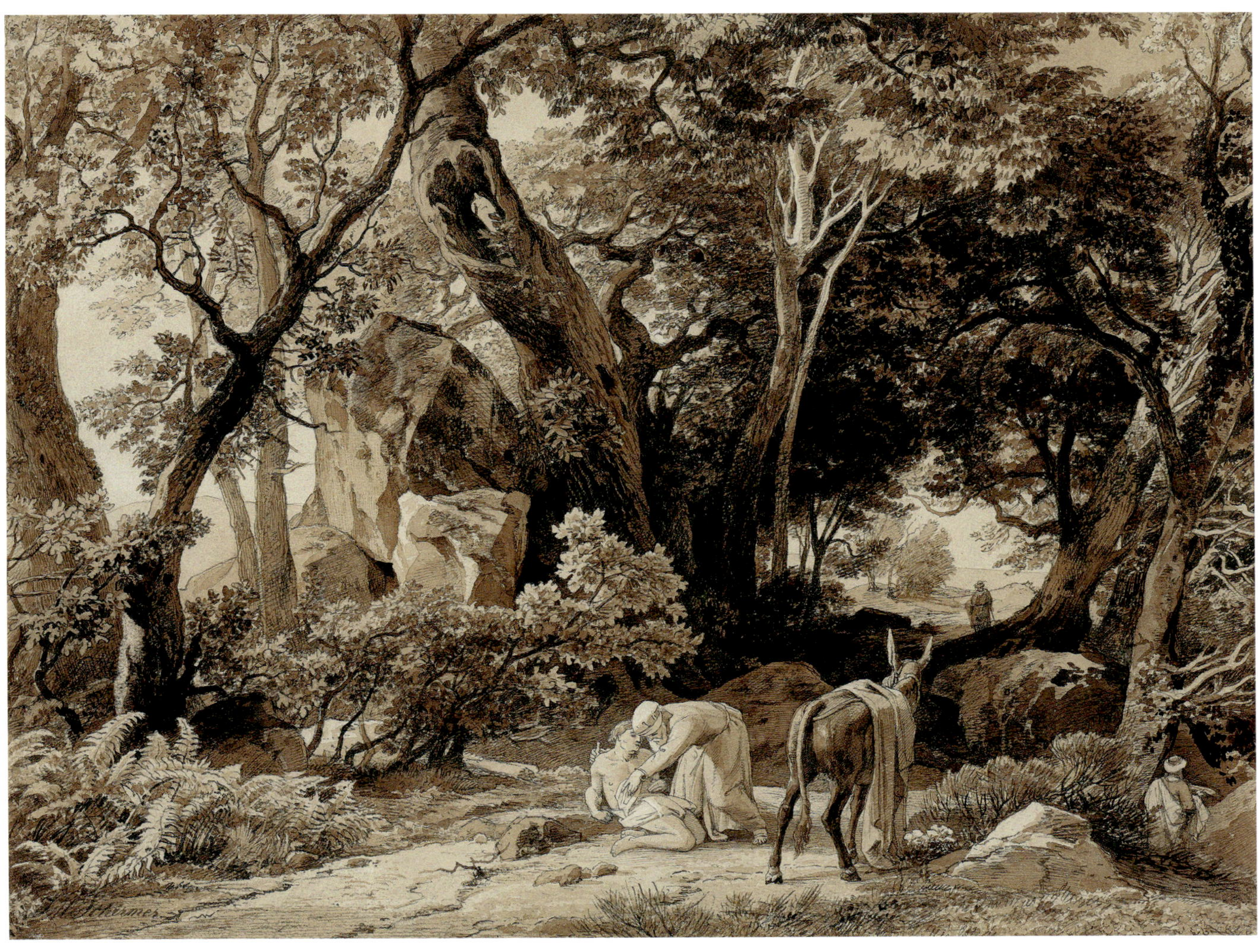

22.

Johann Wilhelm Schirmer

Forest Landscape with the Good Samaritan,
1856–57

Pen and ink with brown wash and black
chalk on paper

In 1856, Johann Wilhelm Schirmer
began a cycle of four paintings depicting the biblical story of the Good
Samaritan. In the parable, a traveler is
robbed, beaten, and left by the road.
Two passersby ignore him, but the third,
a Samaritan, stops to help. After com-
pleting the cycle, Schirmer created additional versions of it in different media
and sizes. This drawing, the third image
in the cycle's narrative, represents the
Samaritan tending to the traveler's
wounds. The massive boulders and trees
surrounding them reflect the majesty
of the forest, but they also intensify the
perilousness of the situation.

The biblical subject and setting had
deep personal significance for Schirmer.
He grew up in a devout family and, as
he explained, "For a long time, I have
striven to give my beloved biblical stories a fitting form through the landscape . . . I have finally dared, through
years of striving and studying this sacred
material, to bear a modest testimony."[5]

5. Andreas Andresen, *Die deutschen Maler-
Radirer (Peintres-Graveurs) des neunzehnten
Jahrhunderts, nach ihren Leben und Werken*
(Leipzig: Rudolph Weigel, 1867), II: 319.

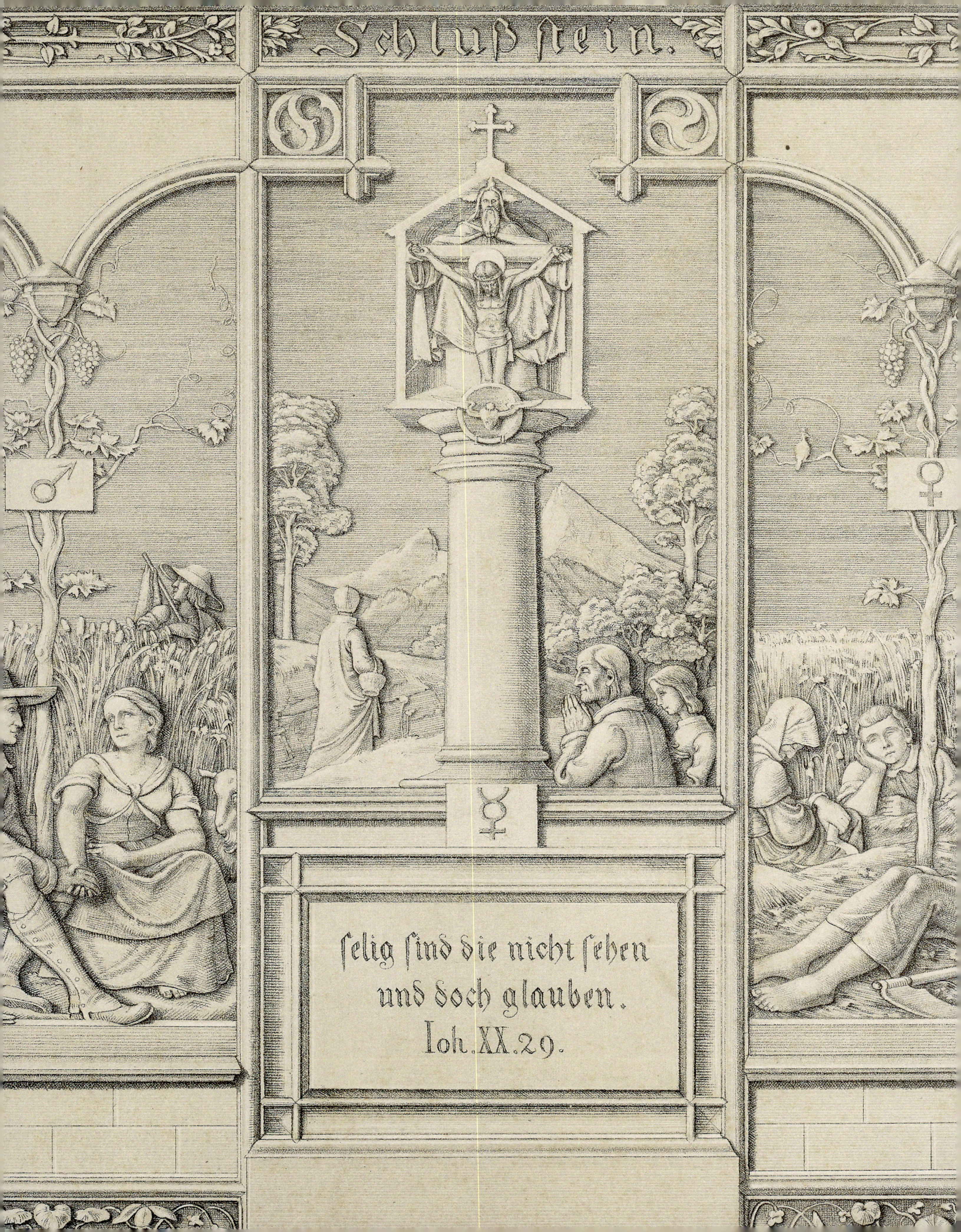
Schluß stein.
selig sind die nicht sehen
und doch glauben.
Joh. XX. 29.

"I AM CONVINCED," Julius Schnorr von Carolsfeld declared in 1860, "that the fine arts have the vocation and the means to participate in the education and formation of Man."[1] Made in the introduction to his *Bible in Pictures* (fig. 1), the passionate statement summarized the mindset of the secessionist artist collective he had joined almost half a century earlier: the Lukasbund (Brotherhood of St. Luke). Founded in Vienna in 1809, the fraternity had banded together to achieve nothing less than a rebirth of contemporary art in the name of Christ and the spirit of the old masters. The tiny coterie of six rebellious art students succeeded against all odds. Once relocated to Rome in 1810, the group quickly grew, forming the nucleus of an international movement of artists later known as the Nazarenes. Fired up by missionary zeal, its members believed in the unity of artistic production, spiritual reawakening, and social regeneration. Art, they argued, should again be embedded in the fabric of society as it once was in the Middle Ages and take its rightful place as the teacher of the people, from the pages of picture Bibles and, as Peter von Cornelius put it in 1814, "from the walls of our high cathedrals, our peaceful chapels and solitary cloisters, from our town halls and warehouses and markets."[2] Although painting was, and would always remain, central to the Nazarenes' production, they wanted to reach beyond the confines of aristocratic patronage and the bourgeois world of the Salon and art unions. This desire took them in two strikingly different directions: the monumentality of fresco painting and the intimacy of the printed page.

If the artists hailed mural decoration as public art, marked by its resistance to circulation and a capitalist market economy, they treasured printed matter for exactly the opposite reason: its capacity to supply affordable images in large quantities for mass dissemination. Unconcerned with the paradox of this twofold orientation, they pursued mural dreams and paper prayers in synchrony. The ensuing relationship between singular original and high-quality multiples was complex, and in more than one case, the Nazarenes' most aspirational autonomous projects indeed only came to fruition in print. Regardless, this relationship, vital to their cause, fostered innovative experiments in both arenas, not least in matters of technique and materiality.

The Lukasbund's first collaborative mural project is a powerful case in point. Originally, their patron, Jakob Ludwig Salomon Bartholdy, had imagined decorative ornamentation for his main living quarters in Rome, maybe a mixture of arabesques and landscapes. The brotherhood, however, envisioned an ambitious biblical cycle, and when they proposed the Old Testament story of Joseph, the Prussian envoy agreed. In the spring of 1816, he officially hired the young artists, and their success affirmed his decision. The first use of fresco by German artists in Rome created a painterly

Paper Prayers

CORDULA GREWE
Professor of Art History
Indiana University Bloomington

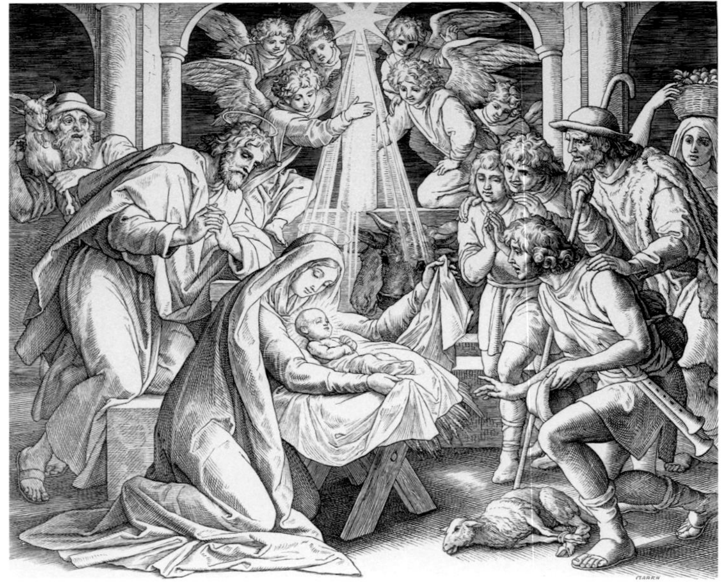

sensation. Finished in 1817, the Joseph cycle earned them a reputation as the pioneers of the era's fresco revival, despite simultaneous Italian experiments, and put the hitherto unknown artists on the international map, not least, as Bartholdy had hoped, back home.[3] Much could be said about the cycle's complex structure, a quintessentially Romantic translation of the text into images with far-reaching social, political, and religious implications, not to mention its notable and long-lasting artistic legacy. But for our purposes, the cycle's afterlife in reproductive print shall take center stage.

Although fresco painting was still very much alive in southern Germany and Austria, this vibrant late-Baroque tradition played no part in the Lukasbund's fascination with mural painting. Instead, their interest was fueled by their obsession with the Renaissance and, above all, their artist-god Raphael.[4] The Casa Bartholdy frescoes reflect a sustained study of the latter's designs, both in terms of composition and color, which points to their further function as a *paragone*, an artistic competition, between German and Italian painting.[5] The pivotal influence of Raphael's Vatican loggia is especially evident in Johann Friedrich Overbeck's *Joseph Being Sold by His Brothers*, in which an Egyptian merchant leads off the young boy while his unscrupulous brothers receive their payment and a group of bystanders wrangles over Joseph's enviable multicolored tunic (fig. 2).[6] Overbeck was more than aware of the commission's critical importance, which explains the attention he paid to the delicate, highly finished pencil drawing now in the Milwaukee Art Museum's collection (fig. 3). A testament to the remarkable artistic abilities of the young Overbeck, it was clearly conceived as an autonomous work of art.

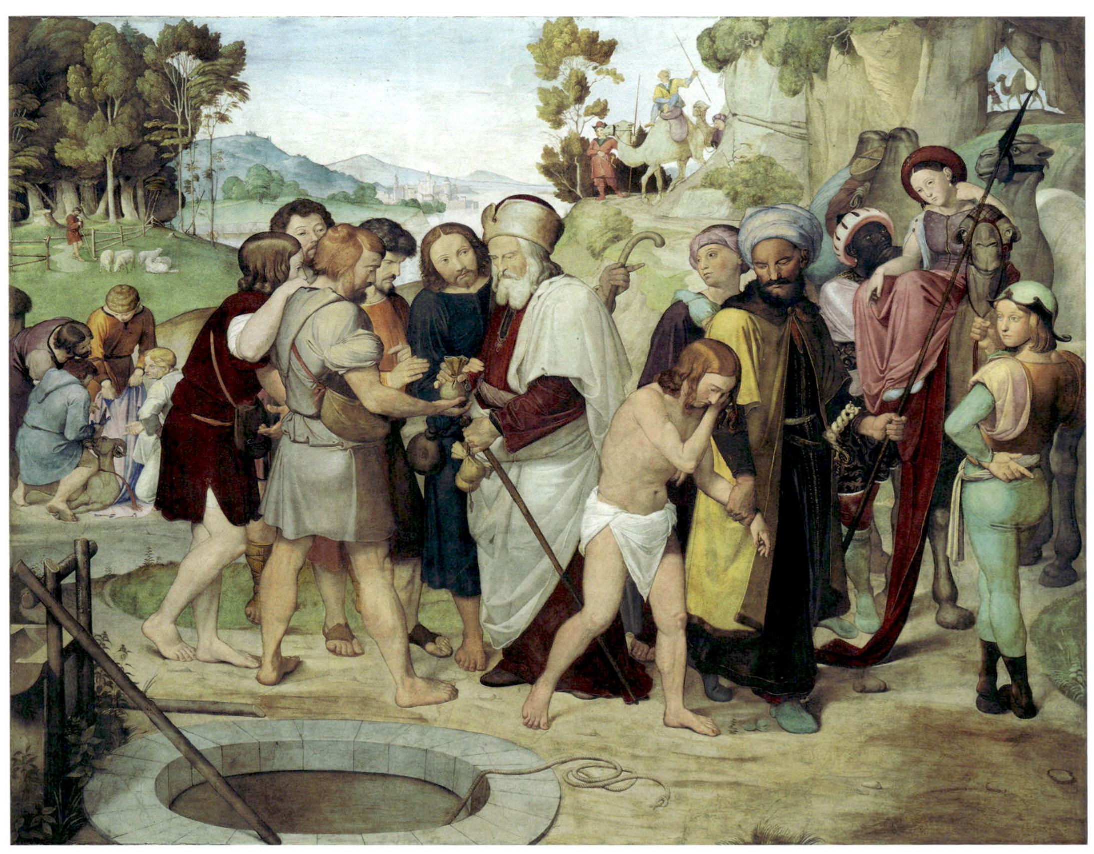

FIG. 2

FIG. 3

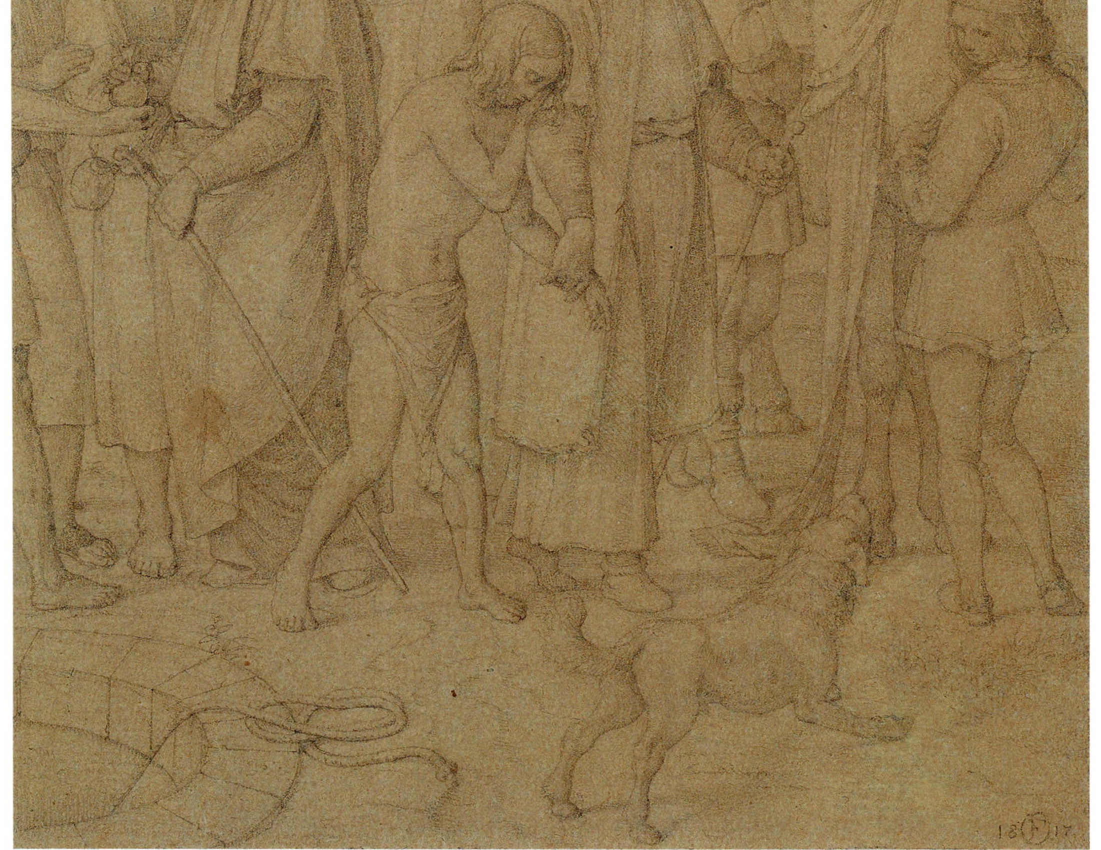

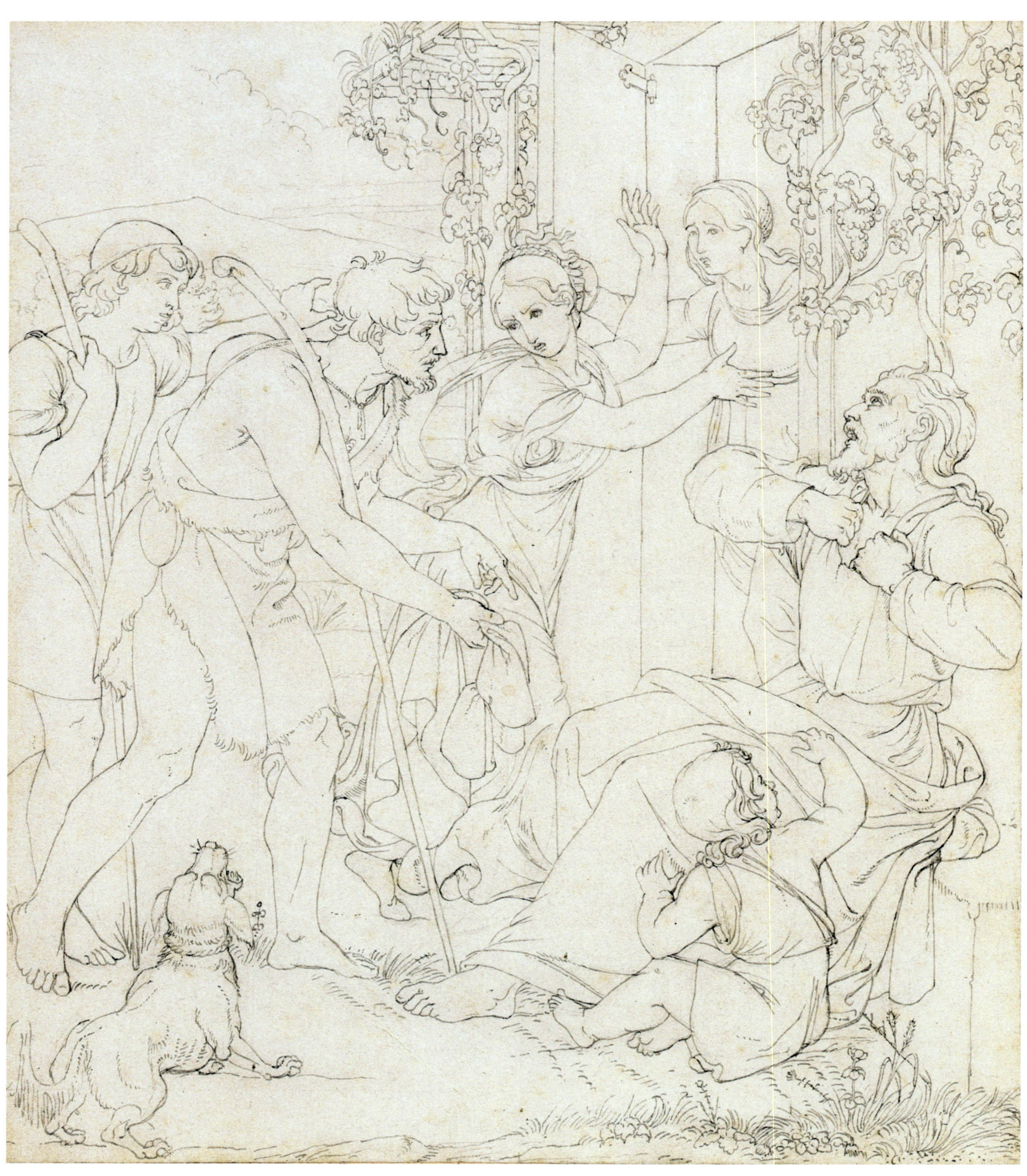

The drawing is a bit of a mystery. It is not mentioned by Overbeck's conscientious biographer, Margaret Howitt, or anywhere else until 1928, when Wilhelm Neuss, a Roman Catholic priest and professor of church and art history at the University of Bonn, published it in his article about the nature of Nazarene art and its significance for German art in the nineteenth century.[7] At that point, the sheet was part of a collection of Nazarene works in the possession of Prince Johann Georg, Duke of Saxony.[8] Despite this notable gap in the work's provenance, there can be no doubt about Overbeck's authorship, and the subtle differences between drawing and fresco support this attribution.[9] When Overbeck began to work up the sheet, he had already finalized the basic composition; yet the overall sensibility of his rendition in pencil is notably more loquacious. Doubtful about the effectiveness of this approach on a monumental scale, he refined the narrative's tone. He settled for a more sober staging, which contributes critically to the mural's hypnotizing power on the wall. He stripped the scene of anecdotal detail, such as the vignette of the woolly sheep to the left, which, pushing around the edge of the water trough, tries to nibble on some tasty weeds; and the cameo of the dog to the right, which, invitingly wagging his tail, tries to lure a young boy into playful action (fig. 3). Alerted by its barking, the slender youth at the far right has indeed turned around and now looks, slightly puzzled, at the excited furball at his feet. Inevitably, we start to wonder what might have prompted the dog's outburst, and as we do, our attention drifts away from the central narrative and its moral lesson. Thus, if these vignettes, precisely for their quiet irreverence, add a lighthearted realism to the pictorial imagination of the biblical passage, they also distract.[10] Overbeck must have quickly realized this, and the dog had to go.

Chased away from Overbeck's composition, the dog (still barking) follows Joseph's jealous brothers back home, and together they enter another moment in the drafted fresco cycle. This repetition might be less surprising if Overbeck had drawn this scene as well. But he did not. Instead, fellow Lukasbruder Wilhelm Schadow was responsible for *Jacob's Lament* (fig. 4).[11] The canine's reprise thus doubles as a powerful testimony to the Lukasbund's programmatic work as a collective; with the medieval workshop in mind, they hailed fresco for its communal spirit and capacity to form community both in terms of artistic practice and audience participation. We do not know for sure who copied whom in the matter of the dog. Yet it seems likely that Schadow was the one who, smitten by Overbeck's invention, cited the motif. This might explain why the dog feels somewhat extraneous to *Jacob's Lament*, while its absence in the final, executed version of *Joseph Being Sold by His Brothers* has created a small but noticeable gap in the narrative structure. Maybe the boy should have gone, too? As it is, the colorful youth now seems somewhat lost, and his pose is so artificial it recalls the arabesques of a circus acrobat or a ballet dancer. Equally puzzling is the absent-minded quality of his gaze, which, devoid of its original focal point, now drifts aimlessly. Is he lost in thought or searching for an object on a distant horizon? Whatever the answer, the figure's narrative motivation is gone and, with it, the boy's naturalness. Fortunately, a new visual allure compensates for this loss: The finely orchestrated contrast of silvery pink, pale turquoise, and soft golden browns in his garments shows Overbeck at his best.

It did not take long before the celebrated fresco sparked interest in the creation of a reproductive print after Overbeck's design. Luckily for the artist, the print published in 1826 after the cartoon of *Joseph Being Sold by His Brothers* matched the mellifluous beauty and outstanding quality of his original, and the ensuing lithograph is a technical masterwork in its own right (plate 35).[12] Already, the print's large dimensions, at nearly 26 by 32 inches, demanded the utmost skill of the papermaker and of the parties involved in preparing the limestone printing block and carrying out the printing process itself. These technical difficulties matched the ambitions of the publisher, Johann Velten, whose firm was still young when he undertook the project.[13] Velten had early on recognized Overbeck's importance, not least for disseminating Nazarene ideas and ideals, and he chose his lithographer accordingly. Himself an accomplished painter, Hans Jakob Oeri did not disappoint: The figures' contours are clear but not harsh, and the individual details—from the wood and plants in the foreground to the shepherd resting in the calm expanse in the distance—are delightfully delicate yet richly textured (fig. 5). Equally bewitching is the lithograph's silvery palette, which, stripped by necessity of color, translates Overbeck's pastel hues into a pleasing oscillation of light and shadow. The publisher was most satisfied, and so was Overbeck.[14]

When Oeri was hired, lithography was still a rather new technique and, as the first planographic (flat-surface) printing process, one of the most immediate and most modern print media available to date.[15] *Lithography* literally means "writing on stone," and the process exploits the simple fact that water and oil do not mix: Marks made with a greasy crayon are applied directly to a smooth stone surface, preferably limestone, and then printed with ink rolled on after the stone has been wetted. Its greatest advantage over competing techniques was the capacity to reproduce the individual style and material characteristics of the original line with unprecedented accuracy. Invented somewhat accidentally by the Bavarian playwright Alois Senefelder, lithography almost instantaneously became a highly sought-after reproductive medium, in particular for musical scores and old master drawings. In contrast to this immediate commercial

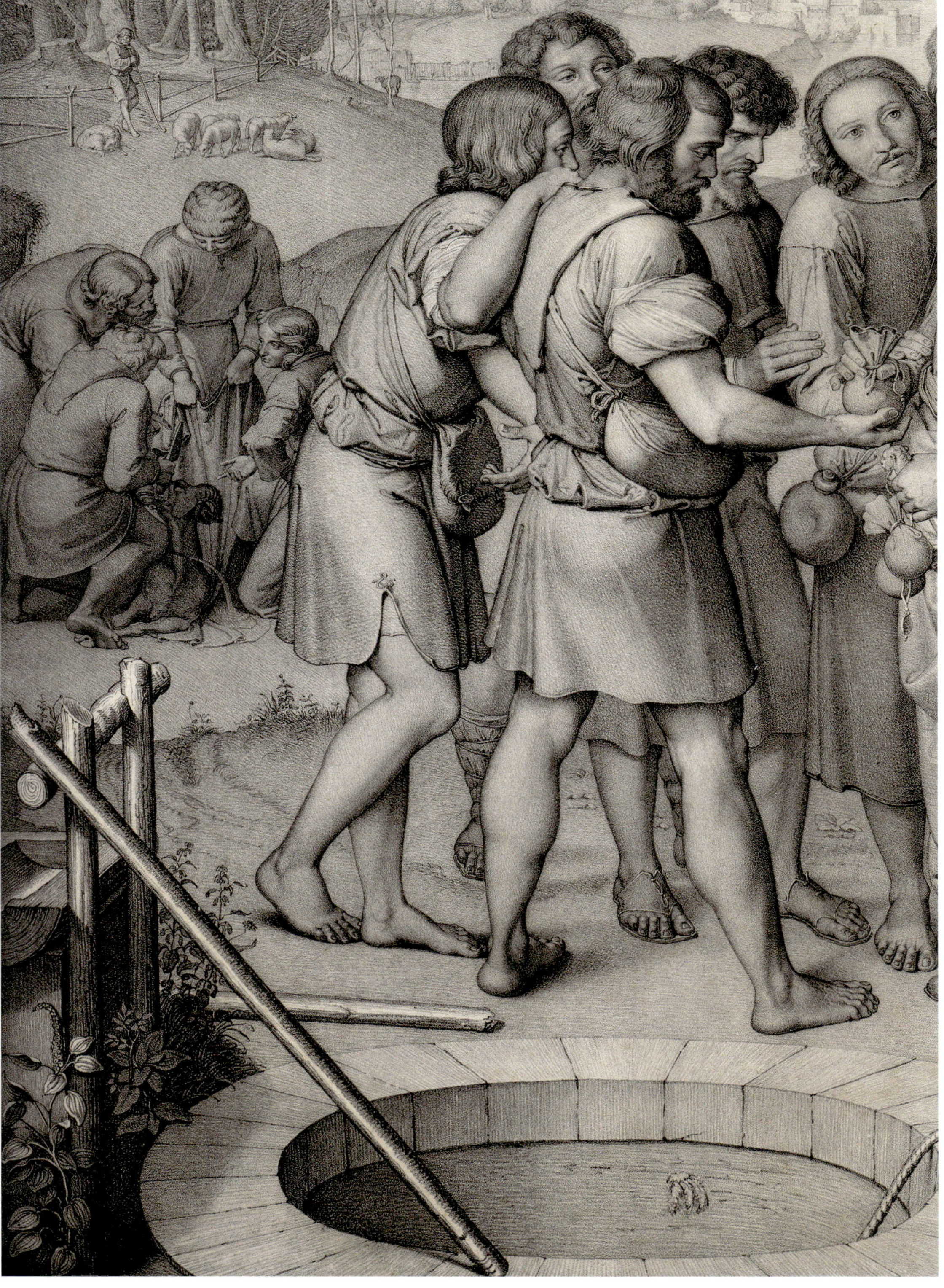

success in reproduction, the earliest attempts at lithography as an artistic medium ended in financial fiascos. Its devotees nonetheless remained undeterred, not least those who, yearning for an authentic national style, considered Senefelder's invention a genuinely German technique. This aspect appealed to Ferdinand Olivier, who would become a venerable trailblazer of the new medium's artistic and aesthetic possibilities.

Born to a family of Swiss-French descent, Olivier spent his youth and early career in Dessau. In 1811, the artist relocated to Vienna and, six years later, still in the Austrian capital, joined the Lukasbund via correspondence, as did his younger brother Friedrich. In contrast to his sibling, however, who left for Italy shortly thereafter to be with his new brethren, Ferdinand never crossed the Alps. He had been tempted a few years earlier when he set out to accompany fellow artist Philipp Veit, who was on his way to Rome.[16] But in the end, Olivier did not even make it to Munich. Instead, he got absorbed in the unexpected beauty of Salzburg and its environs, and when Veit continued his journey on August 24, 1815, he had to travel alone. Two years later, Olivier returned to Salzburg and the landscape that had wooed him so completely, and in 1818, he set out to transform his experience into an extensive cycle of landscape prints (plates 56–64). He first considered etching but, unsatisfied, turned to lithography. Although self-taught, he soon reached a mastery of the new technique that anybody must admire, Schnorr von Carolsfeld enthused, "who understands the mechanism."[17] Regretfully, however, few did. His high hopes crushed, a financially pressed Olivier was bitterly disappointed about the cycle's poor sales.[18] What a contrast to today! How vindicated the artist would have felt had he known that now, two hundred years after the album's release in 1823, curators and collectors alike consider his *Seven Places in Salzburg and Berchtesgaden* an incunabulum of early lithography, which by the end of the twentieth century, was ranked "among the finest landscape prints ever made."[19] Technical prowess is only one factor in this modern appreciation. Equally appealing is the finely calibrated fusion of a new, quintessentially Romantic perception of nature with the period's fascination with folklore and rural religious practices.

For Olivier, his exploration of the Salzburg countryside was at once physical and spiritual, not only a relaxing experience of nature but a pilgrimage, and the album's organization leaves no doubt about its deeply pious quality. Departing from the traditional arrangement of such landscape series, which usually took up the four-partite structure of natural cycles (such as the seasons or the times of day), Olivier's places are arranged according to the days of the week and oscillate between agricultural motifs and vignettes of Christian life. His focus is thereby on ordinary country folk, who, placed into topographically accurate scenery,

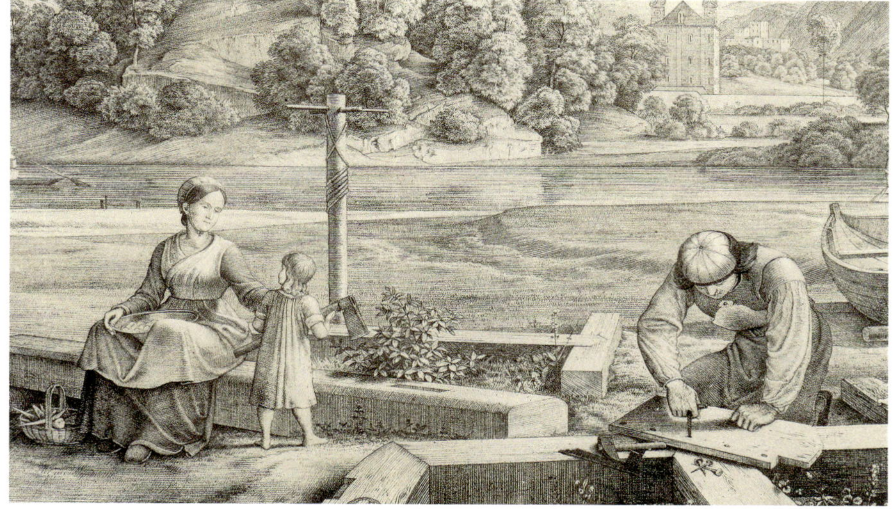

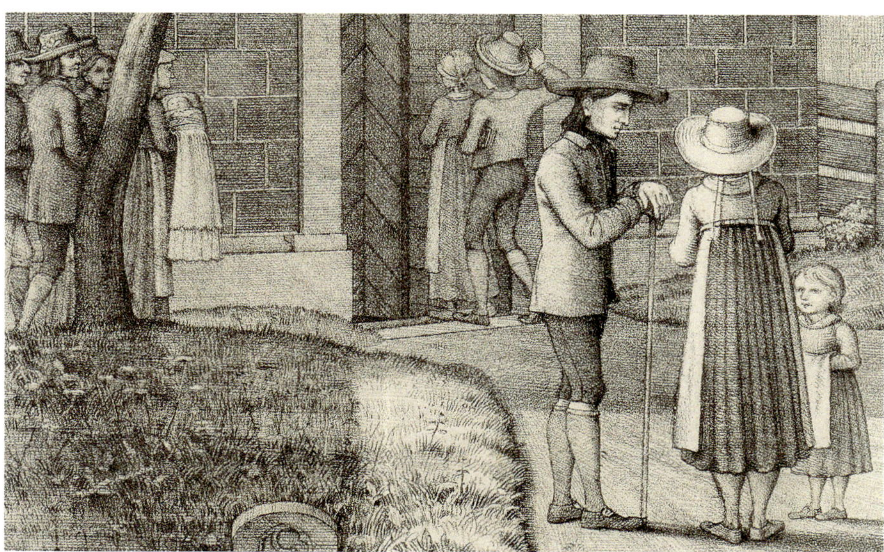

go about their daily lives, here grafting apple trees, there tending to their flocks or harvesting hay, or on another occasion, ministering to those in need. A gentle symbolism provides a Christian gloss to these cultural landscapes, which never depict—and yet often powerfully evoke—a set of biblical figures, like the young family in the *Rosenecker Garden Outside Salzburg* on Monday, which conjures up Mary, Joseph, and the Christ Child (fig. 6). The religious charge of the image was important to Olivier, and he thus set the stage by opening with a key ritual of Christian life: churchgoing on Sunday. This gesture toward the Eucharist articulates a promise of spiritual rebirth, which doubles in the image of new life, here embodied by the newborn on the way toward Baptism (fig. 7). Ultimately,

Olivier's viewer looks from the outside in, occupying (like the artist himself) the peripheral position of the captivated tourist. The countryside, in turn, becomes an idealized space where we moderns can still experience the oneness of humankind, land, and faith, otherwise lost, and that invites a slow form of looking, both aesthetic and spiritual. Olivier's desire to create this kind of devotional gaze is nowhere more palpable than in the final print, *Keystone*. Divided into seven separate fields, it brings together the main protagonists of the week just passed (plate 64). Religion takes shape, once more, as a rural ritual. Yet, this time, the wayside cross at the center faces not the figures in the image but us (see detail on p. 70). As we look at God the Father, presenting his crucified son, we are asked to emulate what we see shown before our eyes: to kneel, to close our eyes, to pray.[20] For as the scripture printed in the image tells us, "Blessed are they that have not seen and yet have believed" (John 20:29).

This desire to translate religious aesthetic into Christian practice would prompt Olivier to turn, in the middle of working on his landscape lithographs, to a very different kind of object: a printed house altar (plate 36).[21] With adoration as its central subject, the Christmas-themed lithograph was meant to aid personal devotion and be folded in the manner of a winged altarpiece. The title, *House Altar*, is description and instruction at once. It evokes the tradition of portable altars, which, first documented in the sixth century, had since become a staple in a variety of religious ceremonies, from

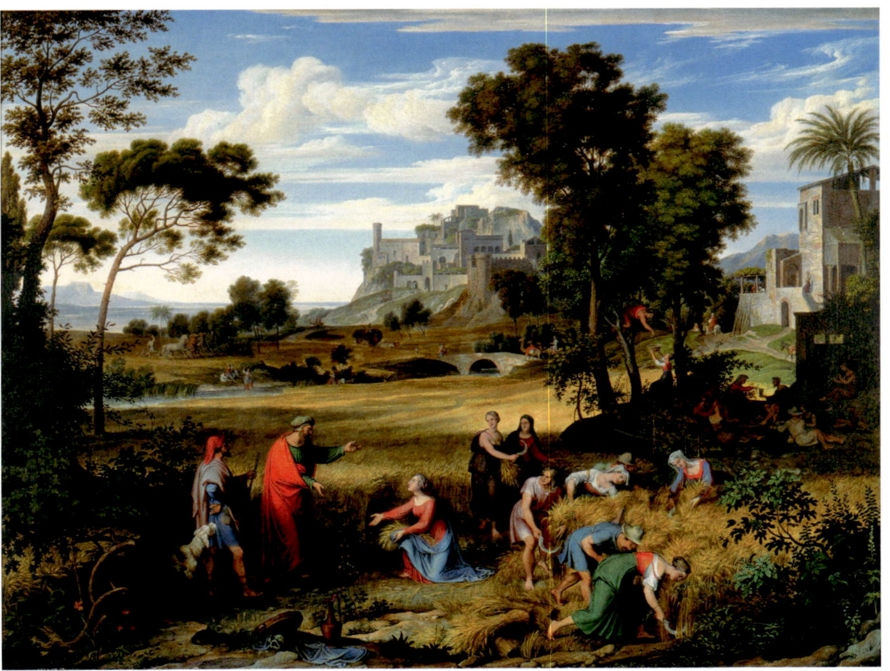

processions and pilgrimages to worship outside the church.[22] Olivier took this tradition a step further, using a medium affordable to most. As such, his lithograph was a visual counterpart to the many Protestant-authored books, often also named *House Altars*, that actively promoted prayer at home. Such collections of Protestant morning and evening devotions would, as one author hoped, transfigure the domestic hearth and family table "into a house altar, before which husband and wife, parents and children, servants and friends will offer their morning and evening sacrifices."[23] How much more desirable if such sacrifices could be made before a real altar, even if made only from paper. Olivier's nineteenth-century audience certainly thought so, and the creases found in this and other impressions testify to the print's intended use and frequent handling before devotional practice yielded to museum protocol. Folded up, this pious artifact could now go with everyone, not only the richest dignitaries, wherever their path should lead—a loyal companion for quotidian travel and life's journey alike.

The figuration in Olivier's *House Altar* fits squarely within the Lukasbund's preference for history painting, in contrast to the focus on landscape that secured the *Seven Places in Salzburg and Berchtesgaden* a position in the pantheon of printmaking. Not surprisingly then, it was not the young secessionists who inspired Olivier's landscape work but one of their mentors, Joseph Anton Koch.[24] Born in Tyrol in 1768, the older artist spent most of his career in Rome, where he met the fraternity in 1811, right after their arrival. Koch quickly formed a bond with the young expatriates before heading to Vienna in 1812. During his subsequent three-year stay in the Austrian capital, Koch cultivated, as he had in Italy over the previous two decades, a circle of like-minded people who would accompany him on his excursions. This experience would prove decisive for Olivier and his artistic development, which, as the Nazarene confessed, had greatly profited from Koch's "extraordinary participation."[25] Three decades later, Overbeck would echo this sentiment when, upon Koch's death in 1839, he fondly remembered how much they all had benefited from "his witty, ingenious acquaintance," "recognition completely free of envy," and "childlike and lively participation."[26] In reality, the relationship was more ambivalent than this posthumous homage suggests. Tensions arose around artistic as much as political differences, and Koch objected fiercely to the brethren's missionary zeal—a passion that, incidentally, had led several of them, Overbeck and Schadow among them, to convert to Catholicism. Overbeck was nonetheless right about the mutually beneficial nature of their rapport, with Koch's *Landscape with Ruth and Boaz* as a masterly case in point (fig. 8).

Based on Nicolas Poussin's canvas *Summer* from 1664, the painting exemplifies the revival of the heroic landscape that the "proto-Nazarene" had become famous for by the time he painted this second version of the

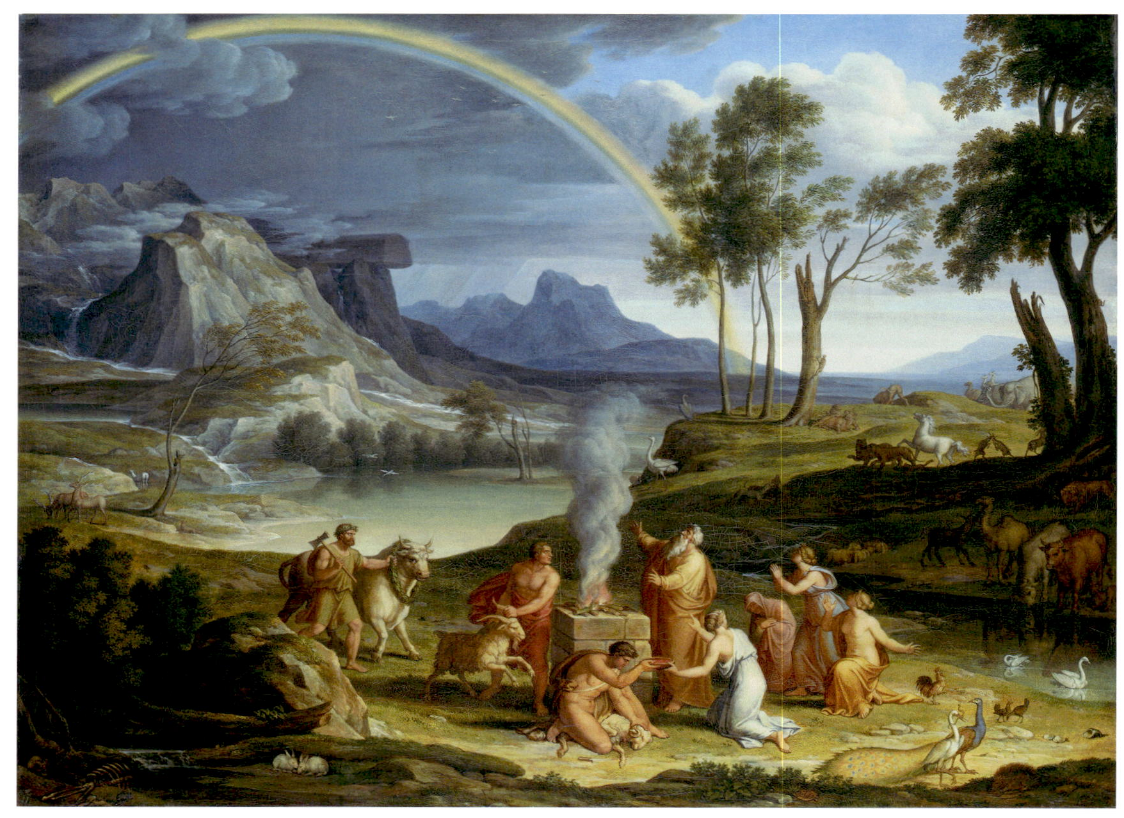

FIG. 9

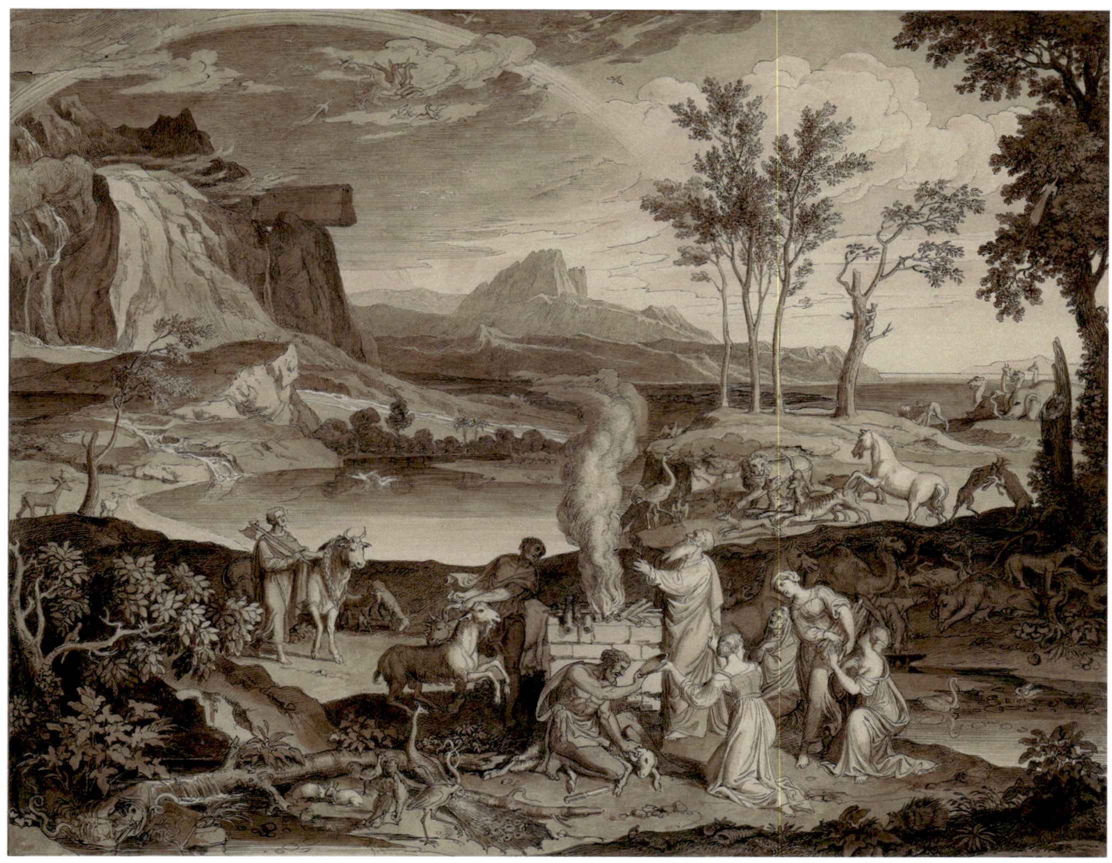

FIG. 10

motif, now in the Milwaukee Art Museum's collection, around 1823.[27] Repeating the original's strict structure—one of Koch's hallmarks—it lives off the artist's new self-confidence in handling paint, with a vibrancy of color and a skillful contrast of bold yet cool hues missing in 1803. Add a greater emphasis on figures and historical narrative and you get a superb example of Koch's mature and most accomplished period, the Roman years between 1815 and 1827. And something else was new, something that had blossomed once his own experiments had found inspiring resonance in the Lukasbund's pursuits: In 1823, the aerial perspective originally gleaned from his seventeenth-century models had morphed into a hyper-clarity that, no longer distinguishing between near and far, bestows a heightened, almost eerie tangibility on every detail. The result is a detail-obsessed, quilt-like rendition of nature, achieving what I have described elsewhere as an "aesthetic of particularity."[28] The ensuing collapse of close-up and distant views into a two-dimensional fabric of lines no longer recalls the painterly logic of Claude Lorrain, Nicolas Poussin, or Gaspard Dughet but rather evokes the graphic principles and abstract pictorial space characteristic of old German prints (think Albrecht Dürer) and Italian frescoes of the Quattro- and Cinquecento.[29] "There could not easily be a better subject for a landscape," a pleased Koch announced in 1826, and then he went on to paint yet another version.[30]

Koch's habit of repeating favorite compositions with few or no changes might seem strange to a twenty-first-century audience, but in his own time, it satisfied a hot market for replicas. Yet commercial calculations were not the only reason for Koch's preoccupation with repetition. He sincerely strove for the most perfect artistic form, which, in turn, led to a small, curated body of subject matter. Through these *Urbilder*, or arche-types, Koch explored the notion of multiples and did so across media, creating them in print and oil, as well as picture-perfect drawings.[31] One of these signature motifs was the rainbow. As a heavenly symbol of peace and restored harmony, it appeared first in yet another heroic landscape of 1803: *Landscape with Noah's Sacrifice* (fig. 9).[32] Among the many reprises that followed, the version he painted in 1813 while in Vienna stood out. Finally winning him a prize at the Munich Art Academy, it proved vital to estab-lishing Koch's reputation as a leading landscape artist of his time. Around 1823, he translated the celebrated painting, later destroyed in World War II, into a large-scale drawing in pen and brown ink (fig. 10).[33] Clearly con-ceived as an autonomous artwork, the piece had a highly finished aesthetic that appealed to a collector in Oxford, England. The buyer was likely influenced by George Frederick Nott, a British theologian and Koch's long-standing patron. Nott acquired the 1823 *Landscape with Ruth and Boaz* for his collection in Winchester; there, it became instrumental in the

Englishman's campaign to popularize this quintessentially German expression of a Romantic Neoclassicism among his British friends.

In the meantime, *Ruth and Boaz* continued their triumphal march on the continent as well, conquering Koch's native Tyrol, where the next version in oil, finished in 1827, would become the first acquired by a local public collection, the Ferdinandeum in Innsbruck.[34] Admittedly, the reception was mixed upon its arrival at the Tyrolean State Museum. Yet it once more embodied compositional perfection for the next generation of Nazarenes, and Joseph von Führich was no exception.[35] Thus, when the Austrian artist reached Rome in the spring of 1827, he immediately sought out the German-Roman circle surrounding Koch. Ultimately, however, encountering Johann Friedrich Overbeck proved life-changing. Soon, as the critic Joseph Beavington Atkinson wryly noted, Führich "literally worshipped the ground on which Overbeck stood,"[36] and he returned home in 1829 as the ultimate Nazarene painter. As such, Führich was committed to public art and educational outreach and worked in all sizes and for all budgets, from standard formats of oil on canvas to the monumental and the intimate, excelling in unmovable public fresco as much as in widely circulated printed matter produced for private consumption. Soon, his artistic output was at the center of the maelstrom of reproduced images that shaped the century's visual imaginary.

Führich had been initiated into mural decoration as soon as he set foot in Rome. The Nazarenes had been working on their second major fresco cycle, the decoration of the Casino Massimo's ground floor with murals after Dante, Ariosto, and Tasso, and when Overbeck decided not to complete his room, the younger artist stepped in.[37] Twenty years later, he delivered his own masterwork, *The Stations of the Cross* (see fig. 11). Executed between 1844 and 1846 and still one of the city's most notable religious murals, the cycle marked a new phase in Nazarene art. Daring to take a neo-Baroque turn, Führich also did not shy away from the more gruesome aspects of Christian iconography.[38] Commercial success followed the aesthetic triumph, and the pictures soon circulated in a variety of reproductions and adaptions, from engravings to oil paintings, not to mention the various plaster reliefs that still adorn churches in such unexpected places as Sioux Falls, South Dakota.[39] Führich's print designs, in contrast, retained a quintessentially Nazarene mellifluous linearity, and even more critical voices praised his late cycles, such as the popular series *The Bethlehemitic Path* from about 1865 (see plates 45–50), for their "genuinely painterly effect" and "solemn magic of legendary poetry."[40]

The simple tone of folk legend and fairy tales, often infused with a sense of nostalgia, also characterized the art of the next generation of Nazarenes who, under the tutelage of Wilhelm Schadow, matured in

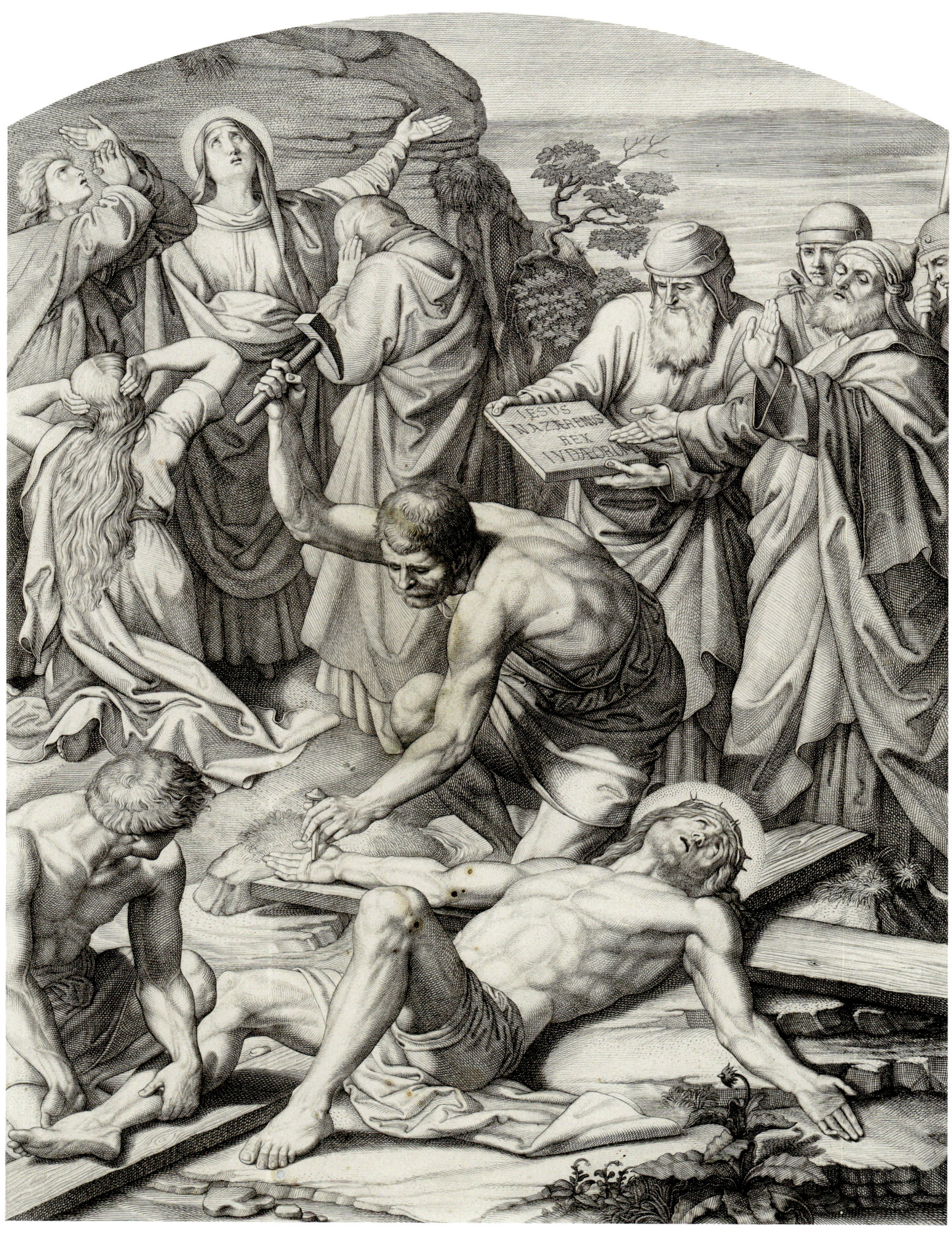
IESVS
NAZARENVS
REX
IVDÆORVM

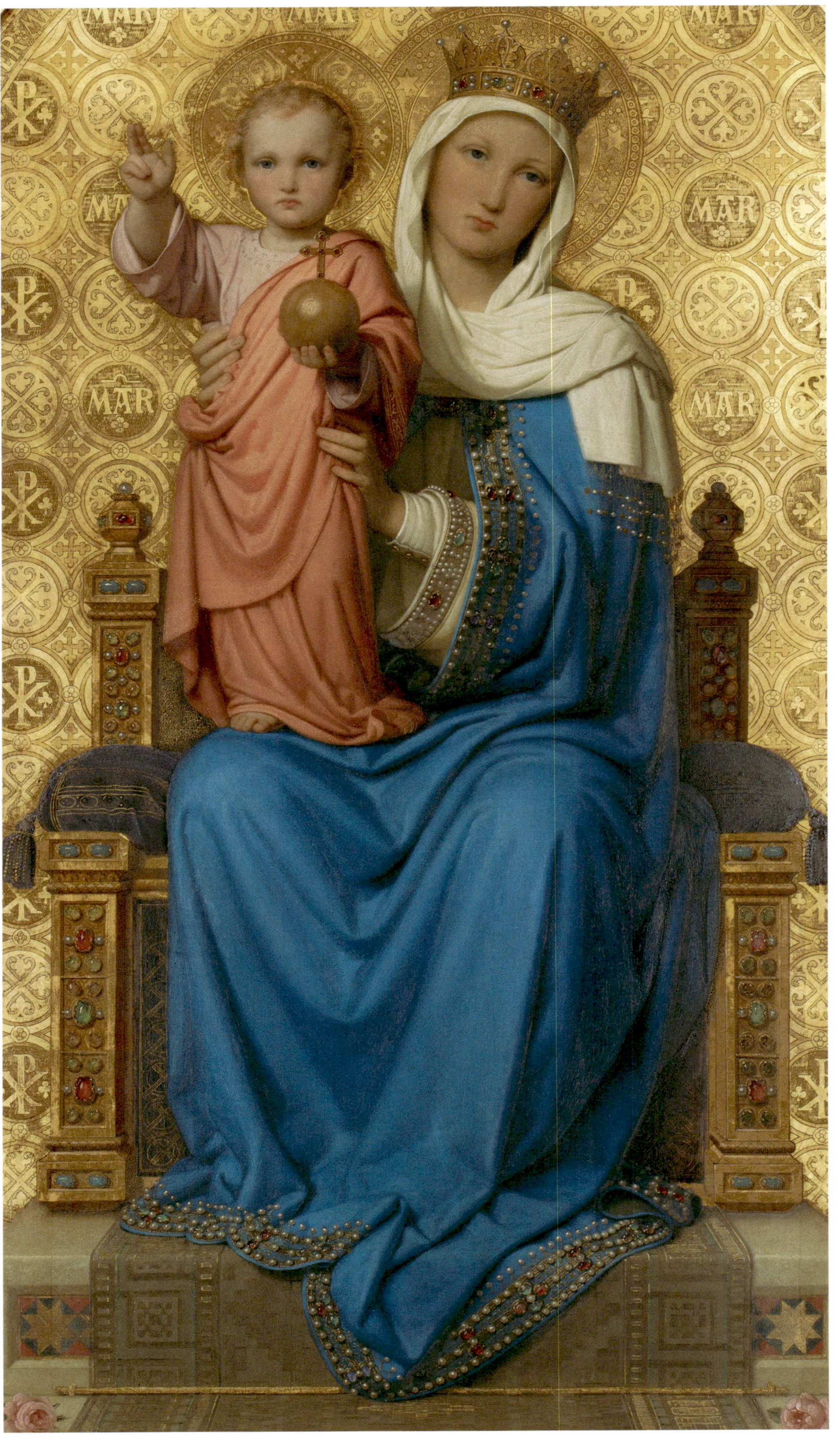

FIG. 12

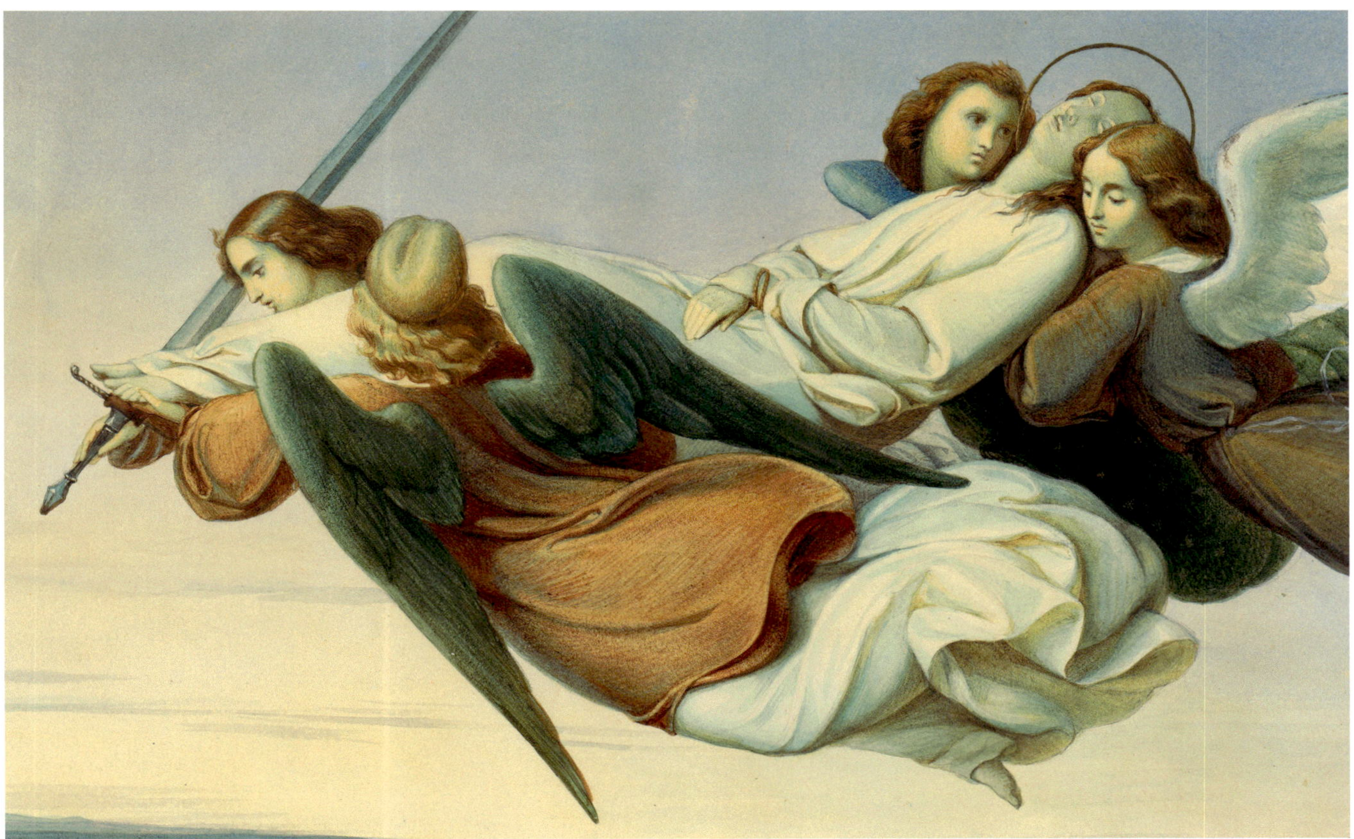

Düsseldorf. Nothing captures their sensibility better than the lyricism of Franz Ittenbach, whose coveted images of the Virgin Mary soon earned him the epithet "Painter of the Madonna" (fig. 12), or the restrained yet heartfelt compositions of Heinrich Karl Anton Mücke, whose popular, often-repeated image of St. Catherine's body being borne to Mount Sinai (fig. 13) alludes to death and martyrdom with poetic, sentimental tenderness. The new direction did not deter the Schadow School from creating stunning murals, such as those in St. Apollinaris Church in Remagen—itself a work of Late Romantic art—which soon attracted tourists from near and far (fig. 14). Yet, when faced with increasing hatred among confessions and a concrete religious crisis, which pitched the Prussian government against the Papal See in 1837, the Catholic establishment, Schadow among them, did not turn to fresco or oil.[41] Instead, the aptly named Society for the Dissemination of Religious Imagery, which the church founded to counter the spiritual malaise, turned to one medium and the most enduring to date: steel engraving.[42] This was no coincidence. Ultimately, the Nazarenes knew and had always known that the battle for modern religious art would be fought on paper.

FIG. 12   Franz Ittenbach, *Queen of Heaven* (detail), 1872 (cat. p. 160)

FIG. 13   Heinrich Karl Anton Mücke, *The Body of Saint Catherine of Alexandria Carried to Heaven by Angels* (detail), ca. 1836 (cat. p. 160)

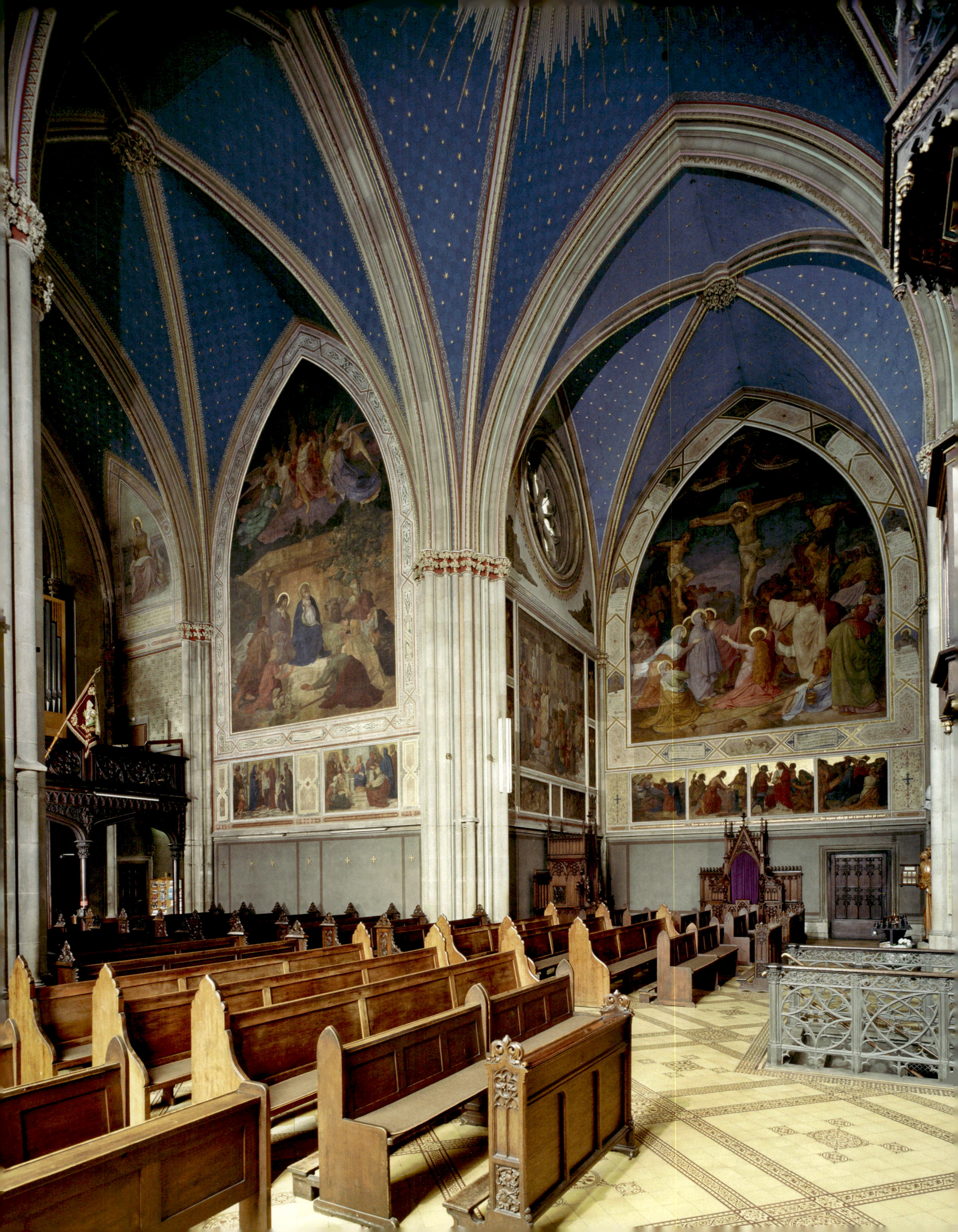

NOTES

1. *Die Bibel in Bildern: 240 Darstellungen, erfunden und auf Holz gezeichnet von Julius Schnorr von Carolsfeld* (Leipzig: Georg Wigand, 1860), VII.

2. Letter from Peter von Cornelius to Joseph Görres, November 1814; cited after Lionel Gossman, "Beyond Modern: The Art of the Nazarenes," *Common Knowledge* 14, no. 1 (2008): 45–104, here 56.

3. Michael Thimann, "'Josephs Trübsale und Herrlichkeit': Der nazarenische Josephszyklus aus der Casa Bartholdy (1816/17)," in *100 Jahre Bibliotheca Hertziana*, ed. Elisabeth Kieven (Munich: Hirmer, 2013), 203–213, esp. 204; Cordula Grewe, *Wilhelm Schadow (1788–1862): Werkverzeichnis der Gemälde mit einer Auswahl der dazugehörigen Zeichnungen und Druckgraphiken* (Petersberg: Michael Imhof Verlag, 2017), 30–36; interpretation, 36–37.

4. See the excellent discussion of the Casa Bartholdy frescoes in Thimann, "'Josephs Trübsale und Herrlichkeit'," incl. the epithet "romantischer Künstlergott" (Romantic artist-god) for Raphael on 212.

5. Thimann.

6. Kristin Makholm, "Friedrich Overbeck (Lübeck 1789–1869 Rome): Joseph Being Sold by His Brothers, 1817," in *Nineteenth-Century German Prints and Drawings from the Milwaukee Art Museum* (Milwaukee: Milwaukee Art Museum, 2002), 16–17.

7. Margaret Howitt, *Friedrich Overbeck: Sein Leben und Schaffen*, 2 vols. (Freiburg im Breisgau: Herder, 1886); Wilhelm Neuss, "Das Wesen der Nazarenerkunst und ihre Bedeutung für die deutsche Kunst des 19. Jahrhunderts," *Kunstwissenschaftliches Jahrbuch der Görresgesellschaft* 1 (1928): 62–86, XV, fig. 19.

8. Neuss, "Das Wesen der Nazarenerkunst," 85.

9. I want to thank Michael Thimann for his expert assessment of the drawing's attribution to Overbeck; private correspondence, February 1, 2024.

10. For a vivid discussion of the "reality effect" as a narrative strategy, see James Wood, "Keeping It Real," *The New Yorker,* first published in print on March 7, 2010; https://www.newyorker.com/magazine/2010/03/15/keeping-it-real-3.

11. I have attributed the drawing, which only surfaced in 2020 and thus too late to be included in my 2017 catalogue raisonné, firmly to Schadow. See unpublished research, available at Ketterer, www.kettererkunst.com/details-e.php?obnr=120001950&anummer=498&detail=1&raumbild=1.

12. Stephan Seeliger, "Friedrich Overbeck: Joseph wird von seinen Brüdern verkauft, 1826," in *Unter Glass und Rahmen: Druckgraphik der Romantik aus den Beständen des Landesmuseums Mainz und aus Privatbesitz*, ed. Stephan Seeliger and Norbert Suhr (Mainz: Landesmuseum, 1994), cat. 32, 90 (with fig. on 91).

13. The son of a milliner from Wetzlar, Johann Sigmund Velten first worked as an art dealer in Basel, before coming to Karlsruhe in 1820; upon arrival, he opened an art dealership (the later Hofkunsthandlung J. Velten) that after his death was continued by his son, Sigmund. In 1826, Velten added a lithography workshop and a book-printing shop to his business, thus creating an in-house publishing house; see René Gilbert, "Johann Velten," posted in 2016 and last revised on September 15, 2022, https://stadtlexikon.karlsruhe.de/index.php/De:Lexikon:bio-1024.

14. Stephan Seeliger discusses the positive reactions of both Velten and Overbeck, which also motivated the publisher and the painter to continue their collaboration. Seeliger, *Unter Glass und Rahmen*, cat. 32, 90.

15. I paraphrase here sections from my book *The Nazarenes: Romantic Avant-Garde and the Art of the Concept* (University Park, PA: Penn State University Press, 2015), esp. 162.

16. Once in Rome, Philipp Veit joined the Lukasbund in 1816; see Norbert Suhr's still seminal study *Philipp Veit (1793–1877): Leben*

FIG. 14 View of the nave and north transept of St. Apollinaris, Remagen. Mainz, Archiv der Landesdenkmalpflege

und Werk eines Nazareners. Monographie und Werkverzeichnis (Weinheim: VCH, 1991).

17. Julius Schnorr von Carolsfeld, cited after Heinrich Schwarz, *Salzburg und das Salzkammergut: Die künstlerische Entdeckung der Stadt und der Landschaft im 19. Jahrhundert* (1926), 2nd ed. (Vienna: Anton Schroll, 1936), 23.

18. For the cycle's reception, see Ute Kuhlemann, "An Artistic Confession: Ferdinand Olivier's Landscape Views of Salzburg," in *German Romantic Prints and Drawings from an English Private Collection*, ed. Giulia Bartrum (London: Contemporary Editions, 2011), 216–226.

19. Antony Griffiths and Frances Carey, *German Printmaking in the Age of Goethe* (London: British Museum Press, 1994), 211.

20. Grewe, "Nature," in *The Nazarenes*, 149–173, esp. 172–173.

21. Stephan Seeliger, "Ferdinand Olivier, *Hausaltar*, 1820," in *Unter Glass und Rahmen*, cat. 24, 70 (with fig. on 71).

22. Not surprisingly, these transportable mini-shrines also played a significant role in the Church's missionary efforts, which explains their global distribution; see the virtual exhibition of the Latin American Institute (Free University, Berlin), esp. Christian Piarowski, *Tragaltäre* at https://www.lai.fu-berlin.de/forschung /lehrforschung/symbolische _repraesentationen/gemaelde_und _tragaltaere/tragaltaere/index.html.

23. Dr. G. W. Maisch, preface to *Der Hausaltar: Evangelische Morgen- und Abend-Andachten für Fest-, Sonn- und Werktage und besondere Verhältnisse des äußeren und inneren Lebens nebst einer Sammlung geistlicher Lieder*, new ed. (Leipzig: Göschen'sche Verlagshandlung), V.

24. Wolfgang Freiherr von Löhneysen, "Koch, Joseph Anton," in *Neue Deutsche Biographie* 12 (1980), 269–270; https://www.deutsche -biographie.de/pnd118724010.html #ndbcontent. For a detailed discussion of Koch as printmaker, see John Ittmann, "Joseph Anton Koch (1768–1839)," in *The Enchanted World of German Romantic Prints:*

1770–1850, ed. John Ittmann and Cordula Grewe (New Haven, CT: Yale University Press, 2017), 307–319.

25. Ferdinand Olivier, cited after Otto Ritter von Lutterotti, "Joseph Anton Koch und sein Wiener Kreis," in *Klassizismus und Romantik in Deutschland: Gemälde und Zeichnungen aus der Sammlung Georg Schäfer, Schweinfurt* (Nuremberg: Germanisches Nationalmuseum, 1966), 43; furthermore Cornelia Reiter, "Joseph Anton Kochs, Skizzenbücher der Wiener Akademie der bildenden Künste: Motivquelle und Musterbeispiel künstlerischer Interaktion," *Römische historische Mitteilungen* 51 (2009): 293–315.

26. Johann Friedrich Overbeck, January 18, 1839, cited after Agnes Thum, ". . . wieviel die neu erwachte deutsche Kunst dem Meister Koch verdankt: Koch und die Nazarener," in *Joseph Anton Koch: Der Erste Nazarener?*, ed. Helena Pereña (Innsbruck: Haymon, 2014), 104-114, here 104.

27. Nicolas Poussin, *Summer (Ruth and Boaz)*, 1660–64. Oil on canvas, 118 × 160 cm. Musée du Louvre, Paris; and Joseph Anton Koch (1768–1839) / Christian Gottlieb Schick (1776–1812), *Heroic Landscape with Ruth and Boas* at https://kataloget.thorvaldsens museum.dk/en/B158. A watercolor (Museum Kunstpalast, Düsseldorf) suggests that Koch had been working on the subject matter of Ruth and Boaz at least since 1799; see Christian von Holst, *Joseph Anton Koch: Ansichten der Natur* (Stuttgart: Staatsgalerie, 1989), 297–299 and 308. For a comparative analysis of the subject's various versions, see Peter Prange, "Zwischen Historie und Landschaft: Joseph Anton Kochs religiöse Landschaften," in Pereña, *Joseph Anton Koch* (2014), 84-104.

28. Cordula Grewe, "Die Geburt der Natur aus dem Geiste Dürers," in *Landschaft am "Scheidepunkt": Evolutionen einer Gattung in Kunsttheorie, Kunstschaffen und Literatur um 1800*, ed. Reinhard Wegner and Markus Bertsch (Göttingen: Wallstein Verlag, 2010), 331–353.

29. Besides studying Albrecht Dürer (1471–1528) and the German old masters, Koch also copied medieval Italian frescoes in situ—and

in the era's fashionable contour style—in 1794, immediately after he arrived in Italy. For a general discussion of this style's cultural and ideological implications, see Robert Rosenblum's pathbreaking 1956 dissertation *The International Style of 1800: A Study in Linear Abstraction*, published twenty years later (New York: Garland, 1976); also, Werner Busch, "Der sentimentalische Klassizismus bei Carstens, Koch und Genelli," in *Kunst als Bedeutungsträger: Gedenkschrift für Günter Bandmann*, ed. Werner Busch, Reiner Haussherr, and Eduard Trier (Berlin: Mann, 1977), 317–343.

30. Joseph Anton Koch, April 19, 1826, cited after Prange, "Zwischen Historie und Landschaft," 85; for the painting, see endnote 34 in this essay.

31. Cited after Holst, *Joseph Anton Koch*, 87.

32. Joseph Anton Koch had been working on the biblical story of Noah's sacrifice since 1802, with a sepia drawing (Kupferstichkabinett, Dresden) preceding the motif's first version in oil, which, executed in 1803, was probably also Koch's first oil painting (today Städel Museum, Frankfurt am Main); see https://sammlung.staedelmuseum.de /de/werk/landschaft-mit-dem-dankopfer -noahs and https://recherche.smb.museum /detail/966576/noahs-dankopfer. For the paintings and preparatory drawing, see Holst, *Joseph Anton Koch*, 194, no. 60, fig. 126 (1802–3, ink and brown wash); 200, no. 64, fig. 131 (1803, oil on canvas); 73, fig. 41 (1813, oil on canvas, destroyed during World War II). See Ittmann, "Joseph Anton Koch," 319, endnote 33.

33. Joseph Anton Koch, March 17, 1814, cited after Otto Ritter von Lutterotti, *Joseph Anton Koch, 1768–1839: Mit Werkverzeichnis und Briefen des Künstlers* (Berlin: Deutscher Verein für Kunstwissenschaft, 1940), 165.

34. Joseph Anton Koch, *Landscape with Ruth and Boaz*, 1826/27. Oil on canvas, 105 × 141 cm. Tiroler Landesmuseum Ferdinandeum, Innsbruck (Austria); Prange, "Zwischen Historie und Landschaft," 85 and cat. 68.

35. Prange, 85.

36. Joseph Beavington Atkinson, *Overbeck* (London: S. Low, Marston, Searle & Rivington, 1882), 21.

37. See the still groundbreaking study by Kurt Gerstenberg and Paul Ortwin Rave, *Die Wandgemälde der deutschen Romantiker im Casino Massimo zu Rom* (Berlin: Deutscher Verein für Kunstwissenschaft, 1934).

38. For a discussion of Führich's neo-Baroque turn, see Cornelia Reiter, "Die Kartons von Joseph Führich zu den Kreuzwegstationen in der Johann-Nepomuk-Kirche in Wien," in *Die Nazarener: Religion Macht Kunst*, ed. Christa Steinle and Rainer Metzger (Frankfurt am Main: Walther König, 2005), 207–213.

39. I refer here to the reliefs in the Cathedral of St. Joseph (Sioux Falls, South Dakota); for the global reception of Führich's *The Stations of the Cross,* see https://www.pfarre-nepomuk .at/nepweb/kreuzweg/kreuzwegliste _aktuell.pdf.

40. Anonymous review of Führich's Christmas and subsequent Easter cycles: "Joseph Ritter von Führich: 'Der bethlehemitische Weg.' ... — 'Er ist auferstanden.' ... " *Die Grenzboten* 27, 2nd semester, vol. 1 (1868): 40.

41. The religious crisis referred to here is the so-called *Kölner Wirren* (the "Cologne Incident" or "Affair," 1837–41), which had erupted between the Prussian government and the Papal See around the insistence of the Roman Catholic Church to consecrate only those mixed marriages that would raise offspring in the Catholic faith; for a recent discussion, which also cites the latest secondary literature, see James Ambrose Lee II, "Issues in Religious Freedom: The Cologne Affair and the 'Kniebeugungsstreit'," in *Oxford History of Modern German Theology*, ed. Grant Kaplan and Kevin M. Vander Schel, Oxford online ed. (June 22, 2023), vol. 1: 1781–1848 at https://doi-org.proxy.library .upenn.edu/10.1093/oso/9780198845768 .003.0038.

42. For Schadow's reaction to the *Kölner Wirren*, see Grewe, *Wilhelm Schadow*, 132–133; for the significance of the *Verein zur Verbreitung religiöser Bilder* concerning the international reception of Nazarene art, see Grewe, "Nazarene or Not? On the Religious Dimension in the Düsseldorf School of Painting," in *The Düsseldorf School of Painting and Its International Influence, 1819–1918*, ed. Bettina Baumgärtel (Petersberg: Michael Imhof Verlag, 2011), 86–97.

Creating Communion
The Nazarenes and Religion

23–26

Philipp Otto Runge
WOLGAST 1777–1810 HAMBURG

Etched and engraved by Johann
Adolph Darnstedt
AUMA 1769–1844 DRESDEN

Etched and engraved by Ephraim
Gottlieb Krüger
DRESDEN 1756–1834 DRESDEN

Etched and engraved by Johann
Gottlieb Seyfert
DRESDEN 1760–1824 DRESDEN

Published by Friedrich Christoph Perthes
RUDOLSTADT 1772–1843 GOTHA

Times of Day (Die Zeiten), 1803/05, published
1807

Series of four etchings with engraving

Between 1802 and 1810, Philipp Otto
Runge conceptualized a cycle of four
scenes representing what he described
as "blossoming, conceiving, giving birth,
and annihilating."[1] These prints are
based on his drawings for the complex
visual program, which features detailed
plants and allegorical figures that refer
to the four times of day, seasons, and
stages of life. Large lilies at the center of
Morning and *Day* evoke innocence as the
world blossoms and ripens, while pop-
pies in *Evening* and *Night* allude to sleep
and destruction. Runge thought of the
works as a repeating cycle, with morning
bringing renewal after sleep and decay.
The divine story of Christ's birth, cru-
cifixion, and resurrection, told through
iconography in each work's margins,

echoes this organic rhythm. The dove in
Night indicates that eternal life will follow death, signified by the cross, crown
of thorns, and nails in *Evening*.

Runge hoped to develop *Times of Day*
into a *Gesamtkunstwerk* (total work of
art) that included music and poetry, but
he did not complete it before dying at
a young age. His ambitious vision for
the project is notable for combining two
subjects typical of Romantic art: careful depictions of plants and Christian
symbols.

1. Richard Littlejohns, "Philipp Otto Runge's
'Tageszeiten' and Their Relationship to
Romantic Nature Philosophy," *Studies in
Romanticism* 42, no. 1 (Spring 2003), 67.

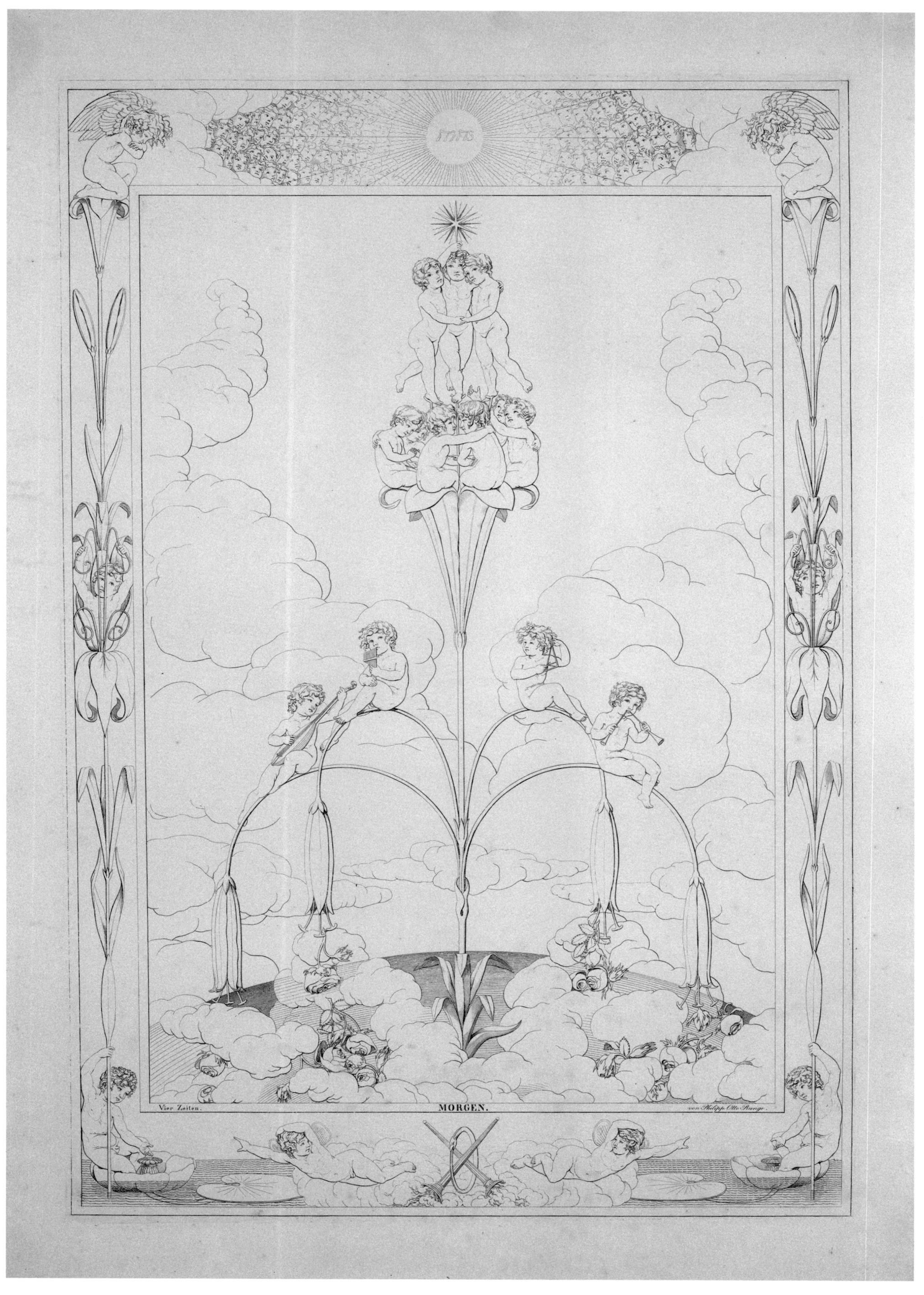

23. *Morning (Morgen)*

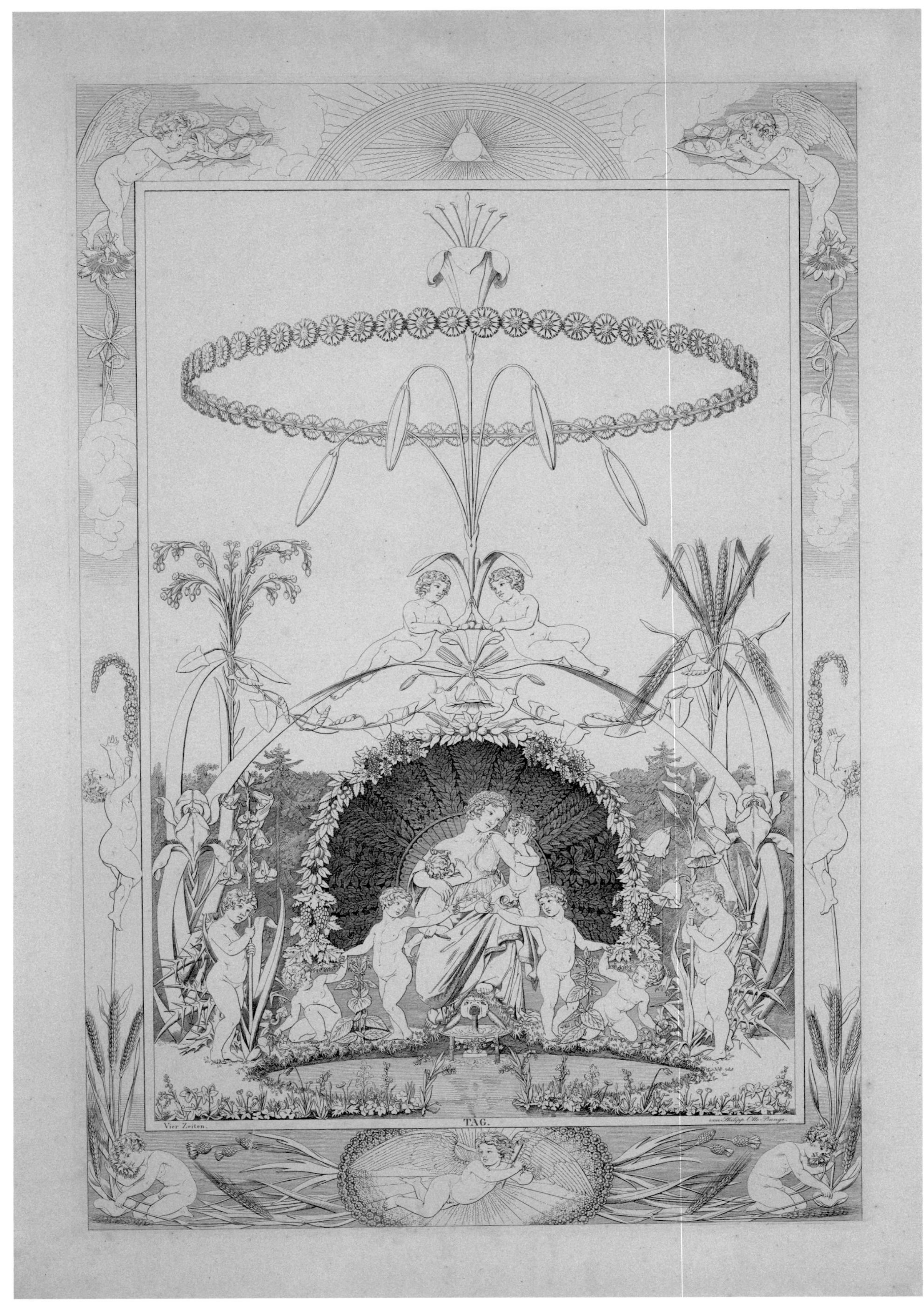

24. *Day (Tag)*

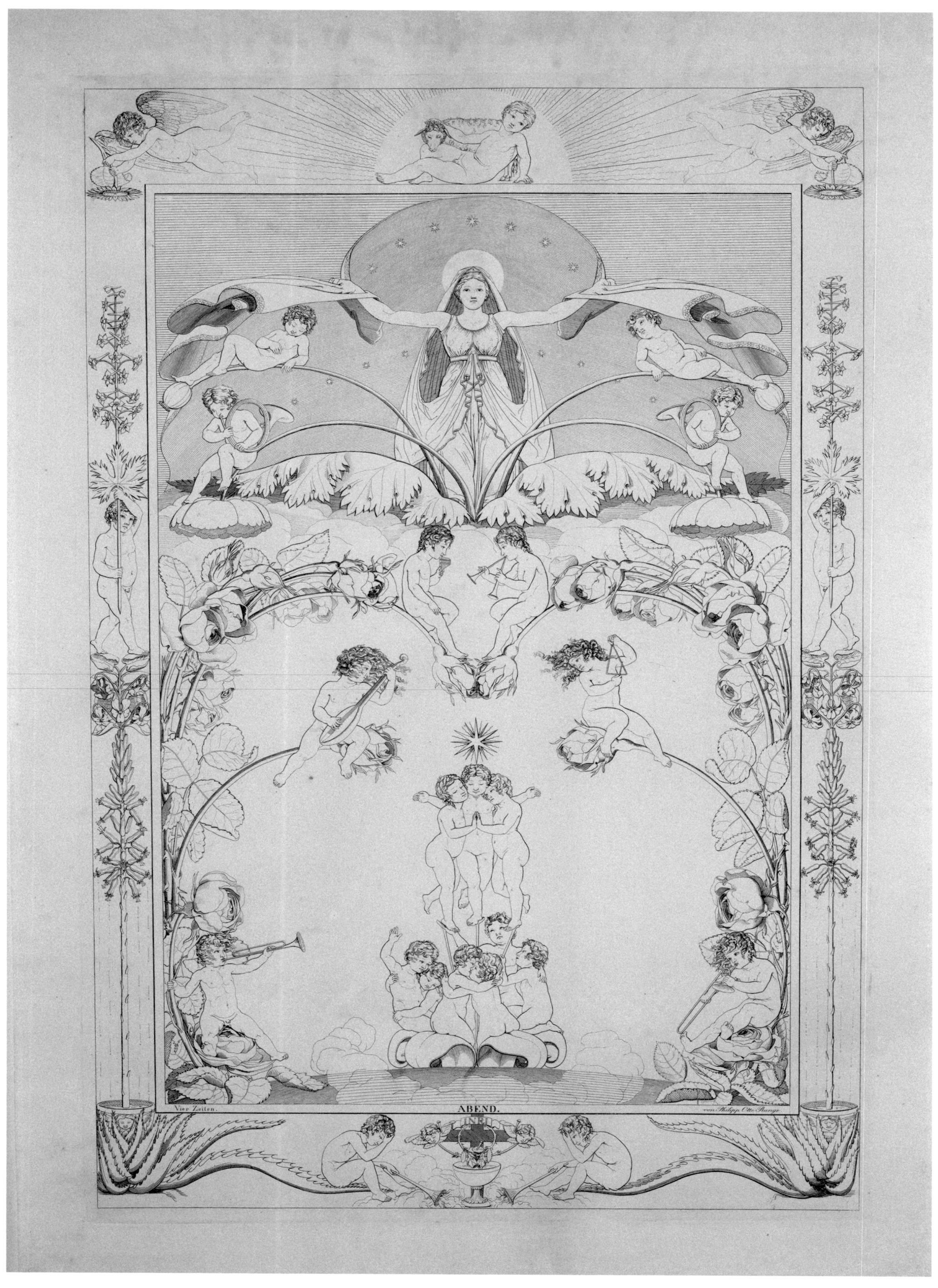

25. *Evening (Abend)*

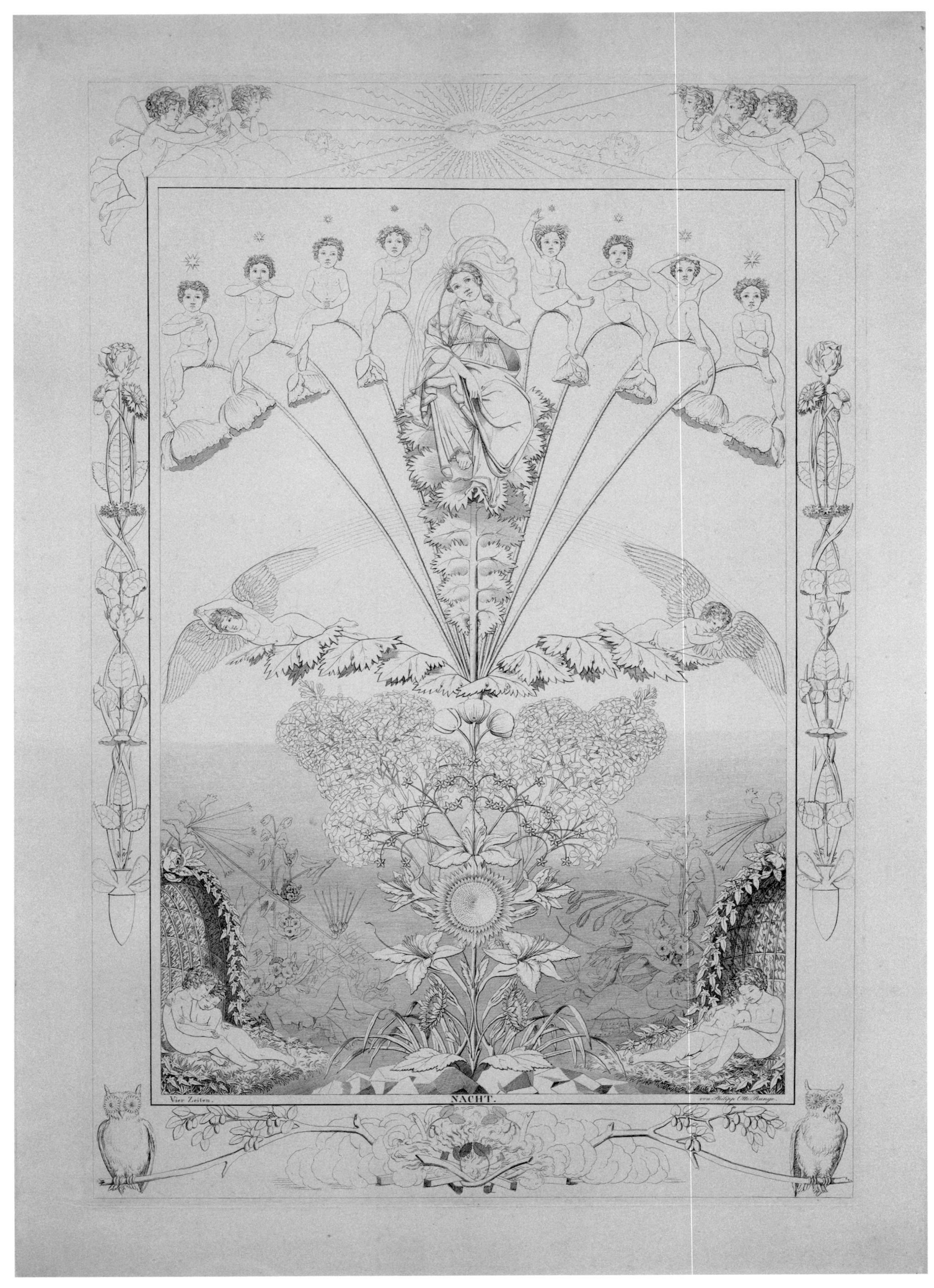

26. *Night (Nacht)*

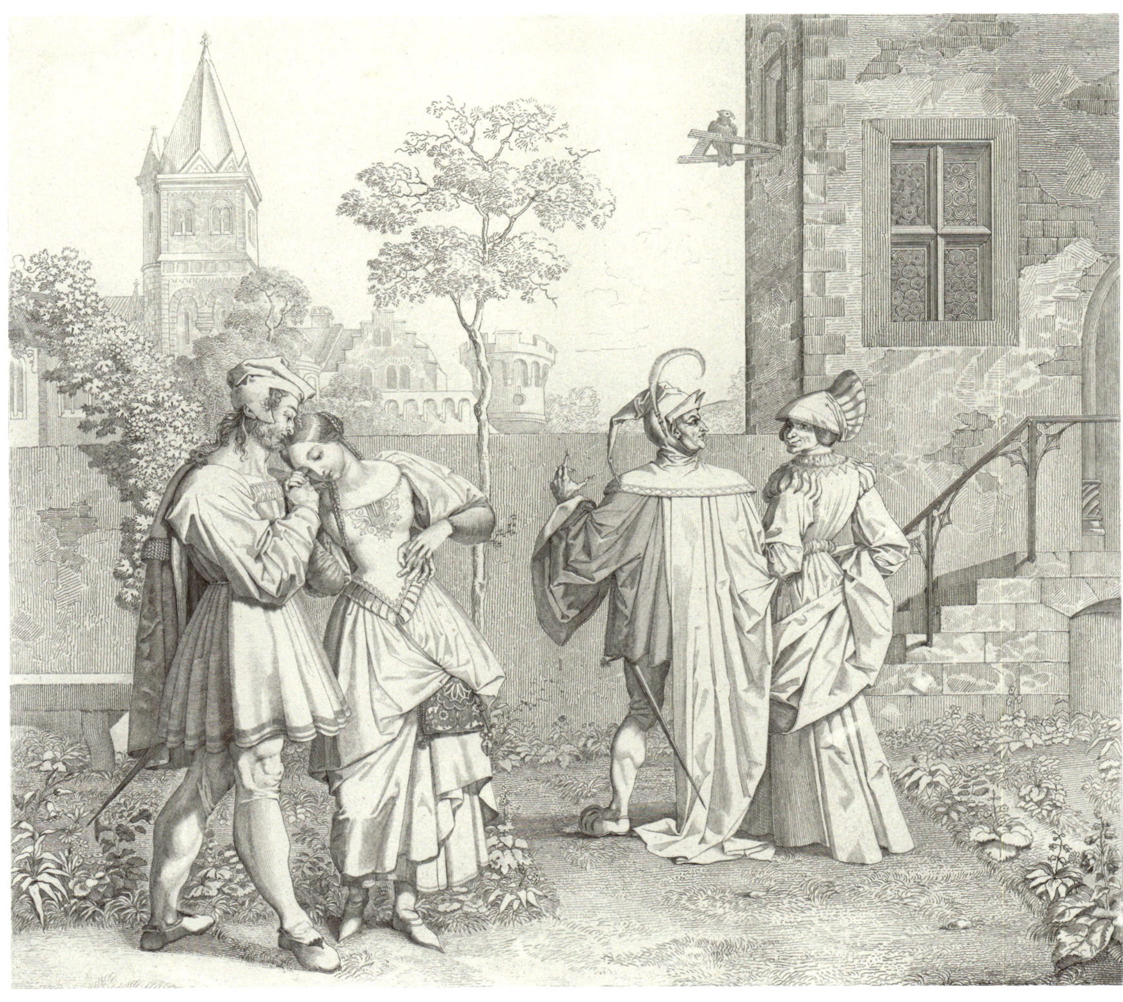

27. *The Walk in the Garden (Der Spaziergang im Garten)*, 1813

27–33
Peter von Cornelius
DÜSSELDORF 1783–1867 BERLIN

Engraved by Ferdinand Ruscheweyh
NEUSTRELITZ 1785–1846 NEUSTRELITZ

Published by Georg Reimer
GREIFSWALD 1776–1842 BERLIN

Illustrations for Goethe's "Faust" (Bilder zu Goethes Faust), 1813–18, published 1845

Series of ten engravings, printed chine collé, with title and dedication pages

Published in 1808, part I of Johann Wolfgang von Goethe's *Faust* tells the tale of a scholar who trades his soul to the devil in exchange for knowledge of life's true essence. Mephisto, the devil's representative who proposed the bargain, encourages Faust to seduce a young woman named Gretchen. She learns that she is pregnant after Faust has abandoned her, and she drowns the child out of desperation. Despite Gretchen's being sentenced to death, her soul is saved when she repents to God. Faust, however, remains beholden to Mephisto.

Peter von Cornelius began his illustrations for *Faust* in 1810. He sent six of them to Goethe, who described them as "truly astonishing."[2] Cornelius then traveled to Rome and completed the remaining drawings there. During this time,

he joined a secessionist group of artists known as the Brotherhood of St. Luke and met Ferdinand Ruscheweyh, who engraved the prints for the portfolio. The two collaborated closely, ensuring Ruscheweyh's delicate silvery lines conveyed the expressiveness of Cornelius's original compositions.

The *Faust* portfolio ultimately exemplified ideals the Brotherhood of St. Luke sought to convey. The narrative of Gretchen's salvation resonated with the group's Christian beliefs, and illustrating a play by Goethe, the country's most renowned writer, elevated German art.

2. Richard M. Meyer, ed., *Goethe und seine Freunde im Briefwechsel* (Berlin: Georg Bondi, 1911), 203.

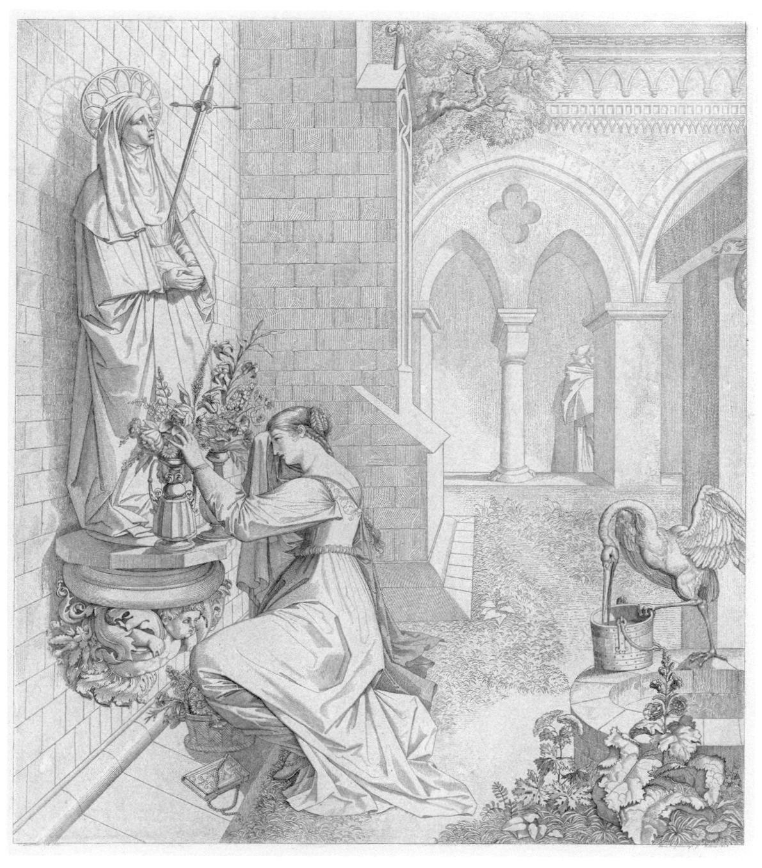

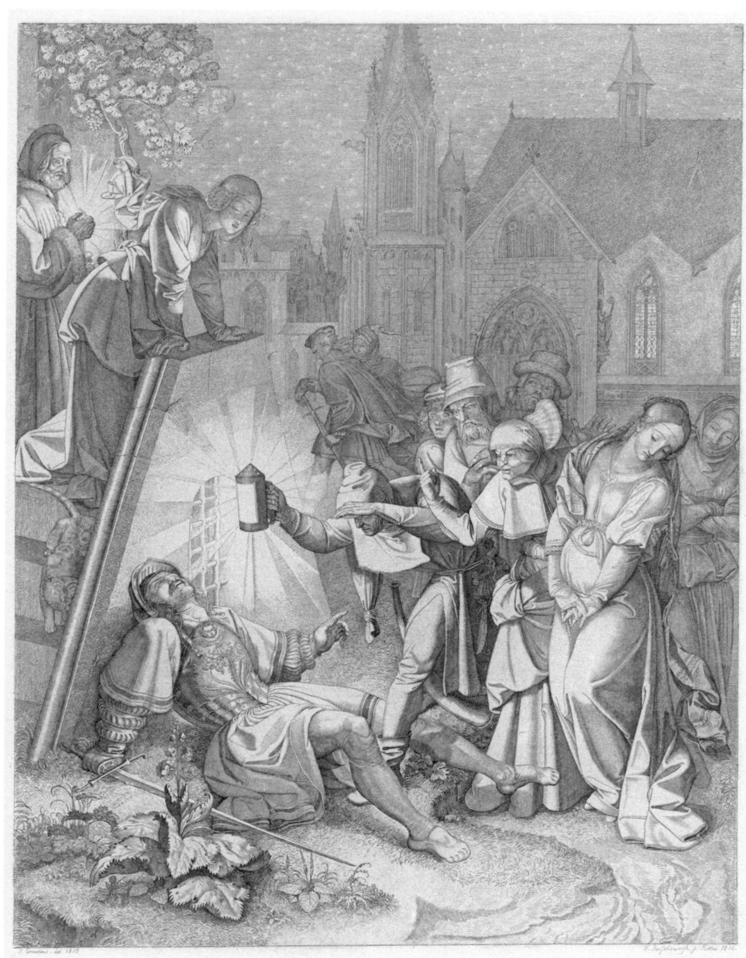

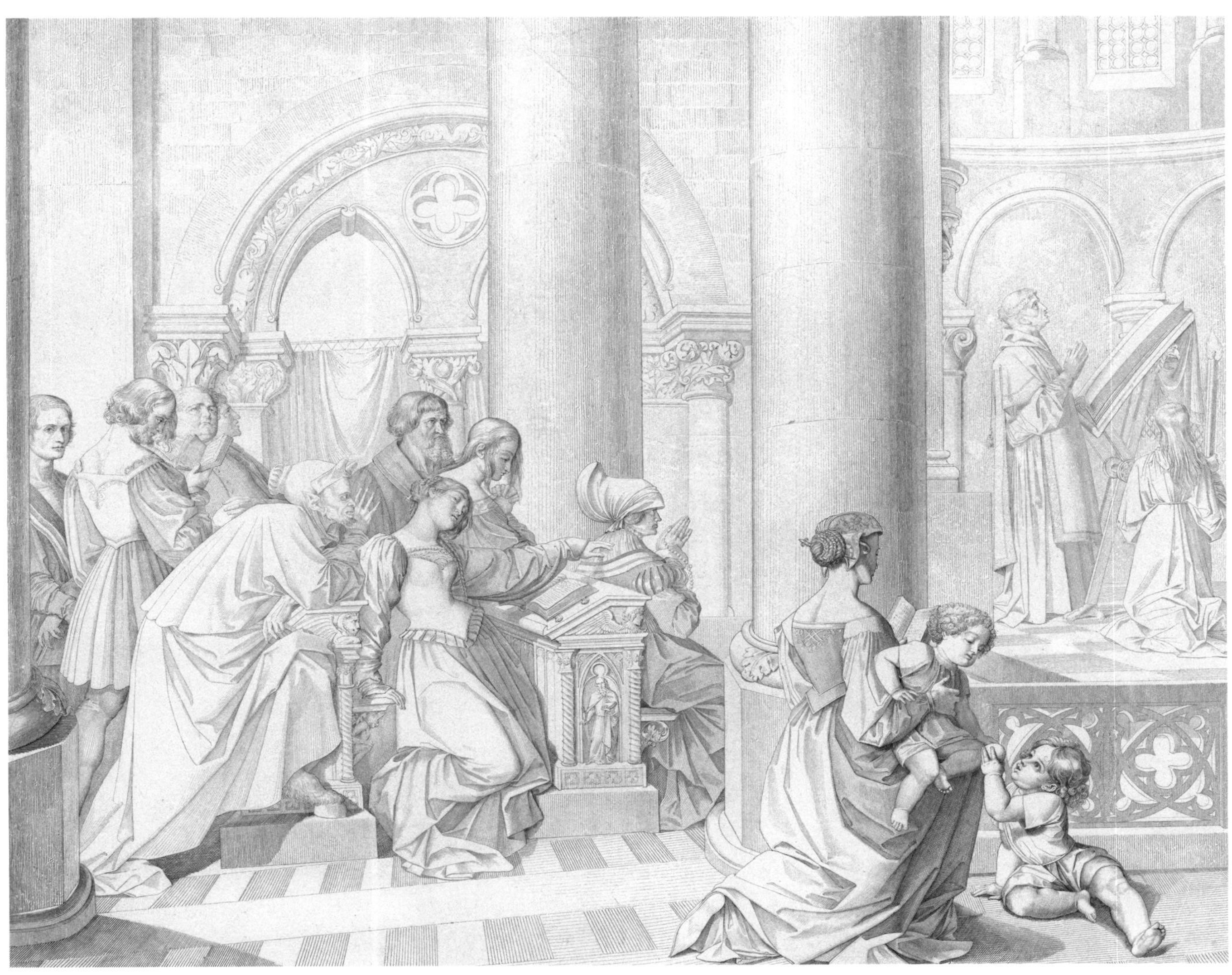

28. *Gretchen Before a Statue of the Mater Dolo-rosa (Gretchen vor der Mater Dolorosa)*, 1816

29. *Valentin's Death (Valentins Tod)*, 1816

30. *Scene in the Cathedral (Szene im Dom)*, 1815

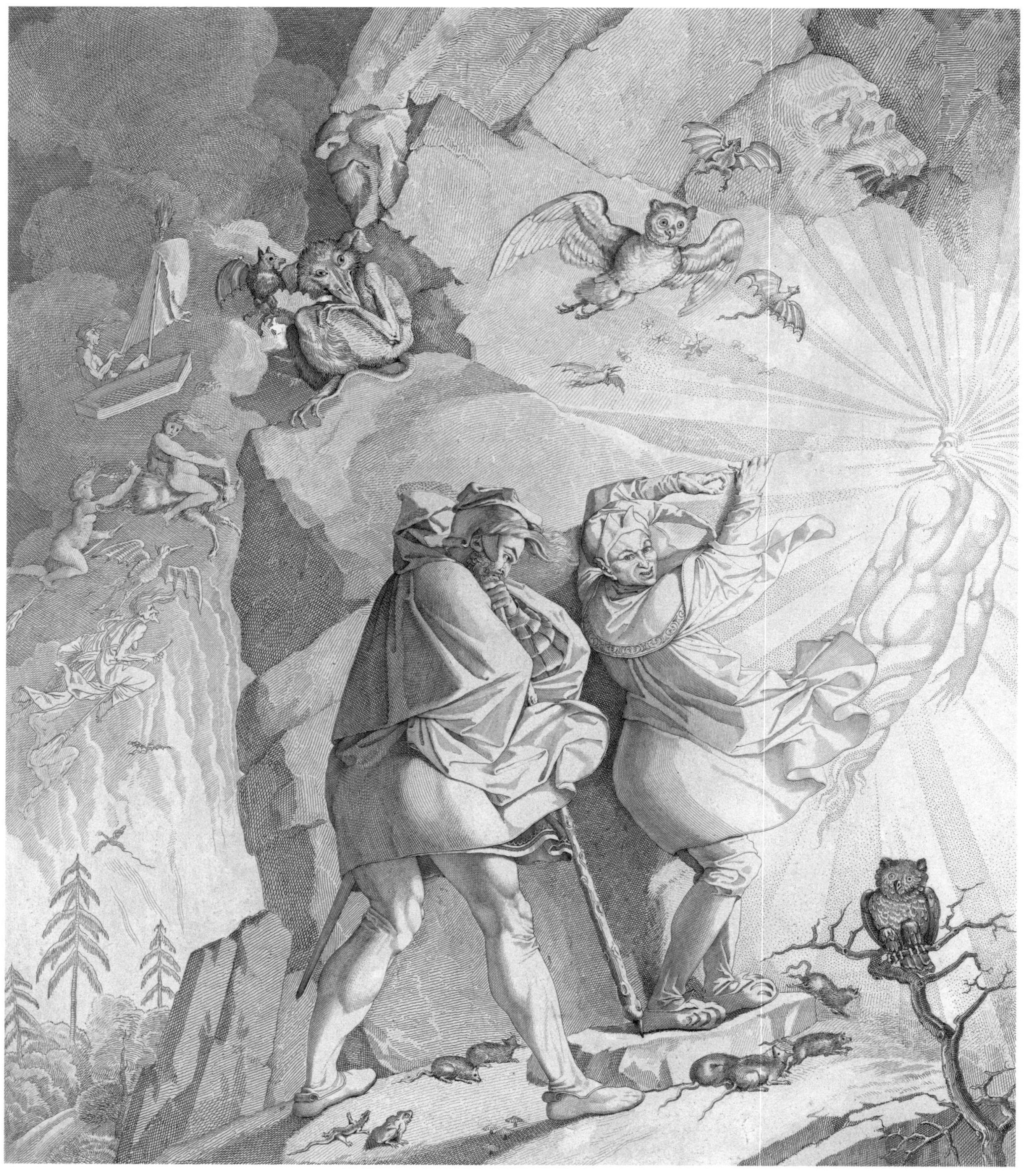

31. *Journey to the Witches' Sabbath (Der Gang nach dem Brocken), 1813*

32. *Vision at the Gallows (Die Erscheinung am Rabenstein), 1814*

33. *Gretchen in Prison (Gretchen im Gefängnis), 1815*

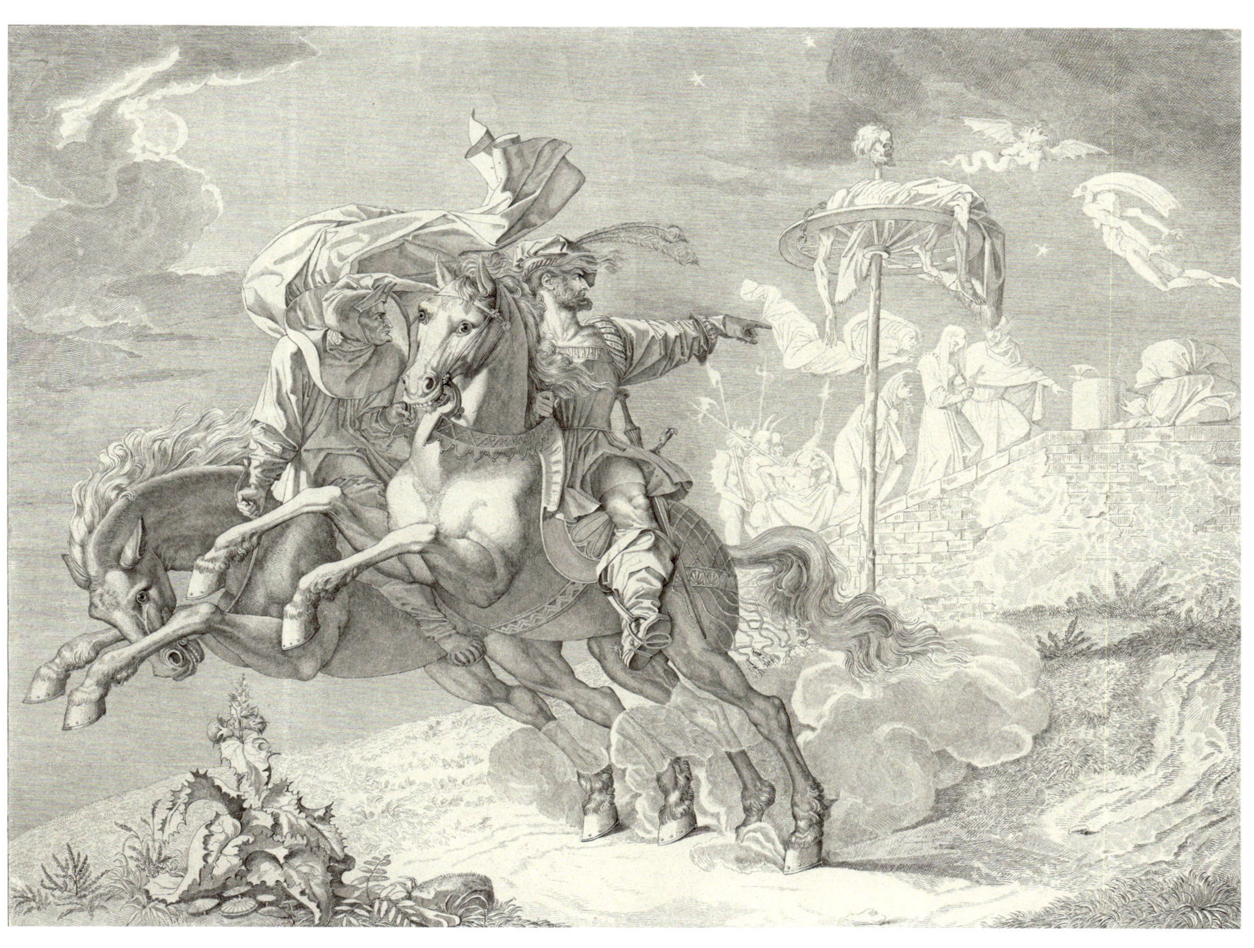

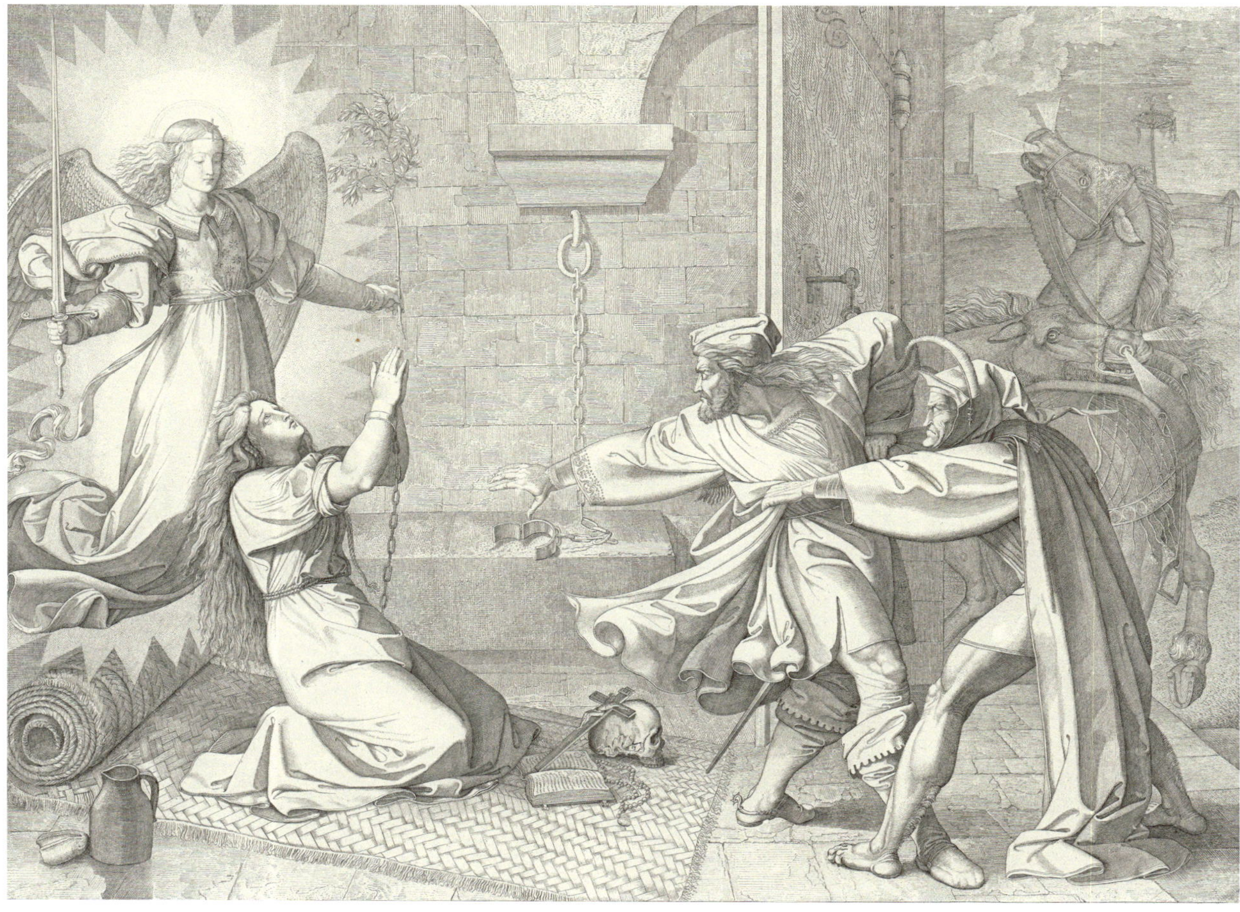

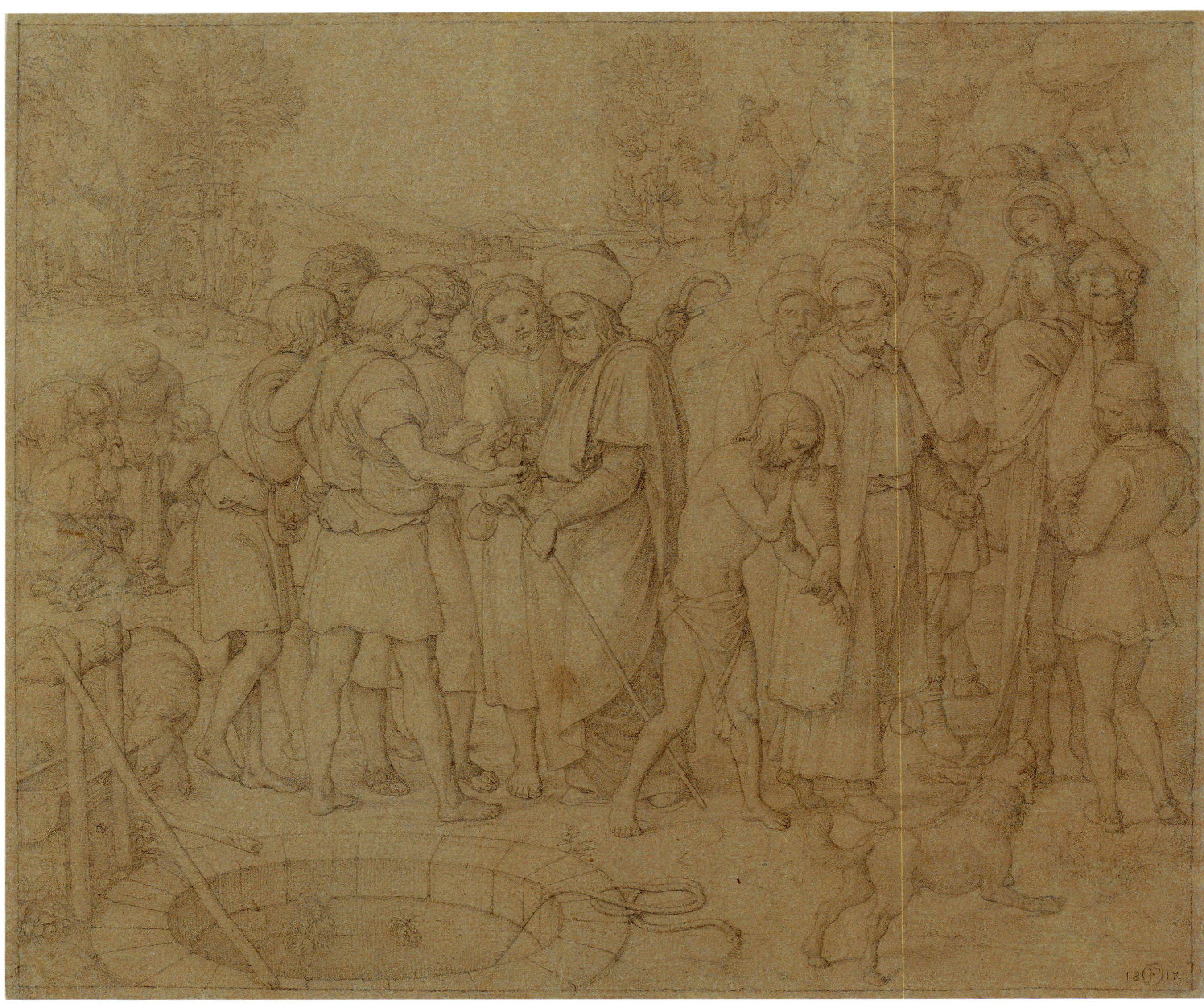

34.
Johann Friedrich Overbeck
LÜBECK 1789–1869 ROME

Joseph Being Sold by His Brothers (Joseph wird von seinen Brüdern verkauft), 1817

Graphite on paper

35.
Johann Friedrich Overbeck
LÜBECK 1789–1869 ROME

Lithographed by Hans Jakob Oeri
KYBURG 1782–1868 ZURICH

Published by Johann Velten
WETZLAR 1784–1864 KARLSRUHE

Joseph Being Sold by His Brothers (Joseph wird von seinen Brüdern verkauft), 1826

Lithograph

This sketch by Johann Friedrich Overbeck is one of several he drew in preparation for a fresco cycle he and four other artists were hired to paint in Rome. Overbeck led a secessionist group of German artists called the Brotherhood of St. Luke, which hoped to forge a new German art grounded in religion. In 1816, Prussian Consul General Jakob Ludwig Salomon Bartholdy gave the brotherhood their first commission: to paint a room in his apartment in the Palazzo Zuccari. They chose the Old Testament story of Joseph as their subject, and Overbeck's contribution featured Joseph's jealous brothers selling him into slavery. The slight differences between Overbeck's drawing and the completed fresco, together with its small scale, suggest he made it before settling on the final composition.

The lithograph by Hans Jakob Oeri is based on Overbeck's full-scale cartoon. Overbeck either referred to or directly transferred the cartoon to create the fresco's outlines, and it captures his most refined idea for the project. It was displayed in Frankfurt in 1818, along with two others from the Joseph cycle, generating public admiration for the frescoes and the artists involved.

Johann Velten, who later published the print based on the cartoon, believed in the Brotherhood of St. Luke's ideals and hoped to increase the group's renown through the sale and circulation of the image. Overbeck's original cartoon was destroyed in World War II, and the lithograph is an important record of the lost work.

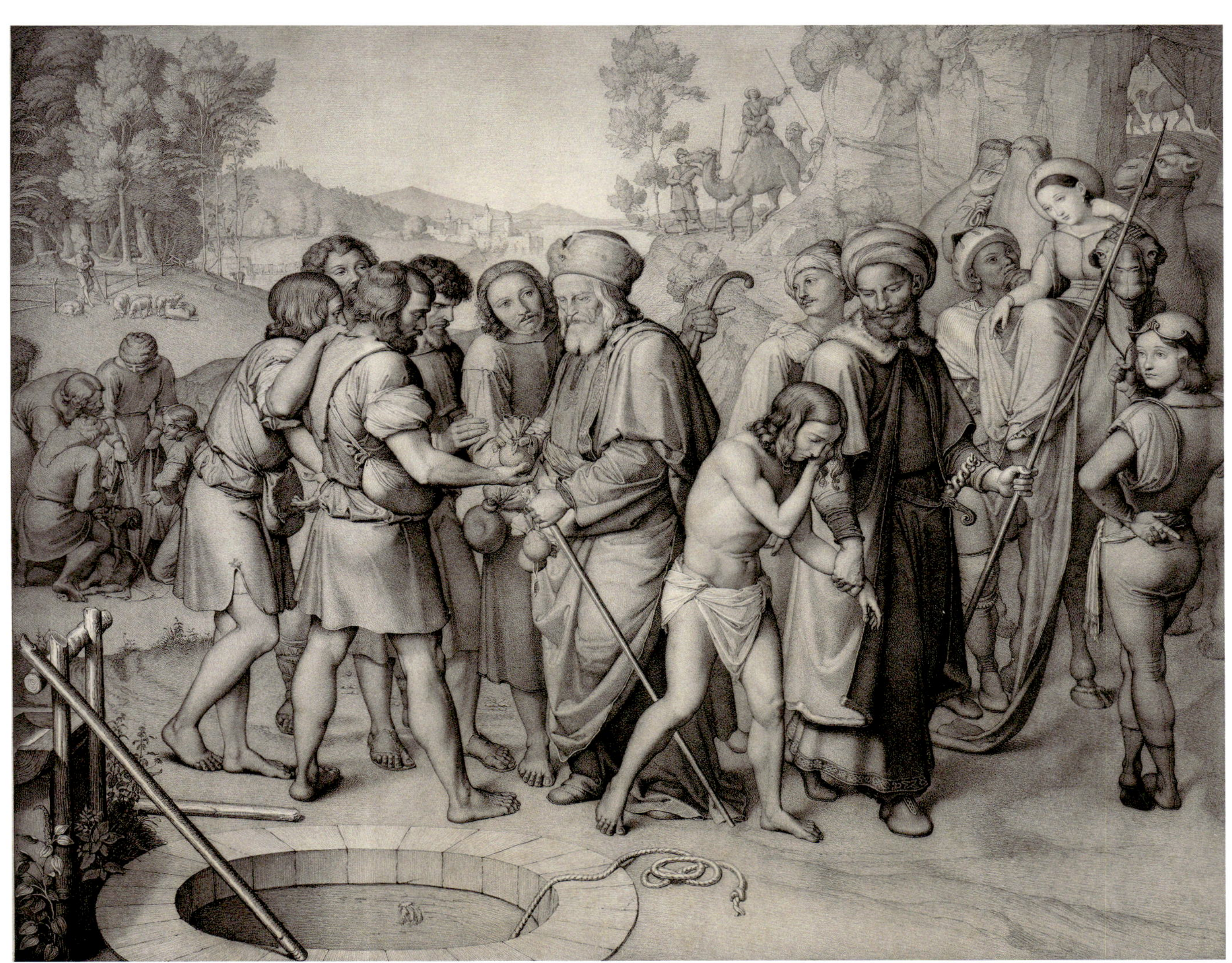

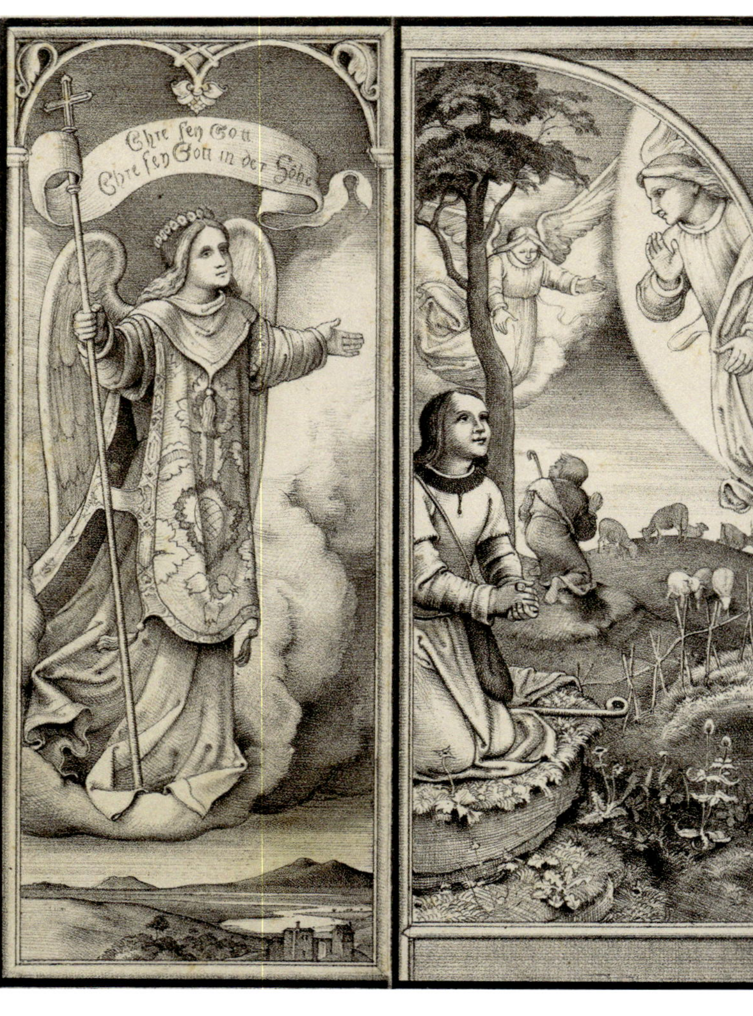

36.
Ferdinand Olivier
DESSAU 1785–1841 MUNICH

Printed by Adolph Kunike
GREIFSWALD 1777–1838 VIENNA

House Altar, 1820

Lithograph

Modeled after winged altarpieces made during the Middle Ages and Early Renaissance, this print by Ferdinand Olivier was designed to be folded and kept in the home. The three scenes visible when the altarpiece is open come from the story of Christ's birth: The center image represents Jesus in the manger, and the left and right panels depict an angel announcing the news to the shepherds and the arrival of the three Magi. When closed, the altarpiece features two angels holding banners, which read "Glory be to God / Glory be to God in the highest" and "Peace on earth / Goodwill toward men." Crease lines visible on the verso of this impression indicate that it was once folded into its intended configuration.

Olivier's lithograph demonstrates the importance of prints in spreading the Nazarenes' beliefs. The group recognized art making as a form of devotion, and this domestic altarpiece encouraged worshippers to actively meditate on the meaning of the biblical story as they handled it.

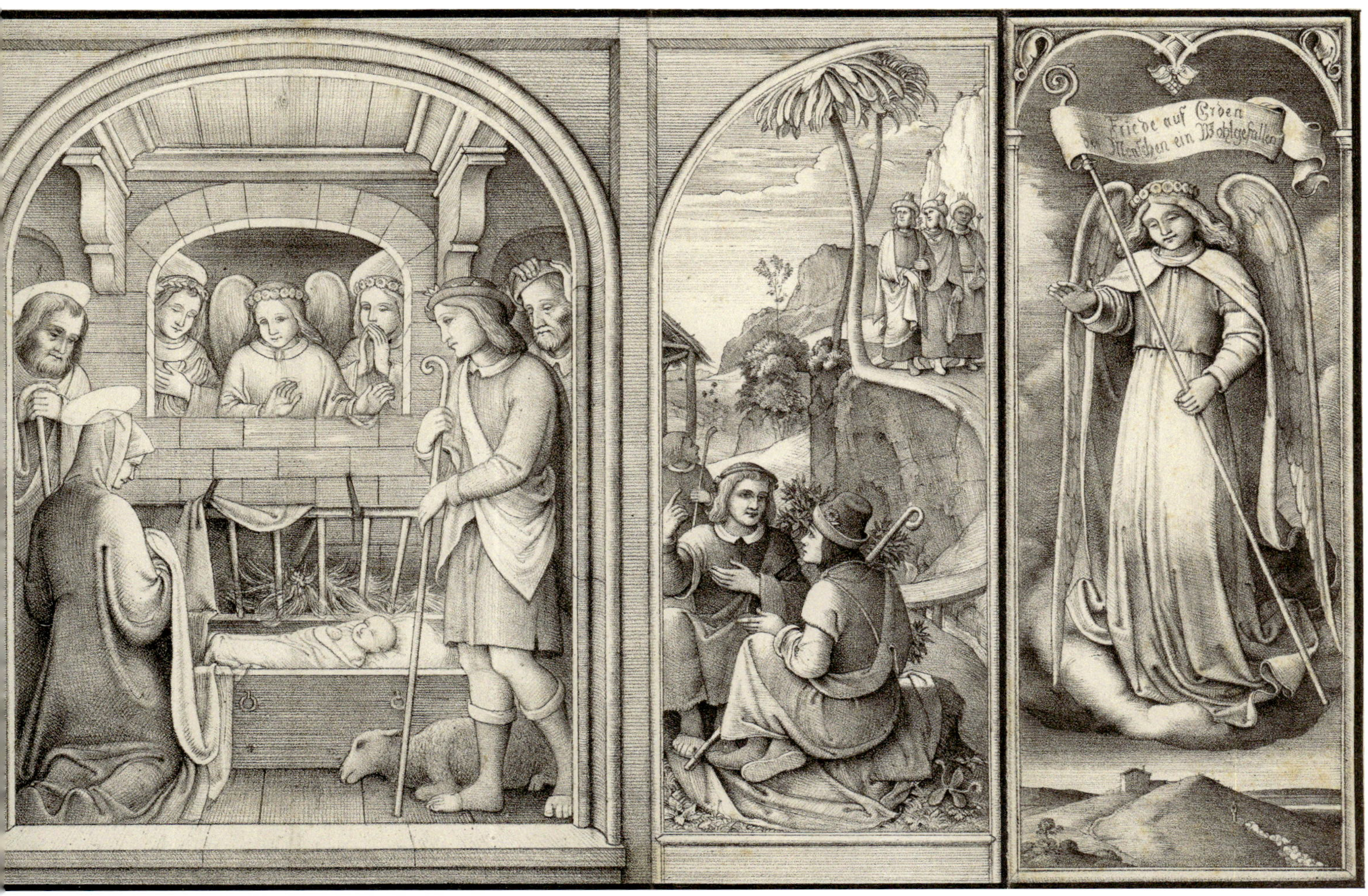

Friede auf Erden
den Menschen ein Wohlgefallen

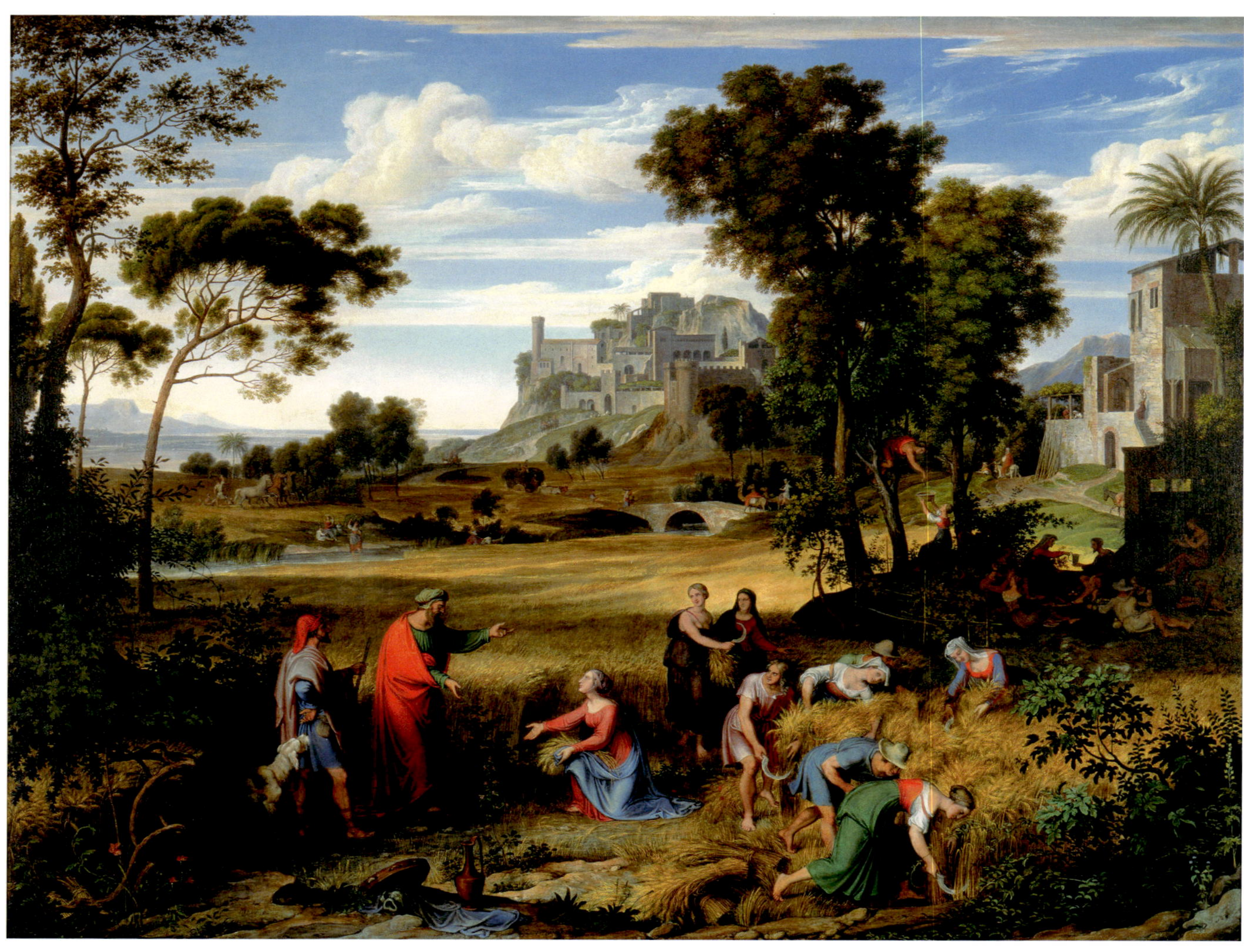

37.

Joseph Anton Koch

OBERGIBLEN 1768–1839 ROME

Landscape with Ruth and Boaz (Landschaft mit Ruth und Boas), 1823/25

Oil on canvas

This painting represents the biblical story of Ruth, who was left impoverished after her husband's death. Ruth is depicted kneeling at the center of the composition, where she had been gleaning wheat from Boaz's fields. Boaz invites her to eat with his workers, gesturing to the group threshing at the right.

Joseph Anton Koch strove to create what he described as "historical or poetic landscape,"[3] where the figures and narrative within the work lend significance to a monumental natural setting. The story of Ruth and Boaz was among his first attempts at this kind of composition; he set the scene in a vast, fecund landscape in front of the distant town of Bethlehem. Koch often created multiple artworks depicting the same subject, appealing to potential collectors by offering different media and various sizes. Between 1803 and 1827, he made five paintings and sixteen drawings of Ruth and Boaz. This version belonged to his English friend and patron George Nott. Nott funded Koch's travel to Italy, where he remained for most of his life.

3. Götz Czymmek, "Johann Christian Reinhart und Joseph Anton Koch als Landschafter," in *Heroismus und Idylle: Formen der Landschaft um 1800* (Cologne: Wallraf-Richartz-Museum, 1984), 26.

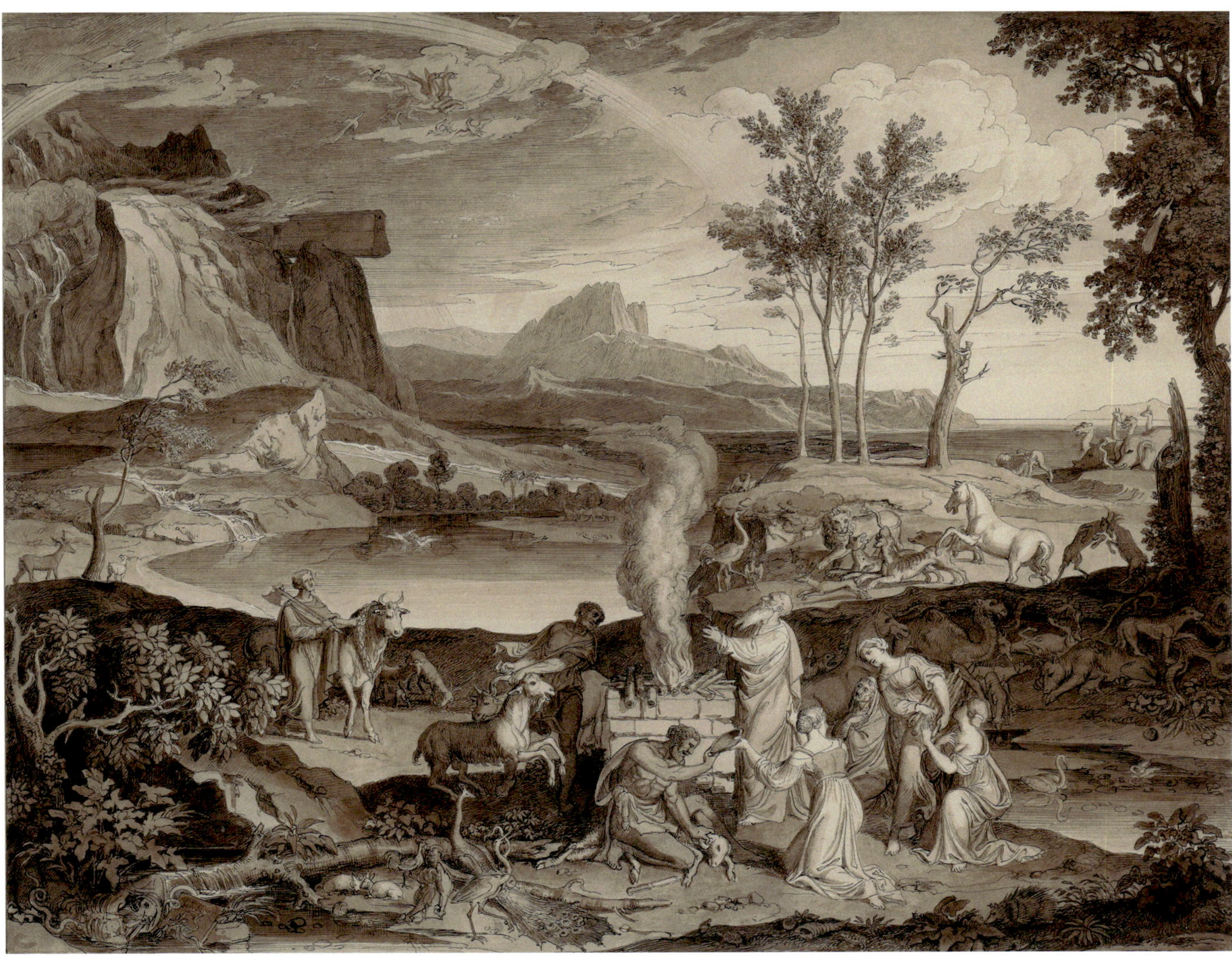

38.

Joseph Anton Koch

OBERGIBLEN 1768–1839 ROME

Landscape with Noah's Sacrifice (Landschaft mit Dankopfer Noahs), ca. 1823/25

Pen and brown ink and wash on paper

Standing in front of a pool of water left after the great flood, Noah prepares a sacrifice to thank God for his survival. In Joseph Anton Koch's drawing of the scene from the book of Genesis, the creatures that Noah's family rescued in the ark roam the landscape. Even mythological creatures appear among the camels, giraffes, lions, and rabbits: A unicorn rears at the right, and two griffons fly with the doves beneath the rainbow.

Koch sometimes treated *Noah's Sacrifice* and *Ruth and Boaz* as companion pieces; this work and a similarly sized drawing of Ruth and Boaz belonged to the same collector in Oxford until they were sold at auction in 1974. The composition is closely related to a painting that Koch submitted to the Munich Art Academy's annual competition in 1814, for which he won a prize. The painting was later lost during World War II, and this drawing is a significant record of the work that earned Koch recognition from his peers.

39.

Johann Friedrich Overbeck

LÜBECK 1789–1869 ROME

Lithographed by Nikolaus Hoff
FRANKFURT 1798–1873 FRANKFURT

Printed by Friedrich Carl Vogel
FRANKFURT 1806–1865 VENICE

Italia and Germania, 1830

Lithograph

An iconic image of the Nazarene movement, this lithograph made after a painting by Johann Friedrich Overbeck reflects the devoted friendships within the Brotherhood of St. Luke. Between 1808 and 1812, co-leaders Overbeck and Franz Pforr created numerous works depicting two women. According to Pforr, the dark-haired figure represented Southern Europe and Overbeck's love of Italian art; her fair-haired counterpart, Northern Europe and Pforr's preference for German aesthetics. Pforr titled a later drawing of the pair *Allegory of Friendship*, basing the women on the biblical brides in a story he wrote. The fictional version of Overbeck weds Sulamith, modeled after Solomon's wife in the Old Testament; her sister, Maria, associated with the New Testament's Virgin Mary, couples with Pforr's double.

Overbeck made Pforr a drawing of Sulamith and Maria around 1811, and publisher Friedrich Wenner commissioned a painting of it. Overbeck abandoned the work when Pforr drowned

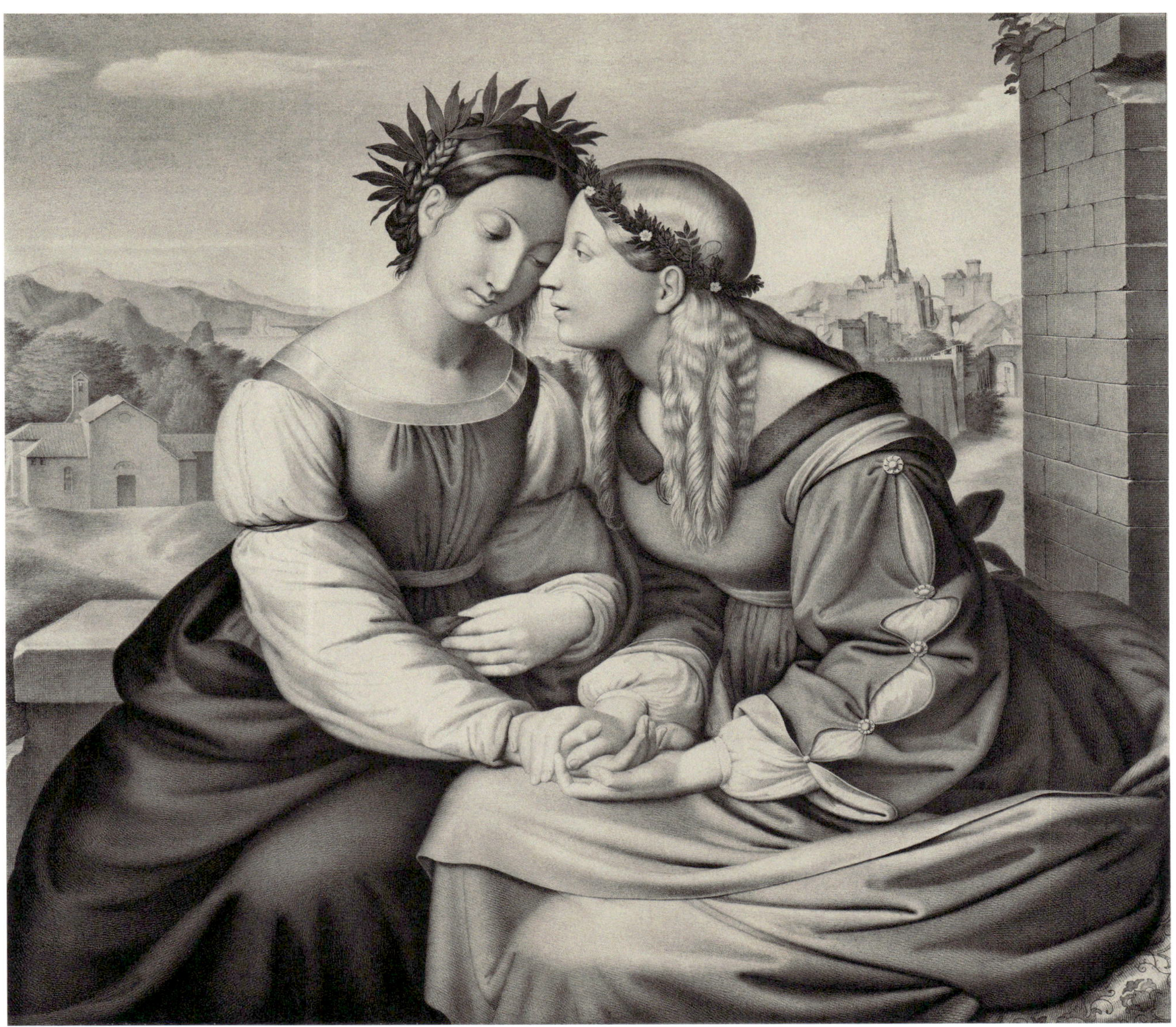

in 1812. He returned to the canvas in 1828 and titled it *Italia and Germania*, explaining in a letter that the two countries are "alien to each other, but which are and should remain my task to merge . . . and which I therefore think of here in beautiful, close friendship."[4] Sixteen years after Pforr's death, the image transformed from an expression of friendship to a statement about an ideal art form that blended influences from Germany and Italy. The painting proved to be popular, and in 1830, the Frankfurt Art Association commissioned print-maker Nikolaus Hoff to create a lithograph of the work for its members.

4. Letter from Johann Friedrich Overbeck to Friedrich Wenner, January 31, 1829. Printed in Eberhard Haufe, ed., *Deutsche Briefe aus Italien von Winckelmann bis Gregorovius* (Hamburg: Christian Wegner Verlag, 1965), 178.

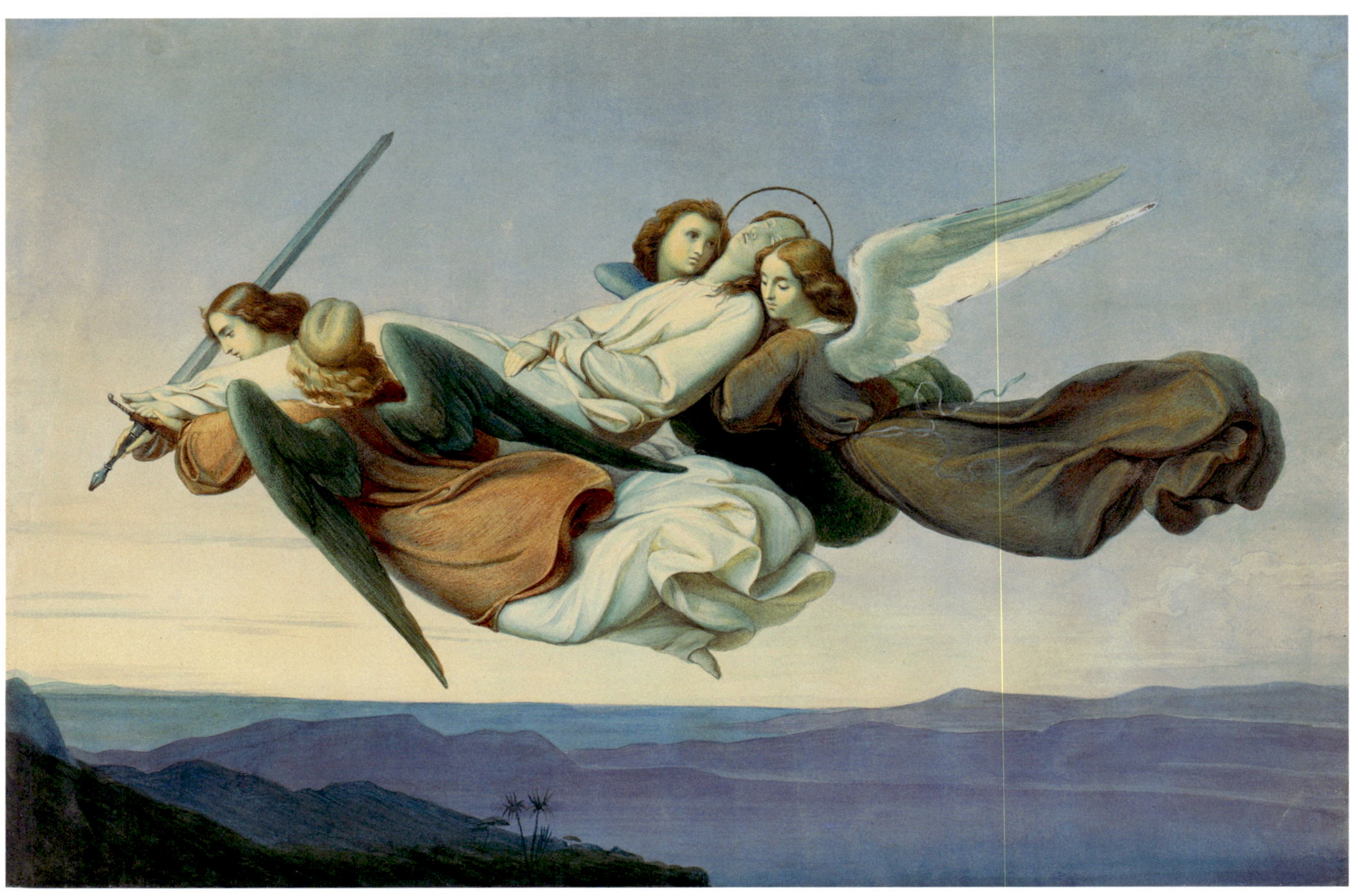

40.

Heinrich Karl Anton Mücke

WROCŁAW 1806–1891 DÜSSELDORF

The Body of Saint Catherine of Alexandria Carried to Heaven by Angels (Der Leichnam der heiligen Katharina von Alexandrien, von Engeln zum Himmel getragen), ca. 1836

Watercolor with touches of gold and lead white on paper

41.

Heinrich Karl Anton Mücke

WROCŁAW 1806–1891 DÜSSELDORF

Published by Julius Buddeus
ACTIVE DÜSSELDORF 1830S–1852

Angels Carrying the Body of St. Catherine to Mount Sinai (Engel tragen den Leichnam der heil. Katharina nach dem Berge Sinai), from the portfolio *Album of German Artists in Original Etchings (Album deutscher Künstler in Original-Radierungen)*, 1841

Etching

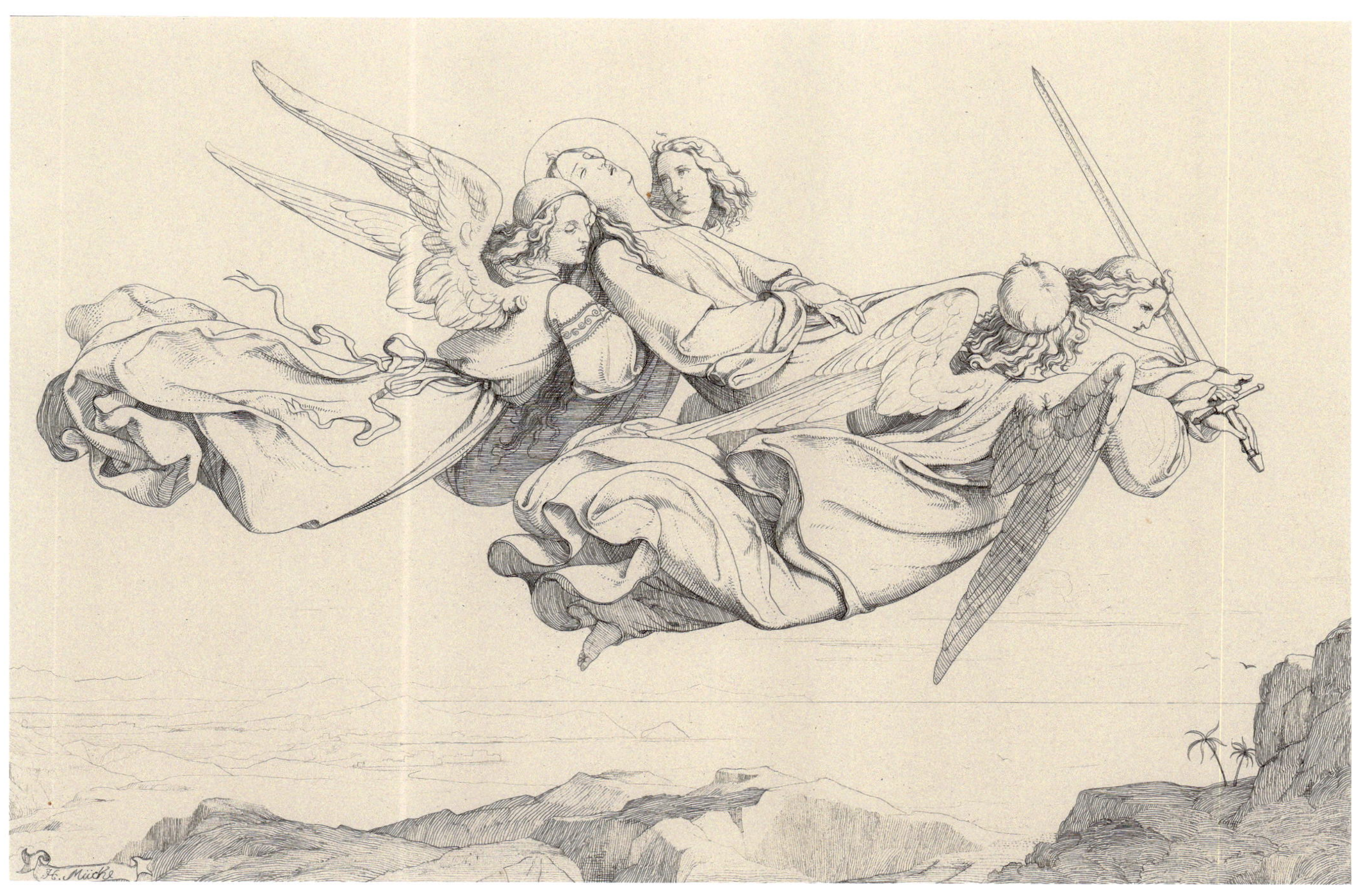

These two works by Heinrich Karl Anton Mücke exemplify how the Nazarenes used multiples to disseminate their artistic ideals. The watercolor is one of at least four that repeat the composition of angels carrying the martyred Catherine of Alexandria to Mount Sinai that Mücke first painted in oil in 1836. That work, which he submitted to the Berlin Art Academy exhibition, was enormously successful. After it was purchased, he created several additional oil paintings for private commissioners. All the St. Catherine images include the same figures, with small variations in the angels' clothing and the landscape below.

In 1841, Mücke etched the subject for a portfolio that featured printed reproductions of German artists' paintings. The figures face the opposite direction from those in the source painting—then in the collection of the hereditary grand duke of Russia—and in all known versions of the work. Mücke made only four prints during his lifetime, and he may not have known he needed to reverse the image on the copper plate to achieve the same orientation during printing.

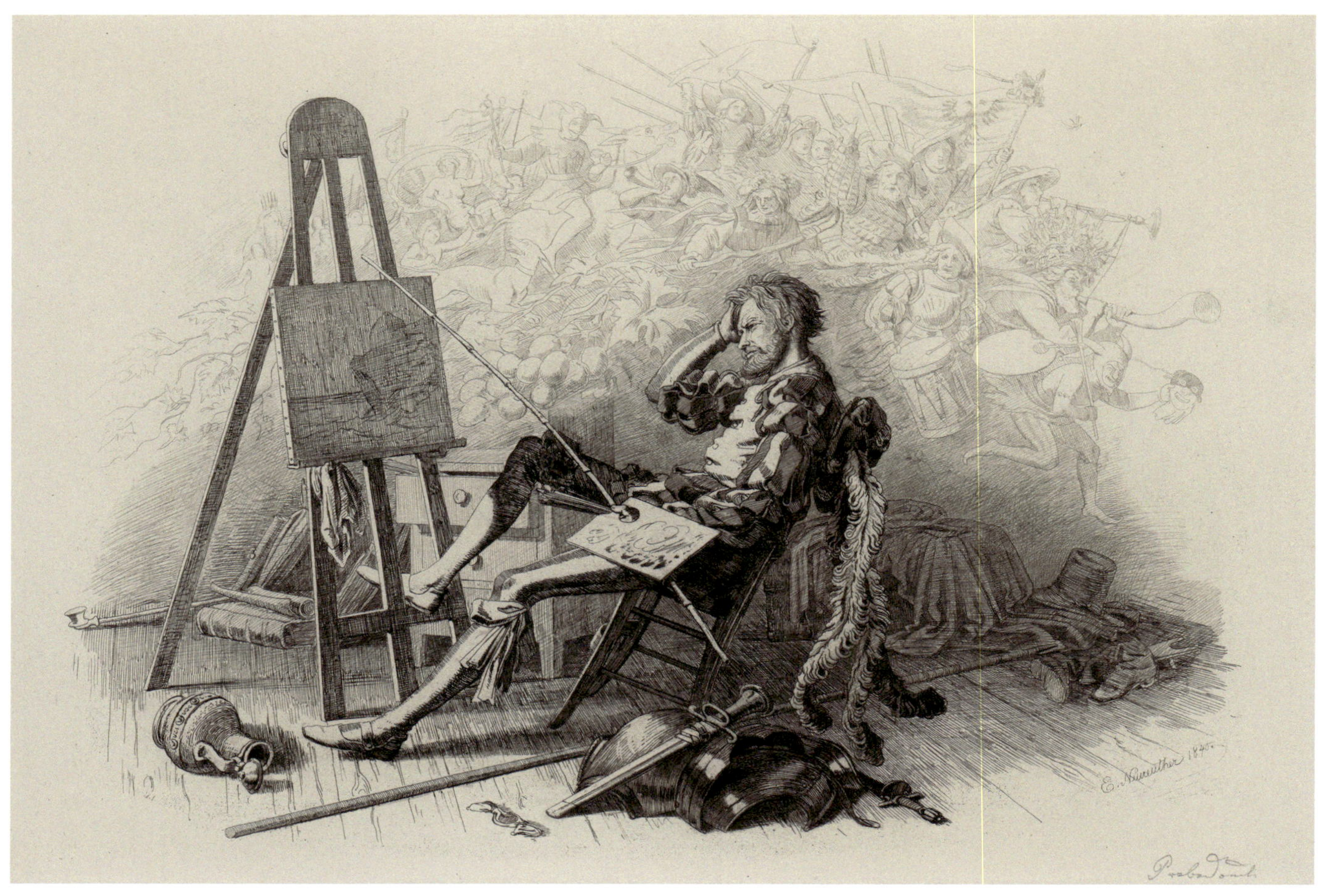

42.

Eugen Napoleon Neureuther
MUNICH 1806–1882 MUNICH

The Morning After the Masquerade (Am Morgen nach dem Maskenfeste), 1840

Etching, printed chine collé

43.

Eugen Napoleon Neureuther
MUNICH 1806–1882 MUNICH

Printed by Carl Mayer
NUREMBERG 1798–1868 NUREMBERG

Maximilian I Presenting the Artists' Coat of Arms to Albrecht Dürer (Artists' Masquerade 1840) (Die Verleihung des Künstlerwappens an Albrecht Dürer durch Max I. [Maskenfest der Künstler 1840]), 1841–43

Etching

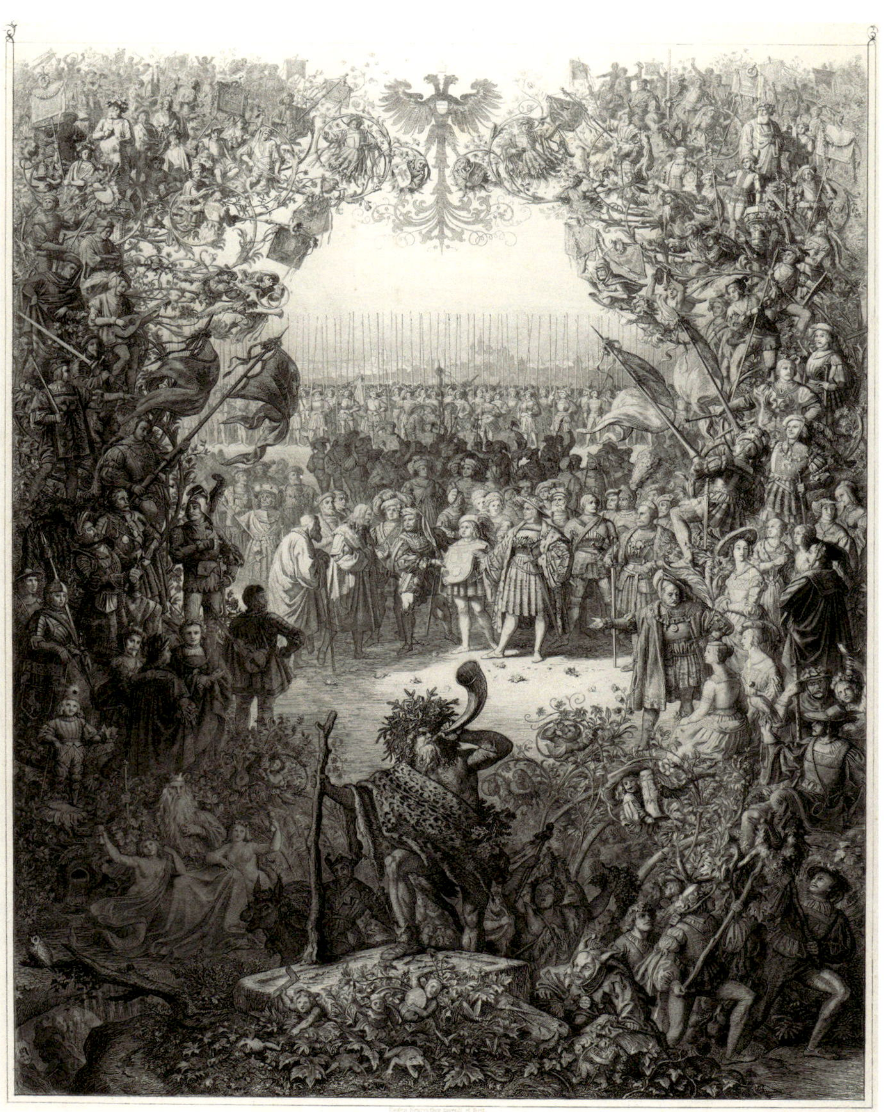

The Morning After the Masquerade depicts an artist in sixteenth-century clothing slumped in front of his easel, struggling to paint. Eugen Napoleon Neureuther was likely referring to the repercussions of the masquerade held to honor Renaissance artist Albrecht Dürer on February 17, 1840, which he helped organize. The event featured artists playing the roles of Dürer and his patron, Emperor Maximilian I, and was followed by a banquet and dance. Neureuther almost certainly participated in all the festivities, leading to a miserable morning like the one he etched.

Neureuther depicted the celebration again a few years later in *Maximilian I Presenting the Artists' Coat of Arms*. At the center of the print, Emperor Maximilian's page presents Dürer with the coat of arms. The margins include references to the 1840 festival, such as a bacchanalian figure blowing a horn, guild members waving flags, jesters, and a float—designed by Neureuther— carrying the Mountain King of Norse legend (lower left). Neureuther etched this print for Munich's Albrecht Dürer Society to commemorate their election year. Several German cities founded art societies (*Kunstvereine*) during the nineteenth century to support artists and instill appreciation for art within the growing middle class. The groups commissioned prints for their membership, bringing affordable, original artworks into homes. Many *Kunstvereine* continue to publish prints today.

44.

Johannes Riepenhausen
GÖTTINGEN 1787–1860 ROME

Raphael and La Fornarina, ca. 1833

Watercolor and ink over graphite on paper

This watercolor depicts the Italian Renaissance artist Raphael painting *La Fornarina*, a work popularly believed to depict his mistress and model. Johannes Riepenhausen imagined the moment when Raphael completed the canvas and invited his sitter to view it. Palette and brush still in hand, the artist looks up to watch her reaction. Despite his reputation for pursuing carnal desires, Raphael was an icon among the Nazarenes. They believed his oeuvre exemplified the classical religious art they hoped to create.

Riepenhausen likely made this drawing around the time he completed a set of twelve engravings representing Raphael's life. In 1833, the artist's remains were exhumed from the Pantheon in Rome so they could be studied. The event prompted Riepenhausen to revisit a series on the same subject he had created with his brother, Franz, in 1816.

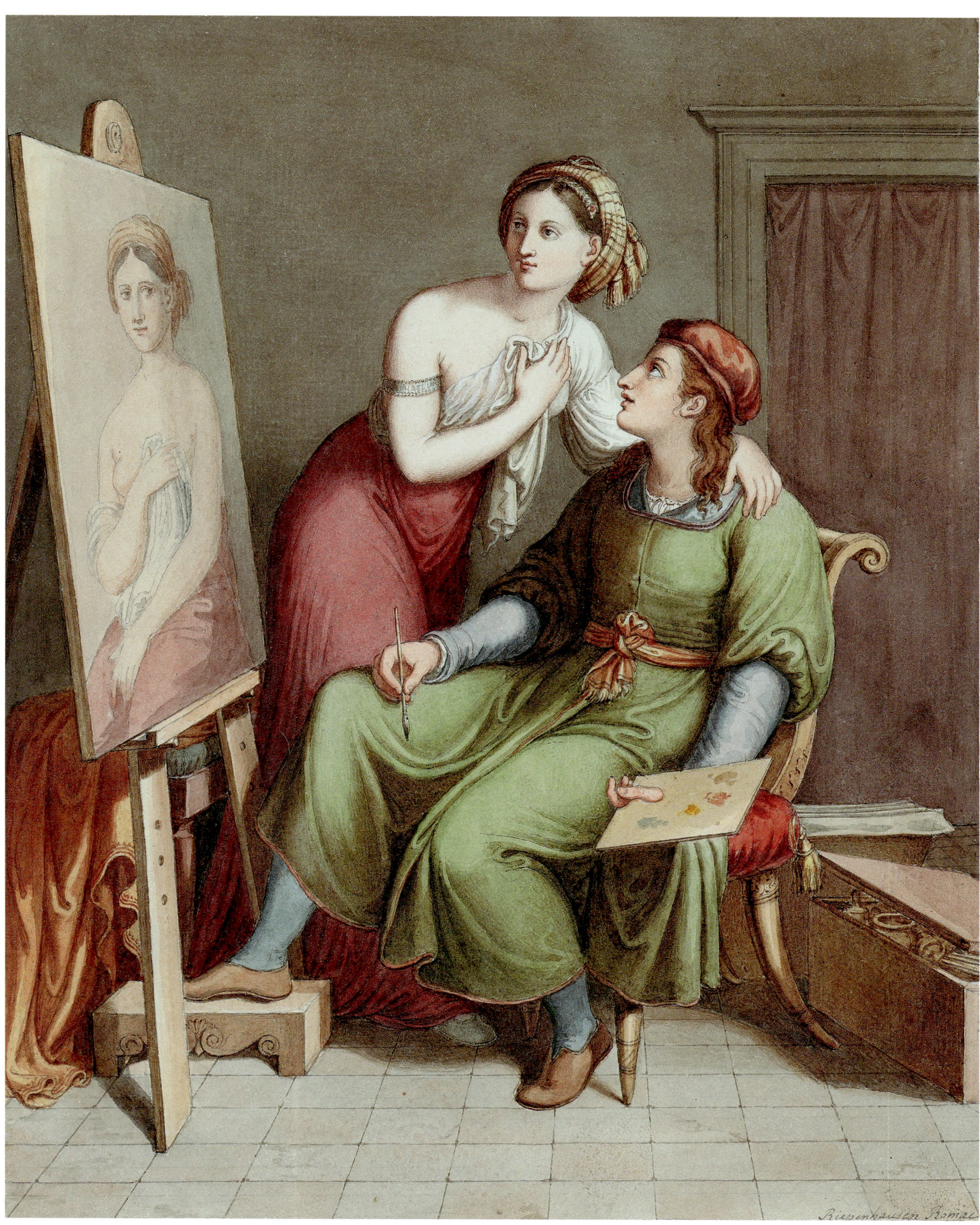
Riepenhausen Roma

45–50

Joseph von Führich
CHRASTAVA 1800–1876 VIENNA

Engraved by August Gaber
KOPERNIKI 1823–1894 BERLIN

The Bethlehemitic Path (Der Bethlehemitische Weg), ca. 1865

Series of twelve woodcuts with frontispiece

The images in Joseph von Führich's portfolio represent milestones from Christ's birth and childhood. A pilgrim wearing a cape adorned with shells leads viewers through the scenes, observing from the periphery. This figure represents the longstanding devotional practice of visiting holy sites, such as Bethlehem. Führich's series offered a substitute for physical pilgrimage; viewers could instead complete a spiritual journey by contemplating each image. The final scene, which depicts Jesus rescuing people from the water with a cross, urges readers to become "fishers of men" who encourage others to follow Christ and spread his teachings.

Führich's project was likely inspired by fellow Nazarene artist Julius Schnorr von Carolsfeld, who released his influential *Bible in Pictures* in thirty installments between 1852 and 1860. Like Schnorr's *Bible*, Führich's portfolio was immensely popular; it was published in many editions and several languages. This impression is a first edition.

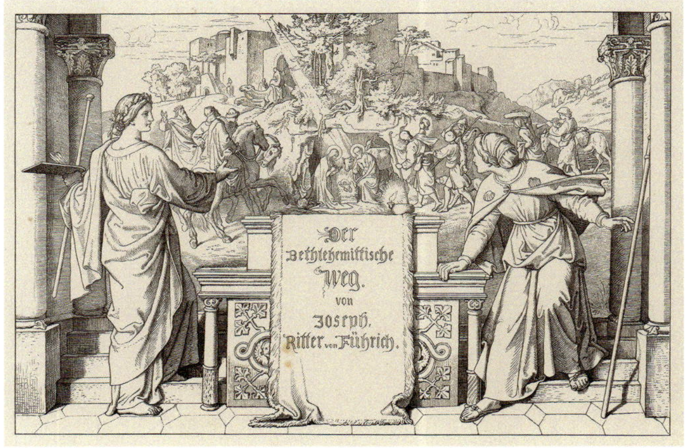

45. *Frontispiece*

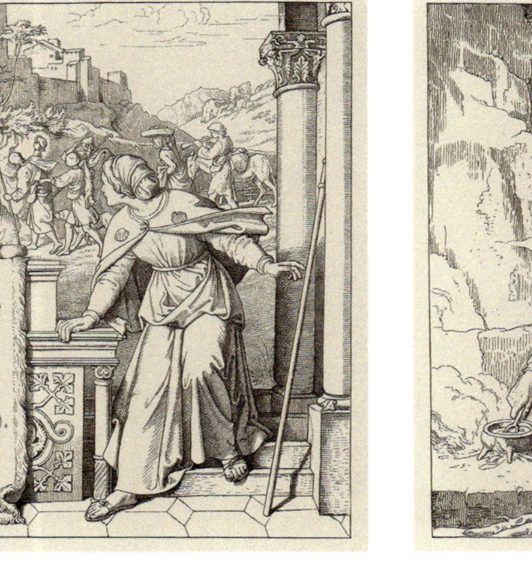

46. *Jesus as an Infant (Jesus als Säugling)*

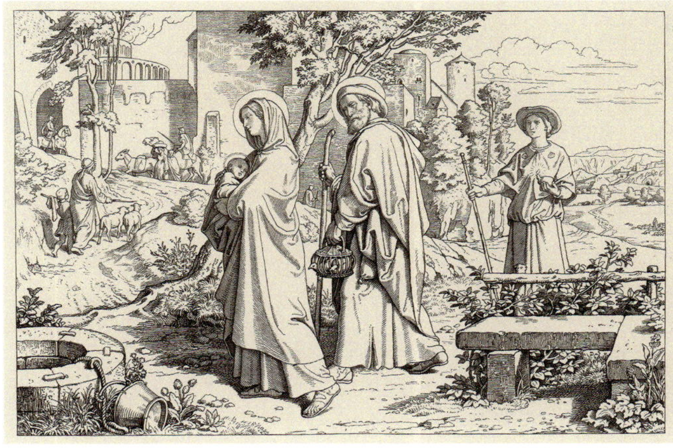

47. *The Sacrifice of Jesus (Jesu Aufopferung)*

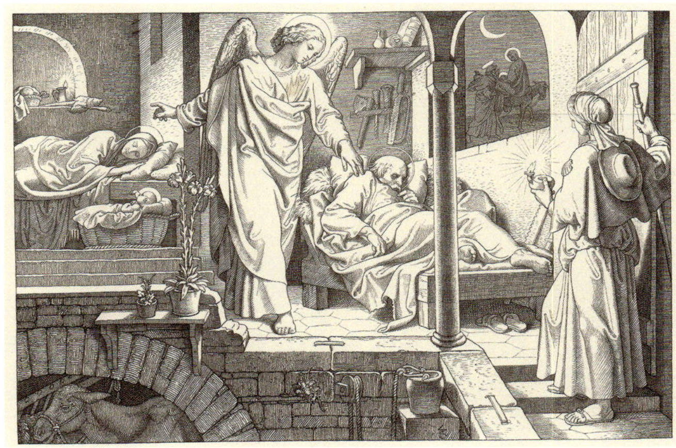

48. *The Flight of Jesus (Jesu Flucht)*

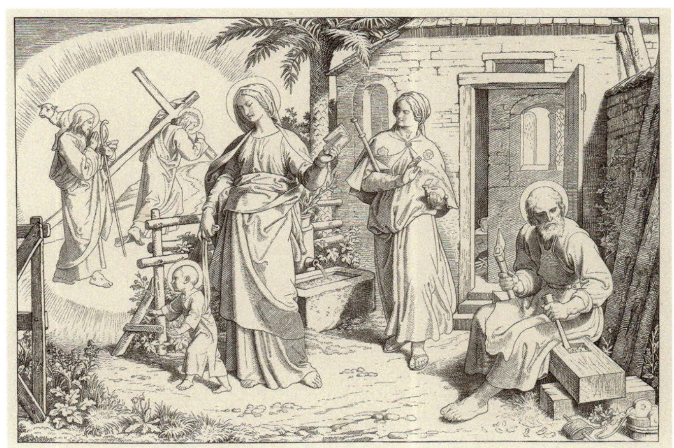

49. *Jesus Walking (Jesus wandelnd)*

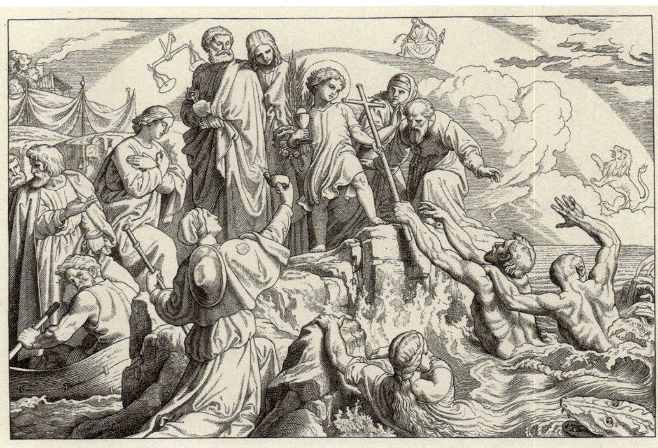

50. *Jesus, a Fisher of Men (Jesus ein Fischer)*

51.

Anselm Friedrich Feuerbach

SPEYER 1829–1880 VENICE

Mother and Child, 1858

Black chalk, watercolor, and
white heightening on paper

This sheet contains a preparatory
drawing of the Madonna and child, a
subject Anselm Feuerbach was working on around 1860. In letters, Feuerbach described his imagination being
overtaken by images of what he hoped
to paint next, and he sketched studies until he had the means to complete
a painting. In *Mother and Child*, Feuerbach depicted the infant Christ with
only faint outlines and focused on the
Madonna figure. He rendered her volu-
minous clothing meticulously, adding
modeling with fine white lines.

Like Franz Ittenbach (see plate 52),
Feuerbach attended the Düsseldorf Art
Academy and was taught by Nazarene
artist Wilhelm Schadow, as well as
Johann Wilhelm Schirmer (see plates
16–22). He traveled to Italy in 1854 and
remained there most of his life. In notes
found after his death, Feuerbach credited his artistic development to his time
in Rome, writing, "A miracle took place,
which can be called a complete trans-
formation of the soul and enlightenment—a revelation."[5]

5. Henriette Feuerbach, ed., *Ein Vermächtnis
von Anselm Feuerbach* (Munich: Kurt Wolff,
1920), 122.

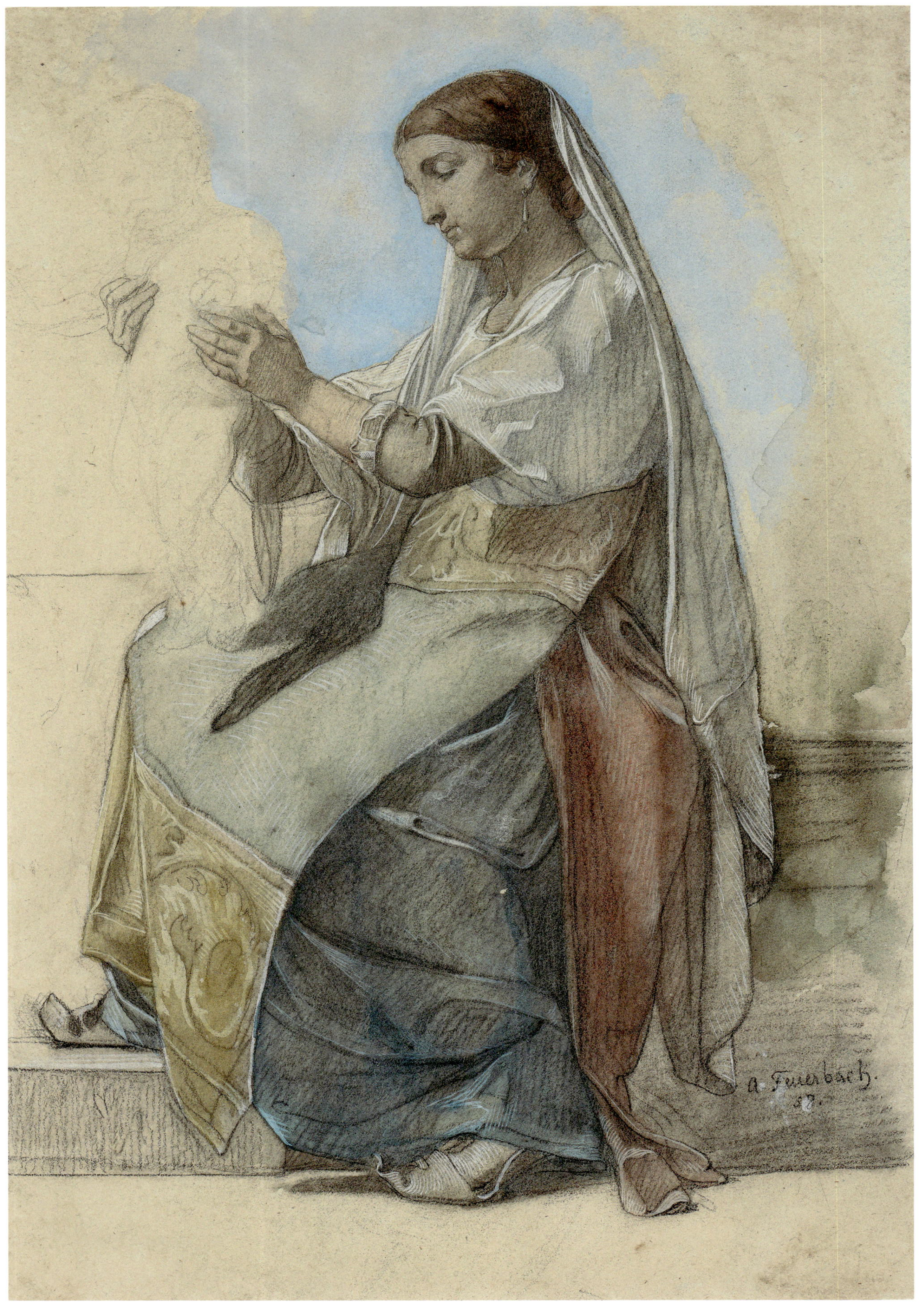

52.

Franz Ittenbach

KÖNIGSWINTER 1813–1879 DÜSSELDORF

Queen of Heaven (Himmelskönigin), 1872

Oil on panel

Franz Ittenbach is best known for painting images of the Madonna for churches and private commissioners. This Madonna is crowned and seated on a throne with the Christ Child on her lap. Christ holds the orb and cross and makes a gesture of blessing, indicating he is the savior of the world. Ittenbach painted at least two other nearly identical versions of this image for places of worship: one for the chapel of a patron in 1872 and the other for a church in Bochum in 1874. The background of the Milwaukee Art Museum's painting is the simplest of the three, with softly gleaming gilt framing the Madonna and Christ Child to emphasize their divinity.

Ittenbach belonged to a later generation of Nazarene artists taught by members of the original brotherhood. He received his training from Wilhelm Schadow, who became director of the Düsseldorf Art Academy seven years after returning to Germany from Rome. Through teaching posts like this, Schadow and other Nazarenes spread their ideals to new believers who would carry them forward.

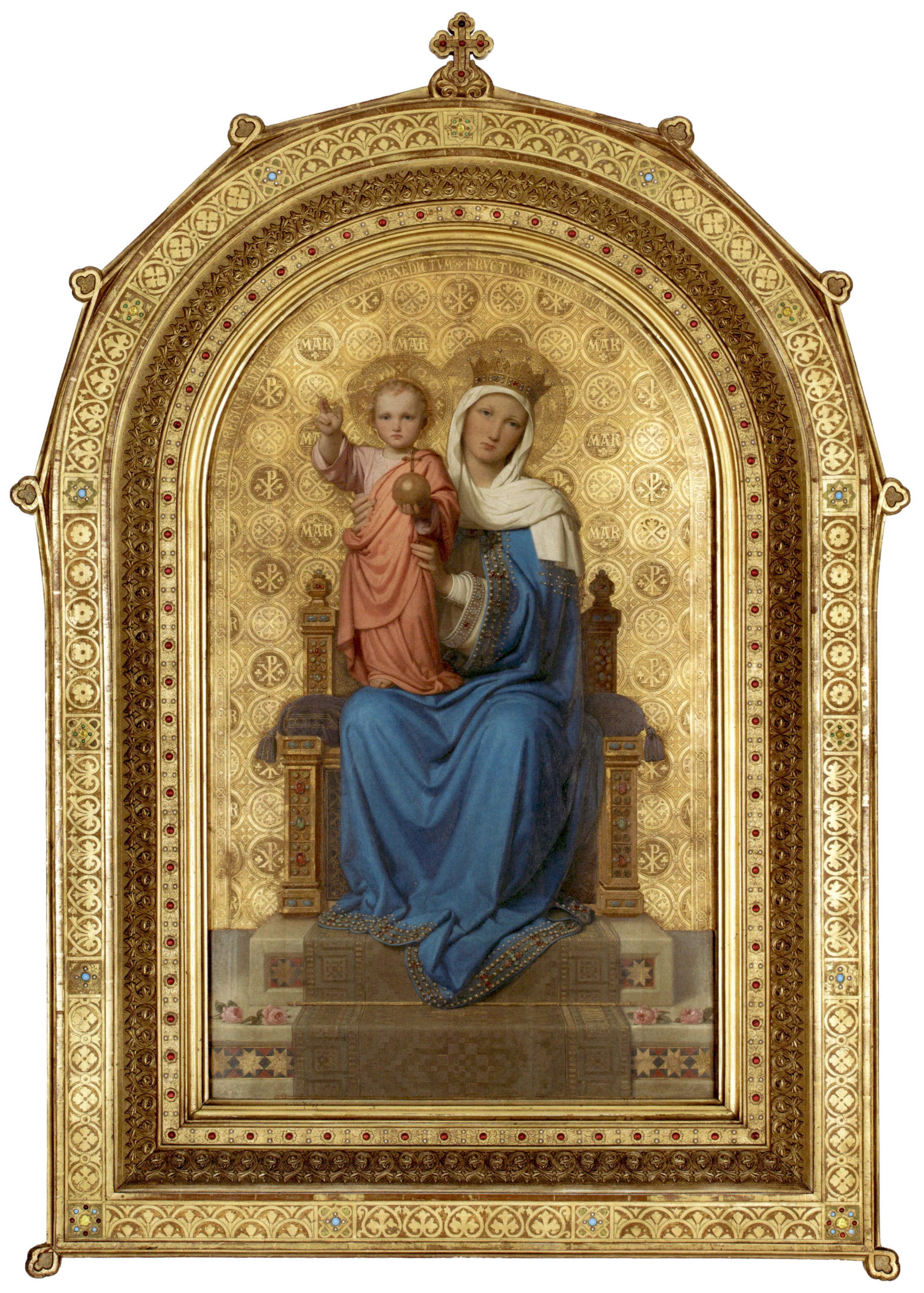

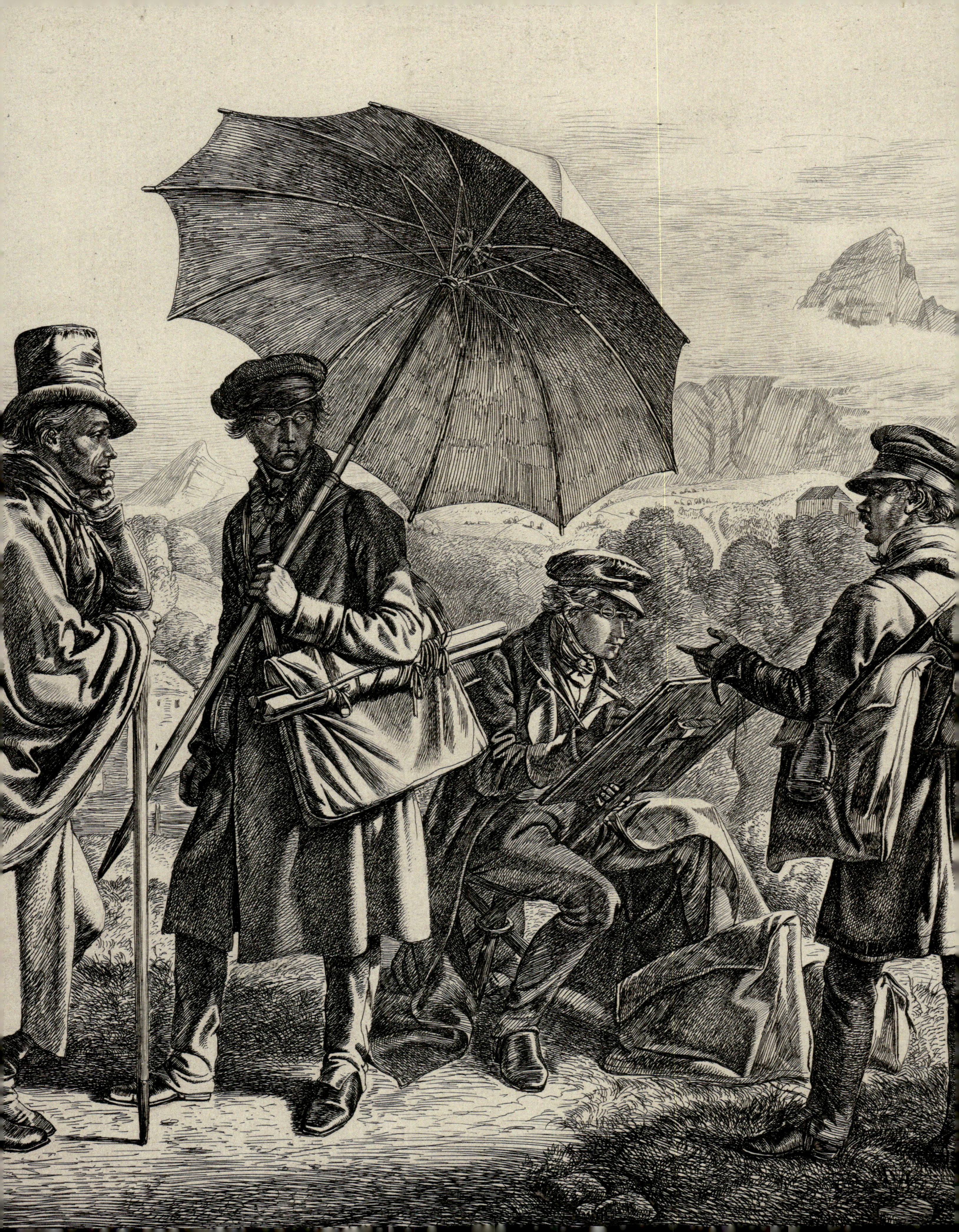

PAUSING IN THE HEIGHTS of the Alps in Berchtesgaden, the four people depicted in *The Artists on Their Journey* take in the beautiful views surrounding them. Friedrich and Heinrich Reinhold stand under the shade of Heinrich's umbrella to the left and listen to Ernst Welker, who gestures toward them while speaking. Christian Erhard sits on a stool, steadying his sketchbook on a portable easel as he draws the landscape. In the distance, the distinctive peaks of the Watzmann mountain emerge above a cloud partly obscuring them. The print, made by Johann Adam Klein in 1819, demonstrates the significance of travel for German Romantic artists. Sketching trips became an important way to experience embodiment in nature, find new subjects for work, and strengthen bonds with other artists, and Klein's etching captures all these aspects of artistic journeys. The print also, perhaps unwittingly, conveys some of the difficulty and tedium of travel during the early nineteenth century. The members of the group are laden with umbrellas, portfolios, stools, backpacks, and water canteens, which they lugged up mountain paths on foot. "We had simplified our luggage very much," Heinrich Reinhold wrote to his brother Gottfried, "but the rest was overly annoying and exhausting for us, especially since it was very hot and humid."[1] Moreover, Reinhold's letter relates that when the artists reached Berchtesgaden after a five-hour journey on foot from Salzburg, they were trapped indoors by a downpour that lasted five days. Klein based this print on the sketches he made of his friends in their room at the inn, transporting them to a more picturesque setting when he etched the scene months later.[2] This might explain the somewhat dour expressions on the Reinhold brothers' faces. Indeed, Friedrich, at the far left, evokes a forlorn traveler standing with elbows propped on the sill of a rain-streaked window far more than an artist transformed by the breathtaking majesty of the mountains. Such disruptions, however, were often integral to the travel experience. Frustrated plans, physical discomfort, and feelings of displacement and longing intensified artists' perceptions and shaped their convictions and sense of self. Heinrich Reinhold summarized his Alpine trip positively despite its challenges: "What wonderful pleasure this journey has given us! What benefit for the artist in spirit and body! These impressions could certainly never be replaced by any to follow. It is a gorgeous country!"[3]

Although individuals had undertaken journeys for centuries, travel proved to be particularly essential to the German Romantic movement. Famed writer Johann Wolfgang von Goethe is credited with proclaiming the benefits of traveling as a process around 1788 in a quotation attributed to him: "One does not travel to arrive, but to travel."[4] Regardless of the destination or primary motivation, traveling created a productive liminal space—a space of perpetual becoming—where artists could grapple with

"One Does Not Travel to Arrive" German Romantic Artistic Journeys

NIKKI OTTEN

Associate Curator of Prints and Drawings
Milwaukee Art Museum

OPPOSITE   Johann Adam Klein, *The Artists on Their Journey* (detail), 1819 (cat. p. 160)

tensions in Romantic philosophy. They explored individuality and self-cultivation while trying to find their place within communities and larger shared identities. They also balanced modernity with tradition and the empirical study of nature with emotion and spirit. Visually representing their journeys, either on-site or after they returned, allowed artists to share these formative events with others. Working on paper, specifically, offered the possibility of capturing not only things they had seen but also some of the sensory effects of travel. Sketches made at breathtaking vistas or in towns along a route were often rendered in a highly spontaneous style, creating a sense of immediacy and conveying the feeling of trying to fully experience a place during a brief pause in a hectic itinerary. More finished and deliberate print series depicting different locations in or around one city introduced a temporal element to travel images, encouraging the viewers who handled them to trace and retrace the pictured paths. These drawings and prints, so easily transportable, also transported viewers on imagined journeys, offering insight into Romantic ideals along the way.

TRAVELING AROUND GERMANY AFTER THE GRAND TOUR

The early nineteenth century marked a transitional moment in the history of travel when perceptions and practices were beginning to change. In the previous century, young aristocratic men—primarily British, but also French and German—completed their education by embarking on the yearslong Grand Tour across Europe. The established routes brought travelers to cities believed to epitomize classical civilization, education, and sociability, such as Paris, Florence, Venice, Rome, Vienna, and German university towns.[5] Because tourism was not yet the well-developed industry it would later become, travel presented many potential dangers at this time. Those on the move faced illness, injury, poor roadways, robbers, and storms, and it could be difficult to find help if they encountered problems. Beyond these physical perils, some people feared that exposure to other cultures and access to drinking, gambling, and sex could result in corruption.[6] Wealthy men on the Grand Tour largely viewed the risks involved as a means of demonstrating honor and asserting masculinity, but most people traveled only when necessary for survival or for religious or professional reasons.[7] Artists undertook arduous journeys to complete commissions, further their training, meet other artists, or seek patronage. Some were hired to accompany aristocrats on their tours, creating works that functioned as souvenirs and also reflected the refined taste of their commissioners. This practice had existed since the sixteenth century and continued into the nineteenth. For example, the Crown Prince of Bavaria (later King Ludwig I) appointed Georg von Dillis to record his 1806 trip

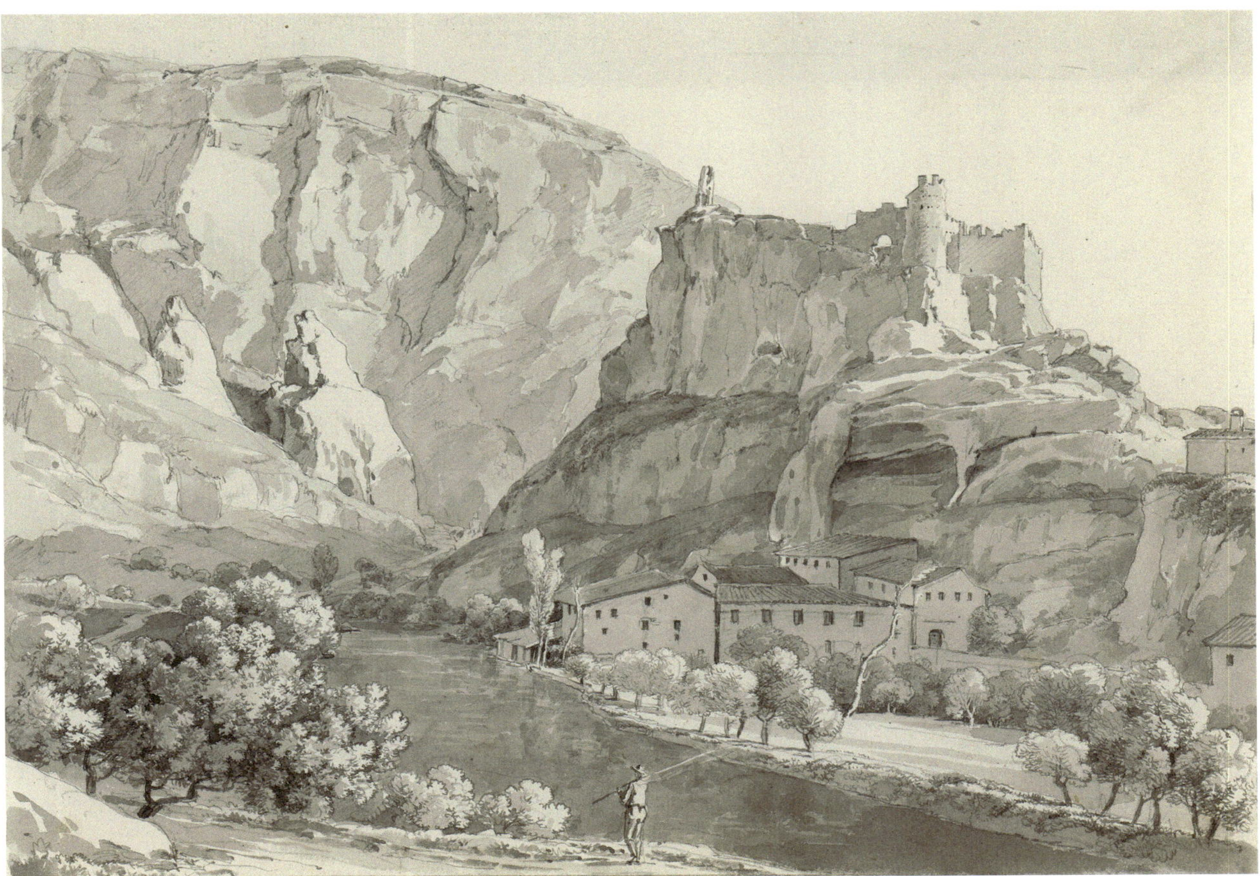

through France, Switzerland, and Italy, resulting in a book of drawings titled *Picturesque Voyage in the South of France*. Several of the sheets depict landscapes with ancient ruins, which were reminders of a lost past for the Romantics (fig. 1).

In addition to participating in long-standing patronage traditions, artists also contributed to new understandings of travel that developed at the turn of the nineteenth century. The Napoleonic Wars (1803–15) created unprecedented danger for travelers, largely bringing the Grand Tour to an end.[8] Around the same time, improving infrastructure made hiking more practical, and the activity gained philosophical significance. As the Enlightenment waned and Romanticism emerged, walking in nature became an important way to confront the boundaries of humanity and reason, commune with the spiritual, and engage in self-discovery.[9] Hoping to experience these effects, many Romantic artists began to take sketching tours around Germany. Caspar David Friedrich, for example, traveled east to hike in the Sudetes Mountains with fellow artist Georg Friedrich Kersting in the summer of 1810. Friedrich often drew trees and

FIG. 1   Georg von Dillis, *Fontaine-de-Vaucluse near Avignon ("Vaucluse")*, from the portfolio *Picturesque Voyage in the South of France Drawn by Dillis (Voyage pittoresque dans le Midi de la France dessiné par Dillis)*, 1806. Graphite, pen and black ink and wash, outlined with pencil on paper. 8⅛ × 11¹⁄₁₆ in. (20.6 × 28.8 cm). Staatliche Graphische Sammlung Munich

boulders in exacting detail, but he rendered the landscapes he sketched on this trip with only the most essential lines. Many, including a page that depicts views of Lausche and Findenkoppe and the Church Tower of Kleinschönau, are labeled with numbers and symbols indicating different types of ecosystems (meadows, fields, young woods) (fig. 2). Such notations may have allowed Friedrich to draw more quickly on his travels, providing him with an abundance of material to transform into paintings once he returned to his studio. Working from unembellished outlines also kept Friedrich from becoming too absorbed in realism, leaving space for him to create evocative depictions of nature infused with spirit.

Carl Friedrich Lessing also took sketching trips, traveling to mountain ranges like the Harz and sites in western Germany such as Eifel and the Mosel region. A drawing he made on one such journey depicts a flat expanse along a body of water with highland formations in the distance and scrub growing from sandy soil in the foreground (fig. 3). Two travelers rest near the side of a road, leaning on a slab of stone or a case containing their belongings. They appear to be at leisure, contemplating the landscape and perhaps pondering their place in nature. Lessing's scene initially seems to lack amenities, but it provides evidence of infrastructure built to ease the burdens of travel. Signposts and roadways both became more prevalent at the beginning of the nineteenth century (although the broken lines Lessing used to depict his road suggest surfaces were not terribly smooth).[10] The drawing also presents a contrast between those who traveled for survival and Lessing's wanderers. In the middle ground, a team of horses pulls a wagon loaded with hay or other goods. The figure walking alongside is likely on the road out of necessity, while the wanderers' primary interests were presumably spiritual and philosophical. Goethe describes the convergence of different types of travelers in his 1816 *Italian Journey (Italienische Reise)*, which recounts his experience living in Italy from 1786 to 1788 in the form of a diary. In entries detailing his route and stops between Carlsbad and Venice, he writes about allowing children to ride in his coach at the request of their parents. One is the daughter of an itinerant musician, and the other he "could get nothing out of."[11] Goethe's travel account may have been an inspiration to Lessing; one of the figures on the left in his drawing resembles a well-known painting of Goethe in Rome by Johann Heinrich Wilhelm Tischbein (fig. 4). With this reference, Lessing evokes cultured philosophical circles and the type of erudite observations and personal revelations Goethe included in his book. At the same time, the artist may have wanted to create the impression that his wanderers were humbler than Grand Tourists. Travelers who chose to hike, rather than ride in carriages, deliberately did so as a gesture of self-fashioning, meant to demonstrate they were anti-aristocratic and aligned with common people.[12]

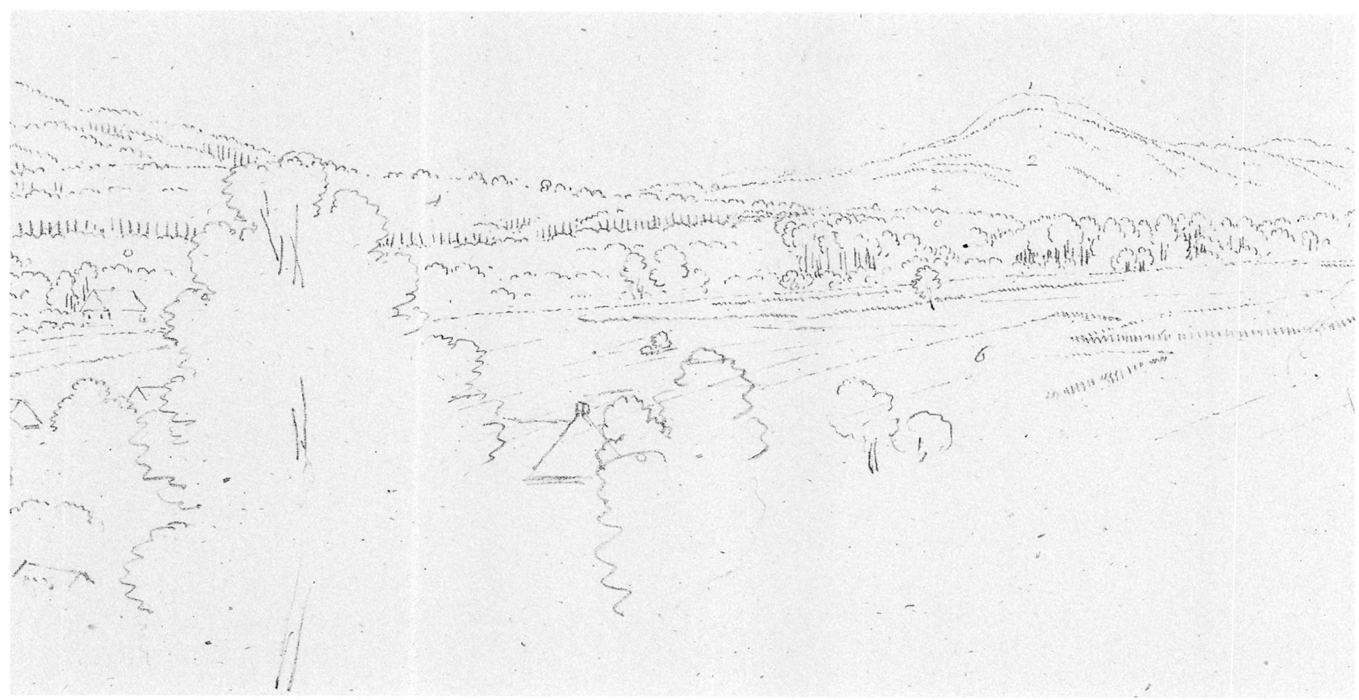

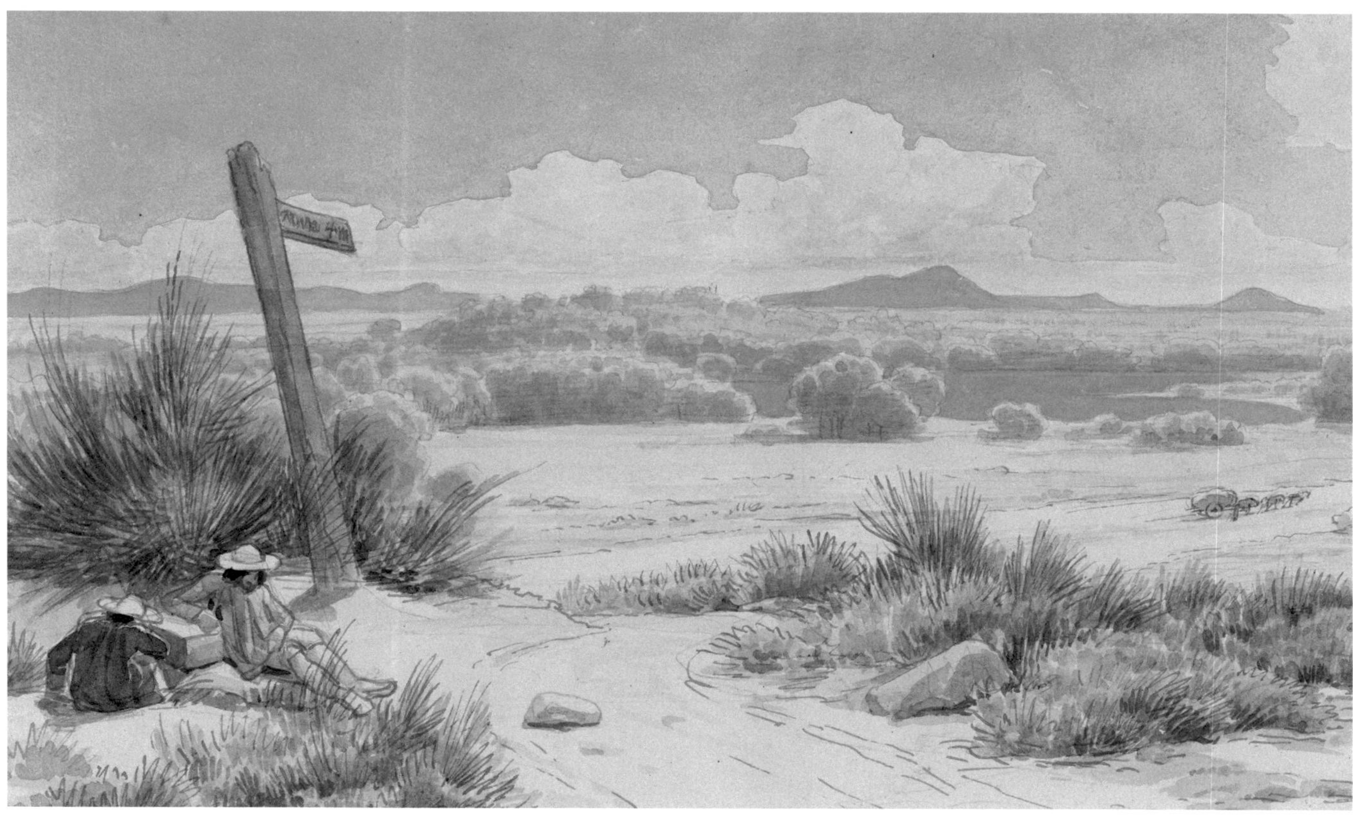

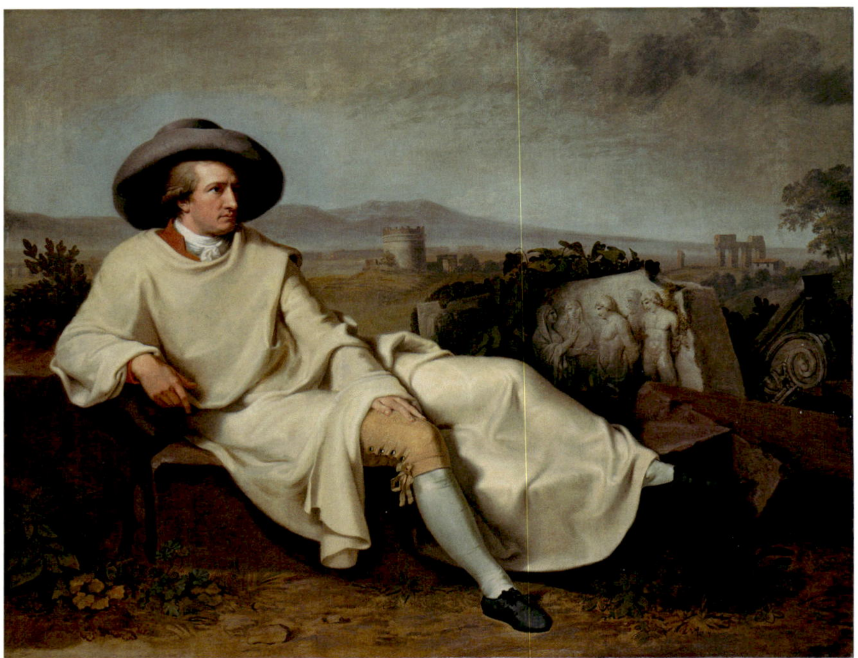

ALPINE HOMELAND: SALZBURG AND BERCHTESGADEN

Within Germany, the Alpine cities of Salzburg and Berchtesgaden
emerged as important destinations for artists. Although many travelers
had previously passed through the Alps on the way to Italy, the difficulty
and perceived danger of the mountainous terrain meant that few lingered.
A new cultural emphasis on the sublimity of nature made the heights
seem less terrifying, and caves, glaciers, and waterfalls became popular
attractions.[13] Some chose to visit the Alps in Switzerland, but others were
interested in exploring the parts of the range that lay within the borders
of the German Confederation, an association of German-speaking states
formed in 1815 after France's defeat in the Napoleonic Wars.[14] Artists who
traveled to Salzburg had the opportunity to depict a place that was virtu-
ally unrepresented. Very few paintings or prints of the city existed before
the 1780s, and those made at the turn of the nineteenth century were
primarily topographical depictions used for practical or illustrative purposes. Ferdinand Olivier was one of the first artists to recognize the
artistic potential of the area. He traveled from Vienna to Salzburg in 1815
and again in 1817. He made the second trip because he had decided to
create a series of etchings that would "make their own unknown splendors
familiar to Germans" and felt that first he needed to gain a better understanding of Salzburg's "new and unknown grandeur."[15]

In addition to the beauty of the natural landscape, Olivier was
inspired by Salzburg's medieval architecture. During the year of his second

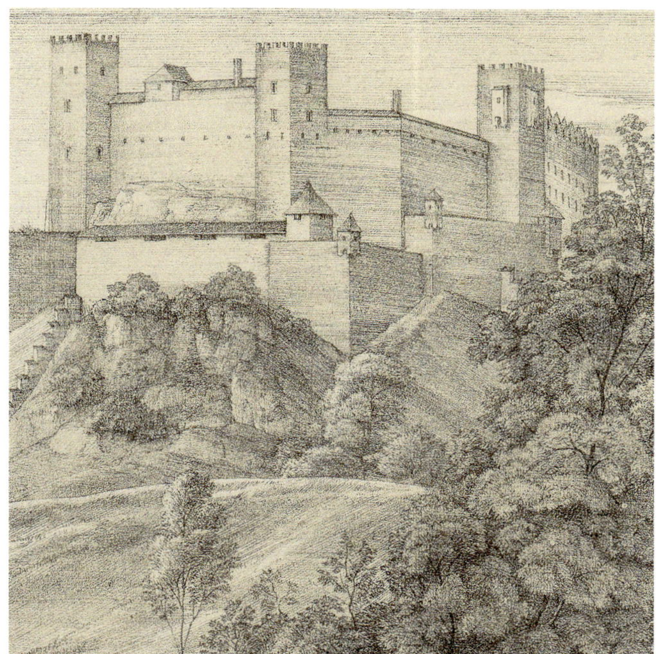 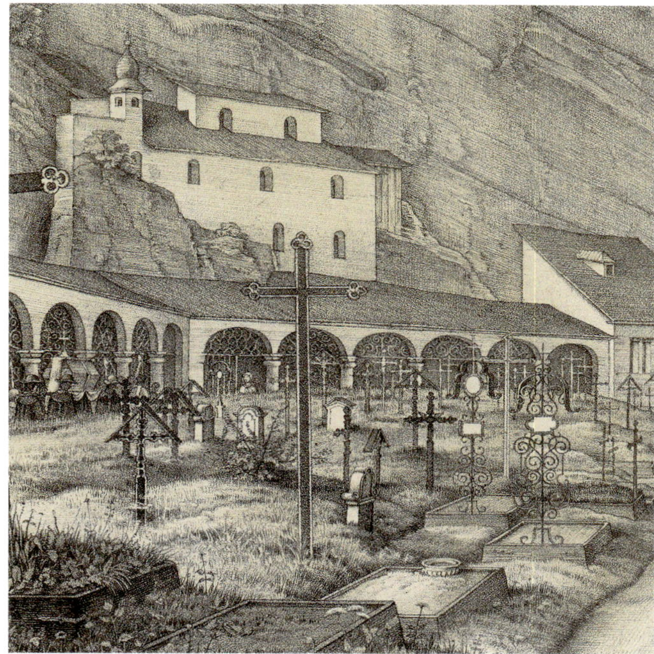

visit, he was invited to join the Brotherhood of St. Luke (Lukasbund), a group of German artists based in Rome who were in regular contact with Olivier's circle in Vienna and shared similar ideas about the direction German art should take. The Lukasbund thought the modern world was corrupt and decadent and hoped to revitalize art by invoking Christianity. They looked to medieval and Renaissance artists for examples that could inform their own approach to uniting art and religion. Olivier applied these ideas when he eventually published his series of Alpine landscapes as a portfolio of nine lithographs titled *Seven Places in Salzburg and Berchtesgaden* in 1823 (plates 56–64). The series is arranged according to the days of the week and presents a vision of people living in harmony with their natural surroundings. The castles and churches that Olivier depicted, such as the Hohensalzburg Fortress in *Tuesday* and St. Peter's Cemetery in *Saturday*, date to the Middle Ages, and he omitted the city's seventeenth- and eighteenth-century buildings (figs. 5 and 6).[16] In addition to the architectural symbolism present in the series, art historians have shown that the landscape is overlaid with meaning related to artistic influence, cycles of life, religious ritual, and time.[17]

National identity also plays an important role in the complex meaning of the work. Olivier represented the newly discovered splendor of the Alps with a printmaking process recently developed in Germany. Lithography was invented in 1796 by playwright Alois Senefelder in Munich, and as Cordula Grewe points out in her essay in this catalogue and elsewhere, the

FIG. 5   Ferdinand Olivier, *Tuesday: Salzburg Castle from the South* (detail), from the series *Seven Places in Salzburg and Berchtesgaden*, 1818–22, published 1823 (cat. p. 161)

FIG. 6   Ferdinand Olivier, *Saturday: Graveyard of St. Peter's in Salzburg* (detail), from the series *Seven Places in Salzburg and Berchtesgaden*, 1818–22, published 1823 (cat. p. 161)

local origins of the technique appealed to Olivier.[18] Moreover, lithographs were typically printed from slabs of limestone, the same rock that formed the characteristic peaks of the eastern Alps. This meant that Olivier drew the series on the very surface he traversed during his journeys. In this way, the cycle features a landscape, process, and material imbued with national significance. Olivier traveled to the Alps during the immediate aftermath of the Napoleonic Wars, when there was much debate about whether the German states should continue to be governed as monarchies or unite as a democracy. At this tumultuous moment, he set out to make a name for himself with a portfolio that not only expressed his ideas about art suffused with historic and religious meaning but also reaffirmed his German identity. The organization of the prints allowed viewers to experience these landscapes day after day, week after week, making the Alps' "unknown splendors familiar" to them as they progressed through the scenes, perhaps as part of a devotional practice.[19]

Several other artists journeyed to the Alps around the same time as Olivier. Friedrich and Heinrich Reinhold, two of the travelers depicted in the Klein print that opens this essay, were friends with Olivier and may have been inspired to visit Salzburg by the drawings he brought back from his second trip. They toured through Salzburg and Berchtesgaden in July 1818, with Klein joining them in early August. Although the rain kept the artists from sketching in Berchtesgaden, they all drew the Alpine landscape at other locations along their journey. A few years later, in 1821, Ernst Fries created a wash drawing of Salzburg and Königssee Lake (fig. 7). The artist, who had recently completed further academic training in landscape painting in Munich, traveled around Germany and Italy over the next several years. The picturesque Alpine views of his drawing are delicate, rendering medieval architecture, the still surface of the lake, and the mountain heights with subtle monochromatic washes. This approach softens the details in the scenes—so crucial to Olivier's landscapes—and emphasizes the atmosphere and light effects. Fries added a dividing line to the paper on which he drew, crowding the two landscapes onto the same sheet. This may have been a paper-saving measure, but for the viewer, it creates the effect of trying to record as many mountain views as possible in a limited time—something Fries likely experienced on his journey.

"A GERMAN PAINTER SHOULD NOT LEAVE HIS FATHERLAND": EXILE IN ITALY

Many, if not most, artists working in the late eighteenth and early nineteenth centuries continued an existing tradition of spending extended periods in Italy. Viewing classical and Renaissance art and learning the techniques of each region were considered essential to artistic training,

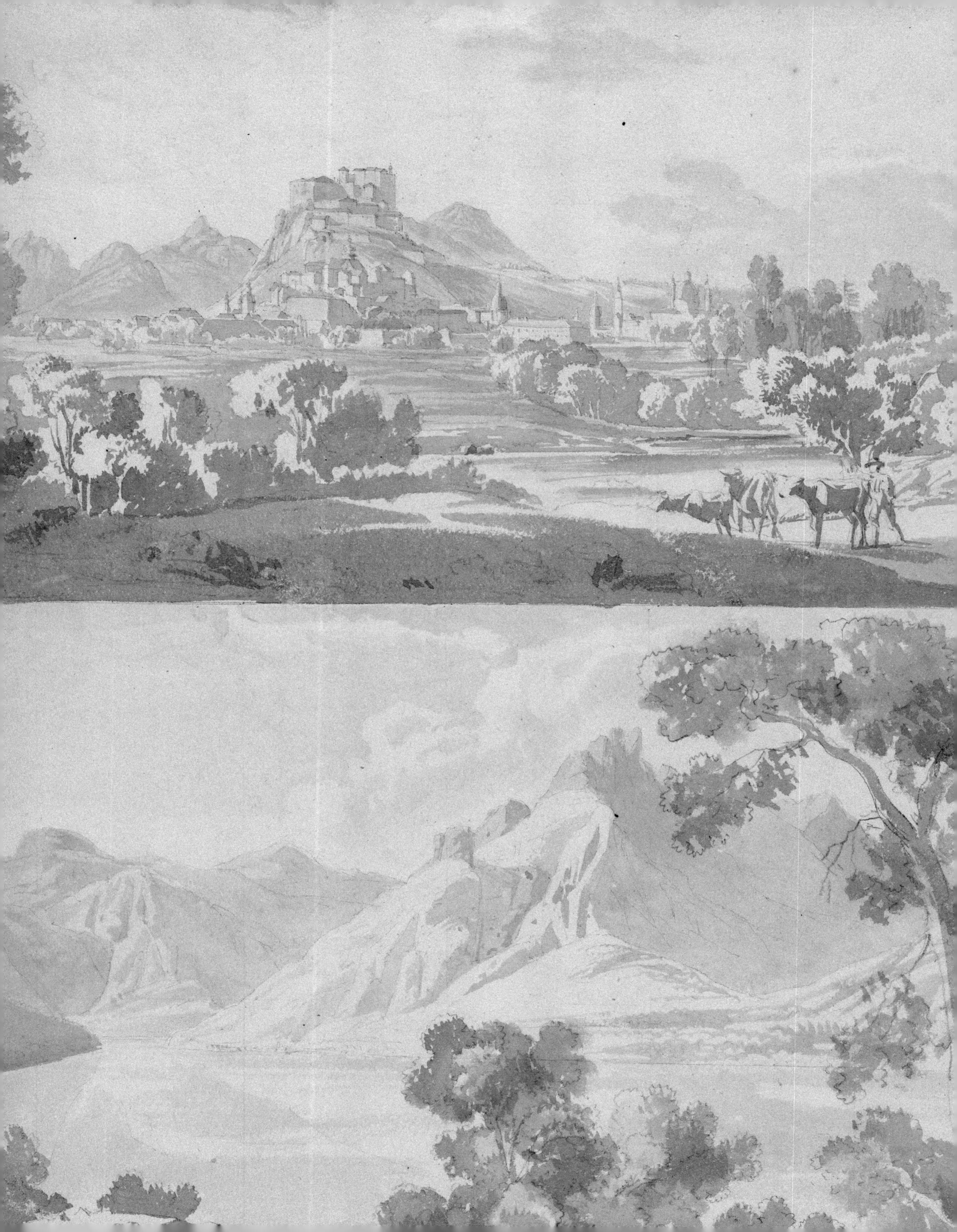

and traveling to cities such as Rome and Venice had been customary since the middle of the seventeenth century. German artists following this convention formed communities in Rome and Naples in the 1780s and 1790s, but many left after Napoleon's French troops seized control of most of Italy between 1797 and 1799.[20] A decade later, a subset of the Brotherhood of St. Luke established a new and important community for Germans in Rome. The six artists from Vienna who founded the brotherhood became dissatisfied with their academic training, finding that it stifled imagination and elevated art they believed was too sensual. The Vienna Academy closed following Napoleon's invasion of the city in 1809, and three members of the brotherhood were excluded when the resource-strapped school limited readmission to Austrians the following year. They, along with one additional member, decided to cross the Alps, traveling through Venice, Urbino, and other cities before taking up residence in an abandoned monastery in Rome.[21] They were drawn to the city because it was the center of Christianity, as well as the site of important Renaissance frescoes by Michelangelo and Raphael, two artists they had adopted as models. Over the next ten years, the group, which became known as the Nazarenes, expanded beyond the original Lukasbund to include additional invited members (like Olivier, who joined in 1817) and artists who were not part of the brotherhood but worked toward the same goals. The Nazarenes maintained a presence in Rome for many years, and Germans who came to the city often visited or studied with members of the circle.

Artists' responses to Italy varied widely. One founder of the Lukasbund, Johann Friedrich Overbeck, remained there for the rest of his life, resisting returning to Germany despite the acclaim he received at home for his contribution to a fresco cycle in Rome's Casa Bartholdy, *Joseph Being Sold by His Brothers* (see plates 34 and 35 and Grewe's essay in this catalogue). He wrote to Joseph Sutter, a member of the Lukasbund who stayed in Vienna, that he found affirmation of his ideals in Rome: "How happy it makes us that we find all of our principles confirmed in these works [in the Vatican]—just as our views have been broadened by the sight of the highest masterpieces since our separation from you, but have not changed in any way."[22] Years later, he completed a painting that became emblematic of his life in the capital city and his artistic philosophy (fig. 8; see plate 39). Originally conceived as a portrait commemorating his friendship with Franz Pforr, the co-leader of the Brotherhood of St. Luke, Overbeck left the work unfinished when Pforr died in 1812. He returned to the canvas in 1828 and titled it *Italia and Germania*. In a letter to the patron who purchased the painting, he explained his decision: "The need naturally arose to give the youthfully unclear idea a more

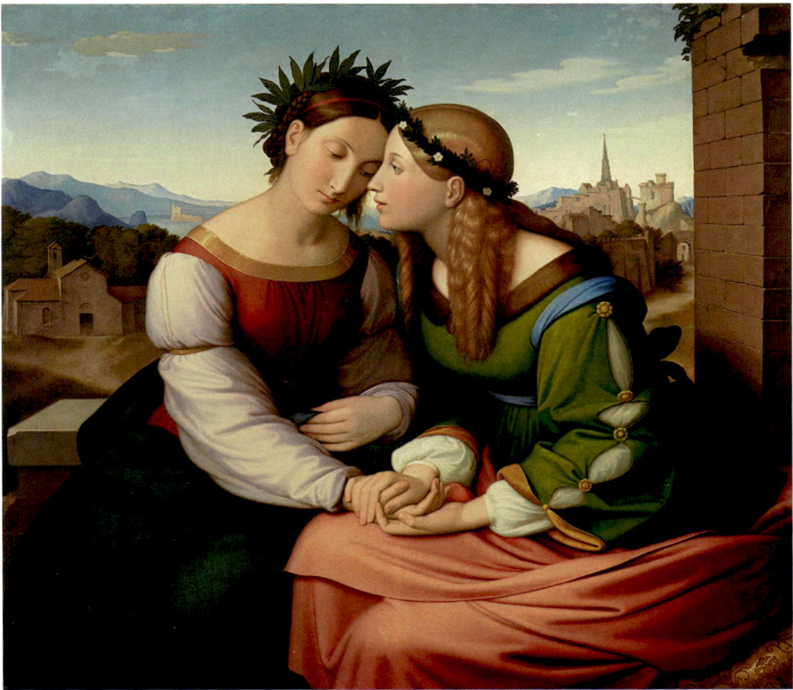

specific meaning. . . . But the fact that I chose the idea of a Germania and Italia is clear from my particular point of view as a German in Italy. They are the two elements, so to speak, which are, on the one hand, alien to each other, but which are and should remain my task to merge, at least in the external form of my work, and which I therefore think of here in beautiful, close friendship."[23] Here we see Overbeck, in true Romantic fashion, reflecting on his foundational experiences and balancing opposing ideas that had become central to his selfhood.

Other members of the Lukasbund were not so taken with the South, but like Overbeck, they found that their time in Rome reinforced their identity as Germans and their dedication to using what they learned to revitalize the arts in their home country. Peter von Cornelius wrote in 1812, "A German painter should not leave his fatherland . . . I feel with pain and joy that I am a German to my core marrow of life," and Julius Schnorr von Carolsfeld proclaimed in 1818, "The German has never been more German than he is here now."[24] Several described their sojourns in terms of being exiled, explaining in letters that they could not yet leave despite desperately wishing to do just that. For most, this exile was self-imposed for the sake of opportunity. In some cases, artists lacked the documents necessary for travel, leaving them stranded. Cornelius, who found himself in this situation, ultimately decided to stay in Rome to work on fresco commissions even after publisher Friedrich Wenner

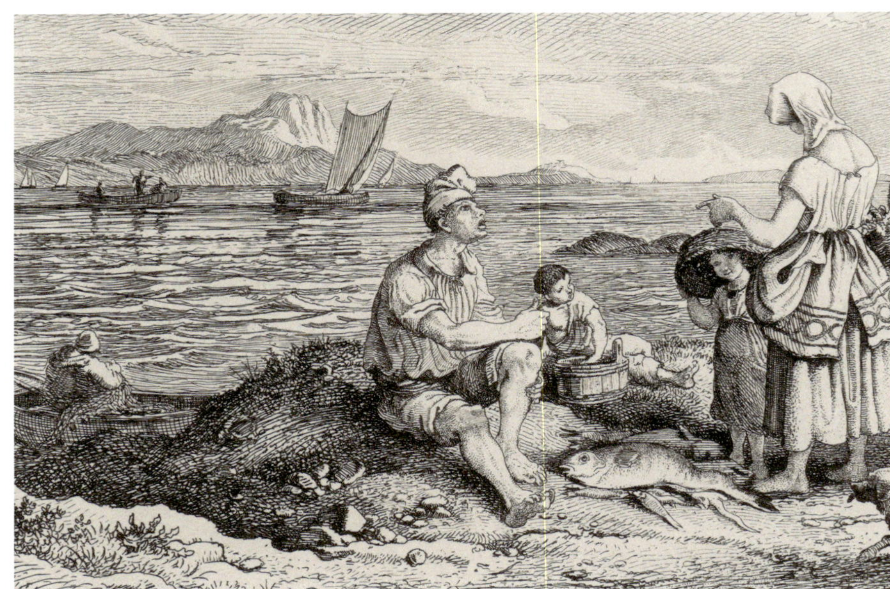

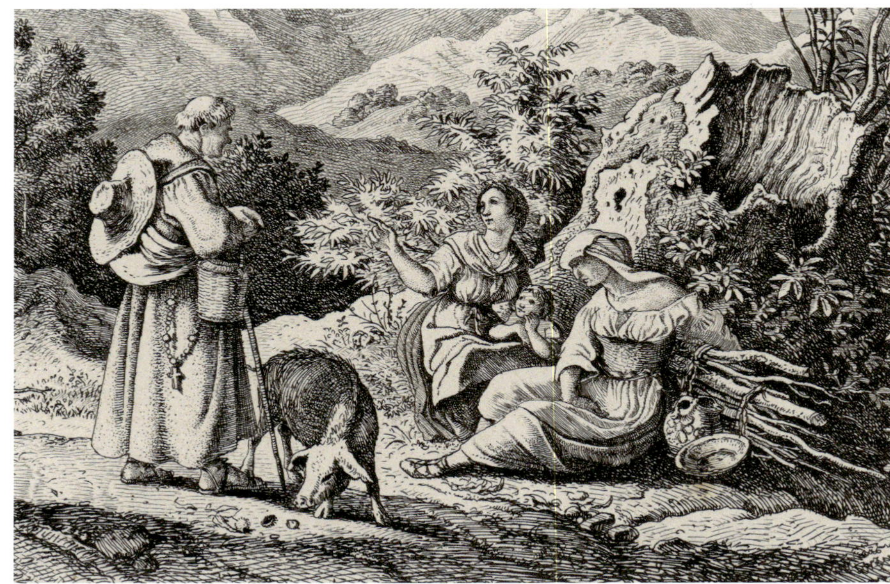

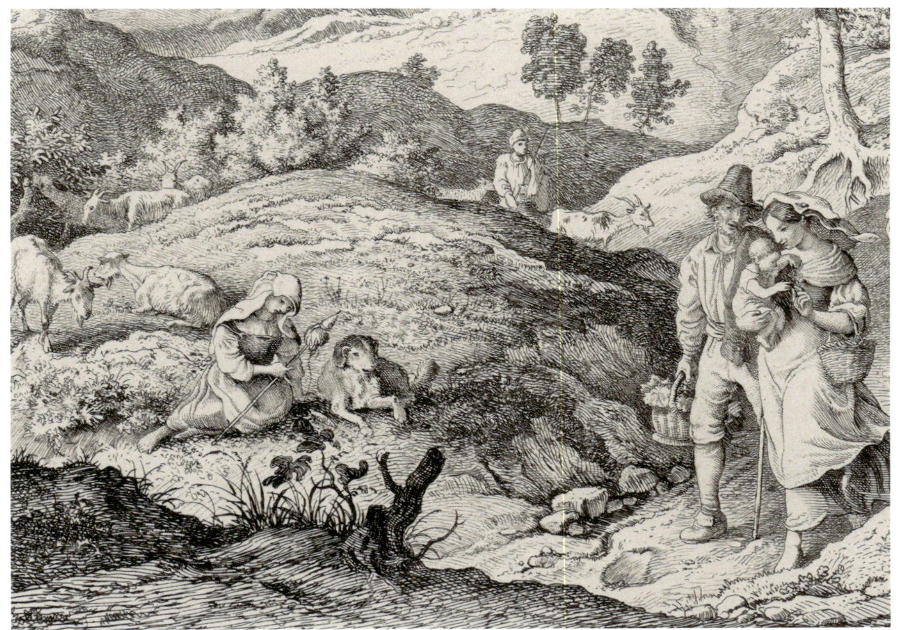

offered to obtain rights for him. "O! that this detour is necessary," he lamented, "that the most beautiful years of my life must first be lost in an endless longing, and then abroad must take up my best energies for a considerable period of time. This is unfortunately also how I recognize that I am a German."[25] Such feelings of displacement and longing were a central component of how Romantics experienced the world. According to sociologist Michael Löwy and literature professor Robert Sayre, a common aspect of Romanticism was the belief that values from the past had been lost in modern times. Many perceived this loss as exile, or as a soul's separation from its homeland.[26] The literal separation from Germany that these artists endured likely compounded a philosophical sense of loss, which they had tried to remedy by communing with medieval and Renaissance art in Rome.

Like Cornelius, many artists remained abroad because they recognized that it would eventually benefit them. Ludwig Richter, who lived in Rome for three years in the 1820s, wrote to the dealer who funded his travel and confessed (after some prevarication), "In a word, I don't like Italy."[27] These views, which Richter expressed during the first nine months of his stay, changed as he became more familiar with his surroundings. He began to describe the city as "beloved Rome" in his letters, though he often mentioned missing his homeland.[28] Indeed, the artist painted several Italian landscapes after returning to Dresden. He also created a portfolio of six etchings titled *Picturesque Views of the Environs of Rome* in 1832 (plates 68–73). It was commissioned and published by the art dealer Carl Gustav Boerner, who founded his business in Leipzig in 1826. The Italian scenes followed Richter's portfolio of six views of Salzburg, published two years before, and Boerner's advertisement for the series positioned it as "an attractive comparison of the beautiful nature of Italy with that of Germany."[29] The locations Richter depicted trace a route that begins more than fifty miles south of Rome and spirals far to the northeast before turning west to reach sites on the outskirts of the city. For each print, he drew a landscape based on sketches he had made during his travels years before, populating it with figures intended to increase visual interest and heighten the picturesque qualities of the scene.[30] Several represent people making use of the resources offered by the land: They are fishing, carrying bundles of wood, and grazing their sheep (figs. 9, 10, and 11).[31] The compositions create the impression of pleasant travels in an idyllic setting that viewers of the prints could experience vicariously. This impression is enhanced by the journey's having been stripped of all the discomforts and hazards that might have accompanied traveling the route depicted, which would have required several days, if not weeks, of walking and carriage rides. The images present only positive aspects of the region for the viewer. And despite Richter's initially conflicted opinion of Italy, traveling helped him gain a better understanding of his German identity and artistic values. Again writing to his patron, he mused, "Only now do I really feel how much I misunderstood my beautiful fatherland," and expressed a desire to create a series of works depicting German geographical features "executed as realistically and delicately as possible so that the educated and common man alike could enjoy it. Art is for the people, otherwise what use is it?"[32] These professed beliefs seem to have remained in place seven years later when the Italian portfolio afforded Richter the opportunity to create multiples for the enjoyment of the people.

TRAVELING THROUGH SPACE AND TIME

On their journeys, artists frequently encountered people undertaking a much older form of travel: the pilgrimage. The Christian practice of visiting the holy sites of Jerusalem, Rome, and Santiago de Compostela reached its peak in the Middle Ages and remained strong through the end of the seventeenth century. By the nineteenth century, travel to these cities waned in favor of local cult sites.[33] Pilgrims were still not uncommon around Germany and Italy, however. Richter included a pilgrim, carrying the recognizable attribute of a staff and adorned with the shells associated with Santiago de Compostela, in a scene from *Picturesque Views of the Environs of Rome* (fig. 12). Three decades later, Nazarene artist Joseph von Führich featured a pilgrim guide in a portfolio of twelve prints representing moments from Christ's childhood (see plates 45–50). The title page of the series depicts an allegorical personification of art with a palette in hand on the left, gesturing toward the birth of Jesus taking place in the background. The figure on the right, dressed in a cape decorated with shells, looks on while reaching for a staff (fig. 13). Described in the text accompanying the portfolio as a "contemplating soul" who is beginning a "holy journey," the individual reappears in every subsequent scene, lighting the events with a lamp. Again, according to the text, the pilgrim is "the symbol of everything we feel when we see such a touching and sublime spectacle as the childhood of Jesus offers us." Führich's choice to treat the portfolio as a pilgrimage introduces a temporal element and allows the viewer to feel as though they are moving through space and time, witnessing the miraculous events of Christ's birth and growth along with their pilgrim guide. Some of the prints collapse chronological time, representing different moments from a biblical story in the same image. *The Flight of Jesus*, for example, depicts an angel waking Mary and Joseph from slumber to warn them that Herod wants to kill the infant (fig. 14). Through the window above the pilgrim's candle, we can see events that took place a short while later: Mary and Jesus ride on a donkey while

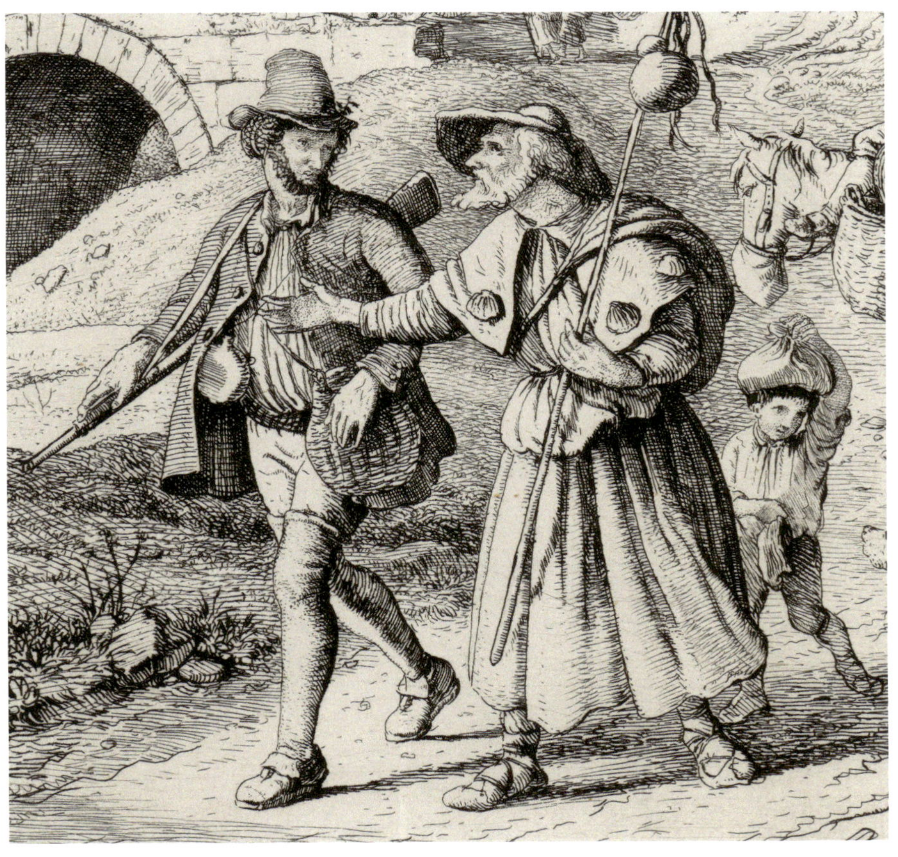

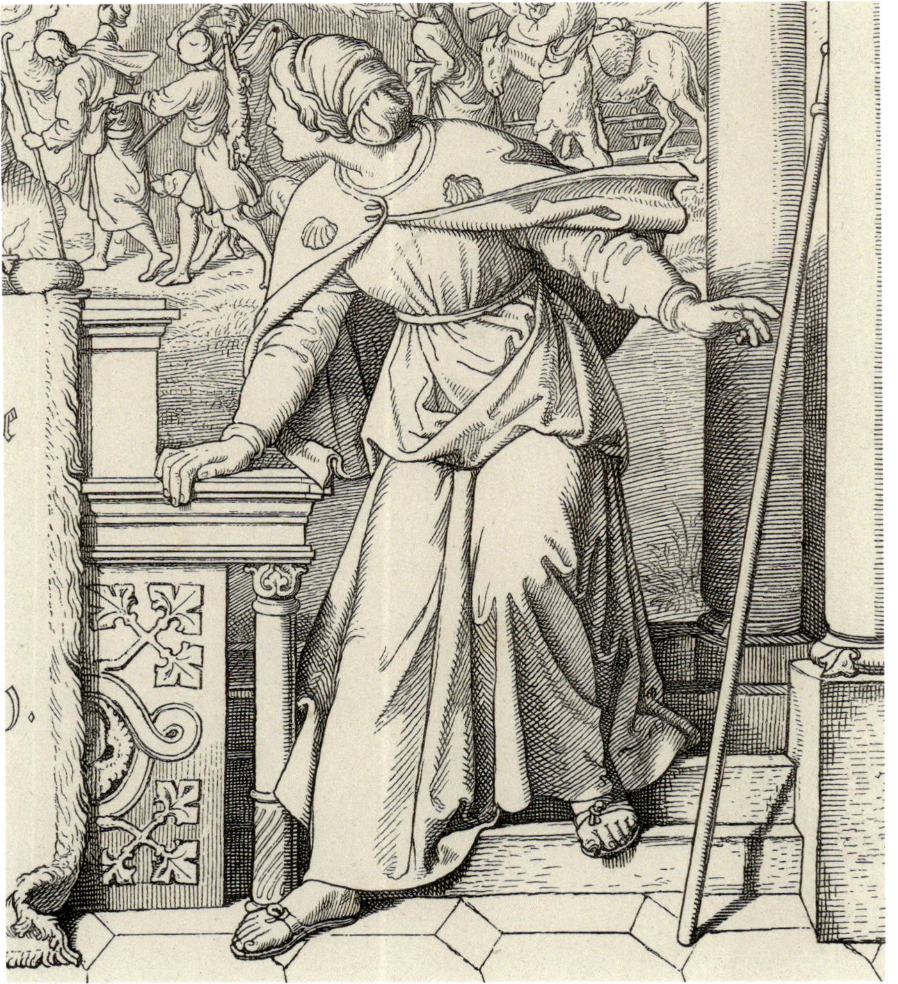

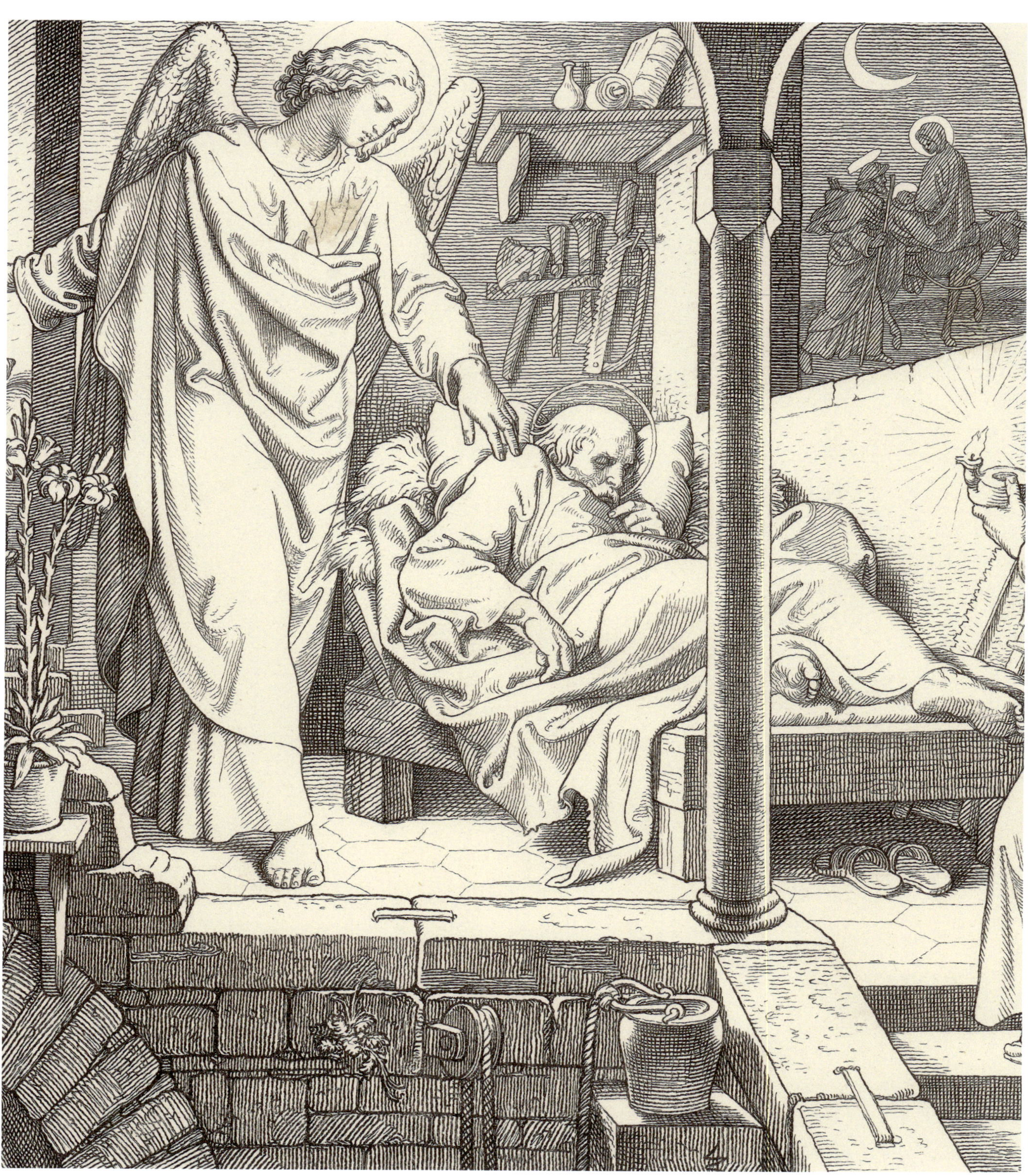

Joseph walks alongside, setting out to seek safety in Egypt. Ultimately, Führich's series made the idea of the spiritual journey central to the story of Jesus's childhood and modeled the devotion that motivated such journeys for the portfolio's middle-class viewers. For his part, Richter may have included a pilgrim in the landscape because he felt nostalgic for his younger self and the time he spent in Italy. In his autobiography, which he began writing in 1869, he referred to himself as a pilgrim numerous times when describing his travels.[34] Richter may also have hoped to evoke a simpler way of life that viewers overwhelmed by a modernizing Germany would find appealing. Both series reference pilgrimage at a time when new developments in mass transit made leisure travel increasingly accessible to more people: The first steamship reached the upper Rhine in 1831, the first train line in Germany was completed in 1835, and the first guidebooks for popular use were published in the 1830s.[35] In their representations of places that had an impact on their art, ideas, and lives, German Romantic artists also captured ways of traveling and engaging with the world that would continue to change in the coming years.

NOTES

1. Heinrich Schwarz, "Heinrich Reinholds Bericht über seine Reise nach Salzburg, Tirol und Oberösterreich im Sommer 1818," *Mitteilungen der Gesellschaft für Salzburger Landeskunde* 67 (1927): 162.

2. Anthony Griffiths and Frances Carey, *German Printmaking in the Age of Goethe* (London: British Museum Press, 1994), 218–219.

3. Schwarz, "Heinrich Reinholds Bericht," 158.

4. A letter by Caroline Herder written in 1788 begins, "Goethe recently said: 'One does not travel to arrive, but to travel.'" Gustav Woldemar Freiherr von Biedermann, ed., *Goethes Gespräche*, vol. 8, 10 vols. (Leipzig, 1890), http://www.zeno.org /nid/20004867017.

5. James Buzard, "The Grand Tour and After (1660–1840)," in *The Cambridge Companion to Travel Writing*, ed. Peter Hulme and Tim Youngs (Cambridge: Cambridge University Press, 2002), 38–42.

6. Wolfgang Kashuba, "Die Fußreise: Von der Arbeitswanderung zur bürgerlichen Bildungsbewegung," in *Reisekultur: Von der Pilgerfahrt zum modernen Tourismus*, ed. Hermann Bausinger, Klaus Beyrer, and Gottfried Korff (Munich: C. H. Beck, 1991), 166; and Sarah Goldsmith, "Hazarding Chance: A History of Eighteenth-Century Danger," in *Masculinity and Danger on the Eighteenth-Century Grand Tour* (London: University of London Press, 2020), 45–55, https://www.jstor.org/stable/j .ctvk3gp1g.7. Buzard has written that many Grand Tourists were badly behaved and attracted criticism, despite being supervised by governors and other attendants. Buzard, "The Grand Tour," 42. Goldsmith points out that fear of moral corruption was not universal, and families tolerated (even expected) different degrees of debauchery from sons on the Grand Tour. Goldsmith, "Hazarding Chance," 55–62.

7. Goldsmith, 62–73.

8. Goldsmith notes that prior to the Napoleonic Wars, war did not necessarily deter civilians from traveling because conflicts were more regulated and limited in geographical scope. The practice of treating people in a given nation as hostile was introduced with the Napoleonic Wars and made wartime travel more dangerous. Goldsmith, 76.

9. Kashuba, "Die Fußreise," 168–169. Adam Rosenbaum explains how the middle-class educational journey (*Bildungsreise*) grew out of the Grand Tour in the early nineteenth century. This form of travel took place over a shorter period and was more focused on self-cultivation than acquiring knowledge. See Adam T. Rosenbaum, *Bavarian Tourism and the Modern World, 1800–1950* (New York: Cambridge University Press, 2016), 32.

10. Kashuba, 172.

11. Johann Wolfgang von Goethe, *Goethe's Travels in Italy Together with His Second Residence in Rome and Fragments on Italy* (London: George Bell and Sons, 1885), 6–7, 17.

12. Kashuba, "Die Fußreise," 170.

13. Buzard, "The Grand Tour," 43–46.

14. Heinrich Schwarz, *Salzburg und Salzkammergut: Die künstlerische Entdeckung der Stadt und der Landschaft im 19. Jahrhundert* (Vienna: Verlag Anton Schroll, 1926), 42–43.

15. "If I could, with quiet effort, dedicate my time and energy entirely to such a venture and thereby give it the proper comprehensiveness, I believe I would be able to deliver a work that, making their own unknown splendors familiar to Germans, should delight and amaze them and is bound to be of decisive benefit to me. For that purpose, however, it is especially necessary that I undertake a second trip there because the first made me only roughly familiar with this new and unknown grandeur, which needs to be assessed accurately to give an account of it." ("Könnte ich einem solchen Unternehmen mit ruhiger Anstrengung meine Zeit und Kräfte ganz weihen und ihm dadurch die gehörige Ausdehnung geben, so glaube ich imstande zu sein, ein Werk zu liefern, das die Deutschen, mit ihren eigenen, ihnen unbekannten Herrlichkeiten sie bekannt machend, in Freude und Erstaunen versetzen sollte und mir von entscheidenden Vortheilen sein müsste. Dazu aber ist vor allem nöthig, daß ich eine zweite Reise dahin unternehme, denn die erste hat mich nur ungefähr mit diesen mir neuen und unbekannten Größen bekannt gemacht, welche, um Rechenschaft davon zu geben, genauer wollen ermessen sein.") Quoted in Schwarz, 20–21. (Translation is mine.)

16. Schwarz, 24–25.

17. For thorough interpretations of the allegorical and symbolic meanings of Olivier's series, see Cordula Grewe, "A Family Tree of German Art: Avant-Garde, Anti-Judaism, and Artistic Identity," in *Painting the Sacred in the Age of Romanticism* (Surrey, UK: Ashgate Publishing, 2009), 253–301; Cordula Grewe, "Nature," in *The Nazarenes: Romantic Avant-Garde and the Art of the Concept* (University Park, PA: Pennsylvania State University Press, 2015), 148–173; Cordula Grewe, "Ferdinand Olivier (1785–1841) and Adrian Ludwig Richter (1803–1884): The Salzburg Albums," in *The Enchanted World of German Romantic Prints, 1770–1850*, ed. John Ittmann (Philadelphia: Philadelphia Museum of Art, 2017), 258–269; and Schwarz, *Salzburg und Salzkammergut*, 21–25.

18. Grewe, "Nature," 162.

19. Grewe introduces the idea that handling the *Seven Places* prints was a form of ritual and spiritual pilgrimage, and I have drawn inspiration from this idea. Grewe also argues that the purpose of realism in landscapes is not to present specific locales but to prime viewers to engage with their symbolic meanings. I do not disagree that the *Seven Places* landscapes exceed mere topography, but here I wish to reassert the importance of the specific sites Olivier chose for the series. See Grewe, "Nature," 169–170.

20. Griffiths and Carey, *German Printmaking*, 123.

21. Mitchell Benjamin Frank, *German Romantic Painting Redefined: Nazarene Tradition and the Narratives of Romanticism* (Aldershot, UK:

Ashgate Publishing, 2001), 11–13; Cordula Grewe, *The Nazarenes: Romantic Avant-Garde and the Art of the Concept* (University Park, PA: Pennsylvania State University Press, 2015), 2–5.

22. Letter from Johann Friedrich Overbeck to Joseph Sutter, July 19, 1810. Printed in Eberhard Haufe, ed., *Deutsche Briefe aus Italien von Winckelmann bis Gregorovius* (Hamburg: Christian Wegner Verlag, 1965), 172.

23. Letter from Johann Friedrich Overbeck to Friedrich Wenner, January 31, 1829. Printed in Haufe, 178.

24. Letter from Peter von Cornelius to Karl Mossler, March 1812, and letter from Julius Schnorr von Carolsfeld to Friedrich Rochlitz, September 12, 1818. Printed in Haufe, 189 and 230.

25. Letter from Peter von Cornelius to Friedrich Wenner, February 20, 1817. Printed in Haufe, 192.

26. Michael Löwy and Robert Sayre, *Romanticism Against the Tide of Modernity*, trans. Catherine Porter (Durham, NC: Duke University Press, 2001), 21.

27. Letter from Ludwig Richter to Johann Christoph Arnold, January 31, 1824. Printed in Haufe, *Deutsche Briefe*, 245.

28. Ludwig Richter, "Auszüge aus Ludwig Richter's Jugendtagebüchern, 1821–1831," appendix in *Lebenserinnerungen eines deutschen Malers: Selbstbiographie nebst Tagebuchniederschriften und Briefen*, ed. Heinrich Richter (Frankfurt am Main: Johannes Alt, 1901), 16, 22, 29.

29. Quoted in Griffiths and Carey, *German Printmaking*, 228.

30. Griffiths and Carey, 228.

31. As Sherman has pointed out, observations about the customs and habits of people in distant places have been part of travel writing since the end of the sixteenth century. Frank notes that such ethnographic imagery appeared in Romantic prints. Richter, however, did not attempt to document or comment upon the Italian people in the series; his Romans do not look obviously distinct from the figures populating the Swiss landscape of the earlier series. William H. Sherman, "Stirrings and Searchings (1500–1720)," in Hulme and Youngs, *The Cambridge Companion*, 30; Mitchell B. Frank, "The Wanderer: Travel Imagery in German Romantic Prints," in Ittmann, *The Enchanted World of German Romantic Prints*, 126.

32. Letter from Ludwig Richter to Johann Christoph Arnold, January 31, 1824. Printed in Haufe, *Deutsche Briefe*, 245.

33. Hermann Bausinger et al., 31.

34. *Lebenserinnerungen*, 124, 133, 186.

35. David Blackbourn, *The Conquest of Nature: Water, Landscape, and the Making of Modern Germany* (New York: W. W. Norton, 2006), 118; Rosenbaum, *Bavarian Tourism and the Modern World, 1800–1950*, 25; Hulme and Youngs, *The Cambridge Companion*, 48.

Journeys

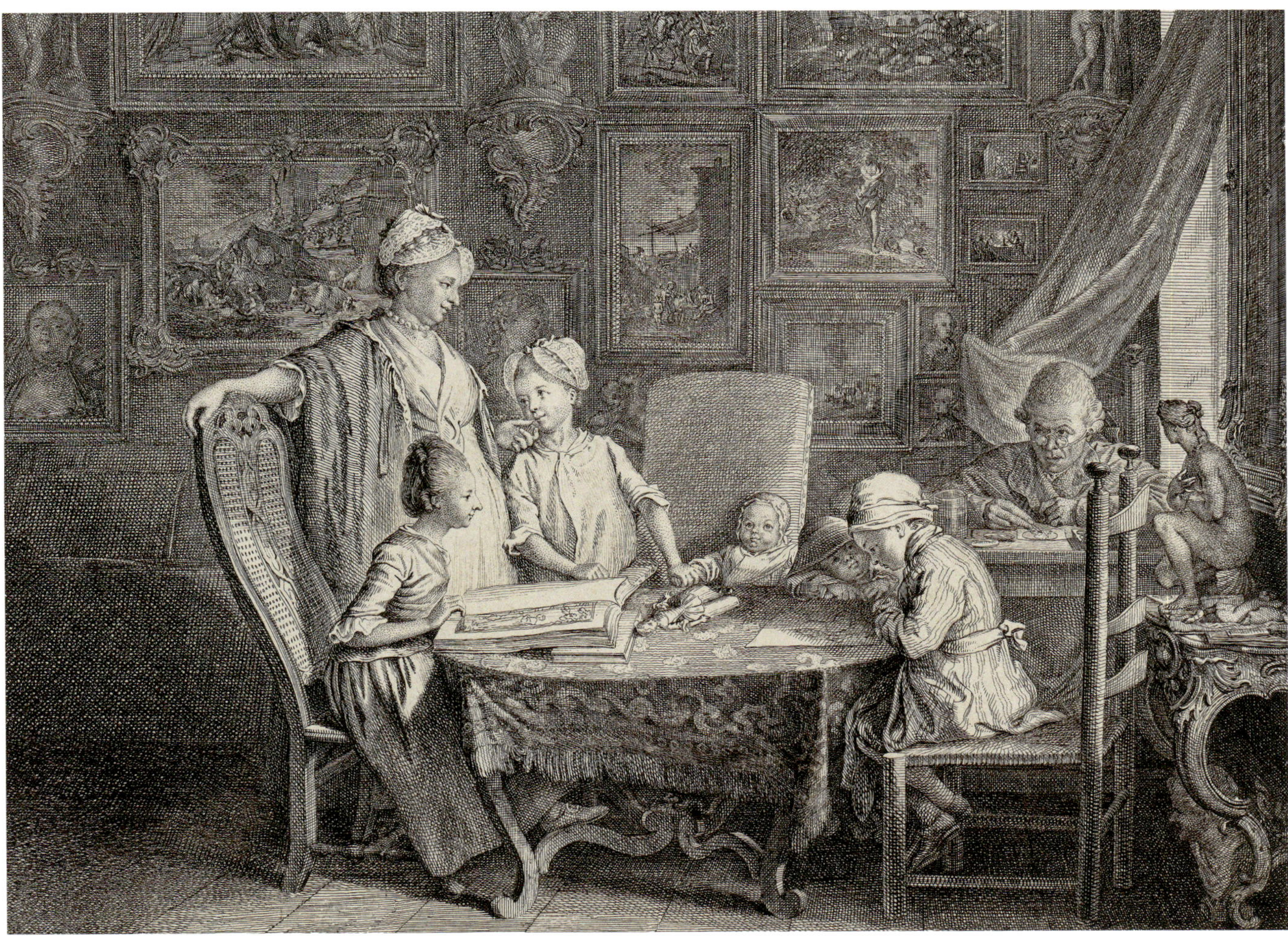

Daniel Nikolaus Chodowiecki

The Cabinet of a Painter (Cabinet d'un peintre),
1771

Etching

When Daniel Chodowiecki etched this scene of himself and his family, he was living in Berlin. He moved there from Poland shortly after his father died in 1743 and had not returned since. The inscription dedicates the print to his mother, who had never met his wife, three daughters, or two sons. Such a long separation reflects the difficulty of travel during the eighteenth century; when Chodowiecki finally visited his homeland in 1773, the journey took eight days and included bad terrain, rain, and scarce food.

Chodowiecki represented his family as happy and loving, gathered around a table where the older children dutifully pursue educational activities. The artworks on the wall and comfortable setting attest to his success as an artist, collector, and dealer. In addition to reassuring his mother that he led a fulfilling life, Chodowiecki's image of bourgeois domestic harmony was highly sought after by collectors.

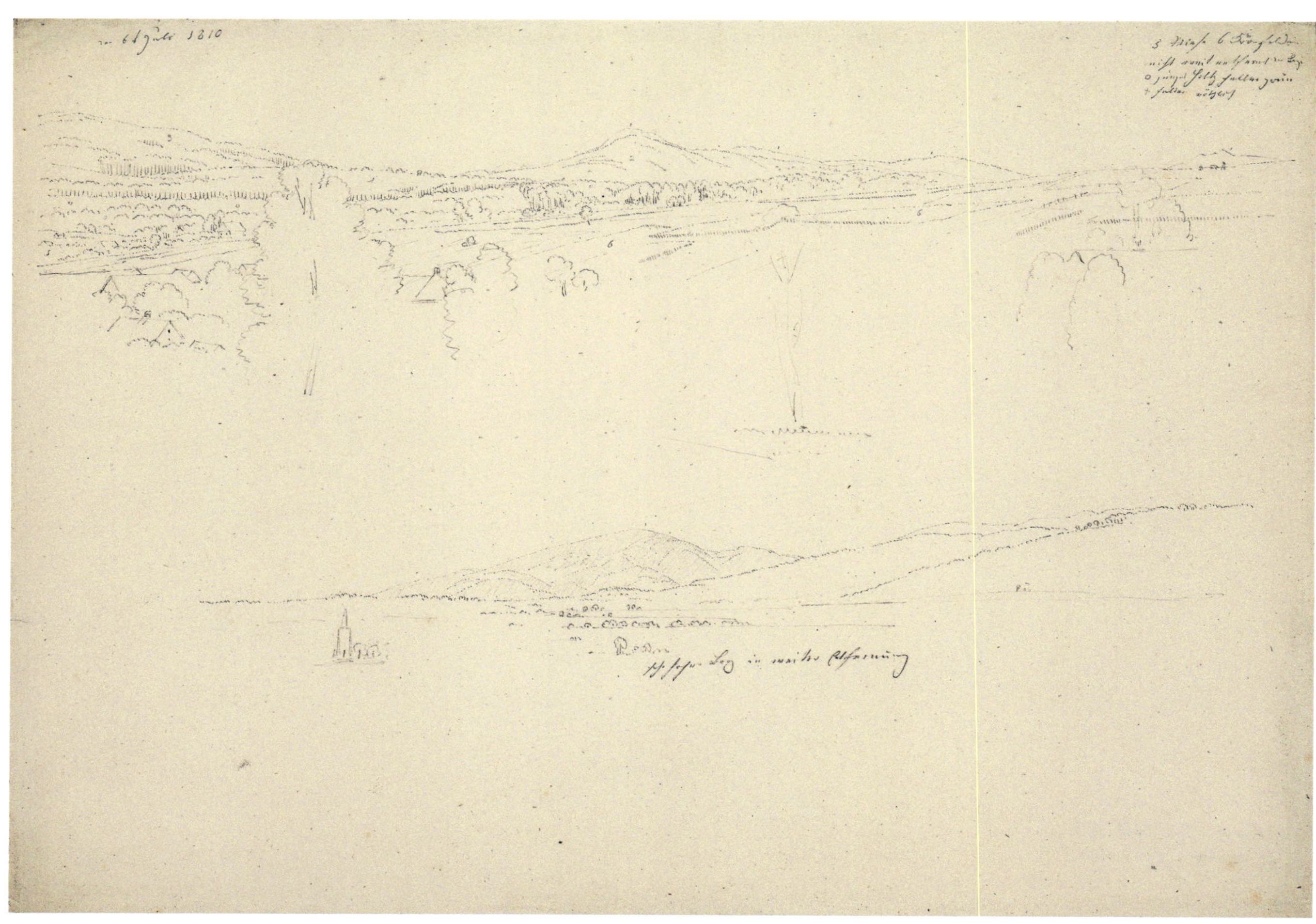

54.
Caspar David Friedrich
GREIFSWALD 1774–1840 DRESDEN

Two Landscapes in Oberlausitz (Zwei Landschafts-skizzen, 6. Juli 1810), 1810

Graphite on paper

Caspar David Friedrich drew the two views on this sheet while hiking from Oybin to Zittau on July 6, 1810. He was traveling from Dresden to the Giant Mountains on the border of what are now Czechia and Poland with his friend and fellow artist Georg Friedrich Kersting. The journey took about two weeks, and the artists sketched along the way. With a spare graphite line, Friedrich captured the mountain peaks, trees, grasses, church tower, and houses. A key at the upper right decodes a set of symbols he added throughout the composition: The numbers 5 and 6 refer to meadows and cornfields, respectively, while O and X indicate young woods and fields. Friedrich used his sketches as source material for paintings he made in his studio, sometimes referencing them many years later, and his quick notations helped him recall how the landscape appeared. Scholars have identified at least one work for which this drawing served as a model.

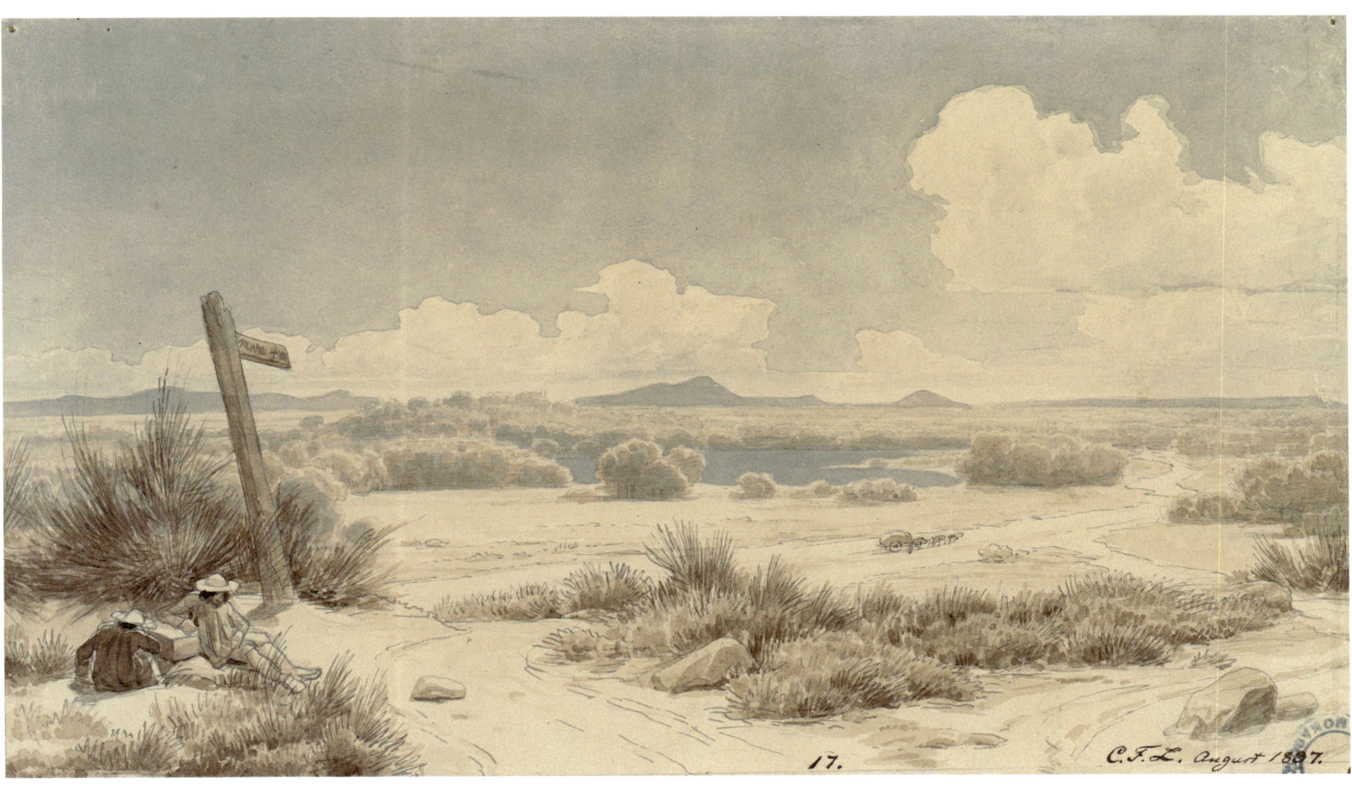

55.
Carl Friedrich Lessing
WROCŁAW 1808–1880 KARLSRUHE

Landscape with Wanderers, 1837

Pen and brown ink and watercolor over graphite on paper

The exact location of this sketch is not known, but it may be the Eifel region in western Germany, which Carl Friedrich Lessing depicted in other works around this time. It features similar sandy expanses dotted with rocks, low trees, and distant highlands. The artist became known for his work portraying the low mountains (*Mittelgebirge*) stretching across the central German lands. Here, two travelers recline next to a road sign that points the way to their next destination.

Traveling to distinctive national sites was important to German Romantic artists, especially as landscape painting attained greater significance. Lessing was at the forefront of this development; he studied at the Düsseldorf Art Academy under Wilhelm Schadow, a Nazarene and member of the Lukasbund. He also co-founded the Society of Landscape Painting with Johann Wilhelm Schirmer (plates 75 and 76) and helped build the school into a leader in the genre.

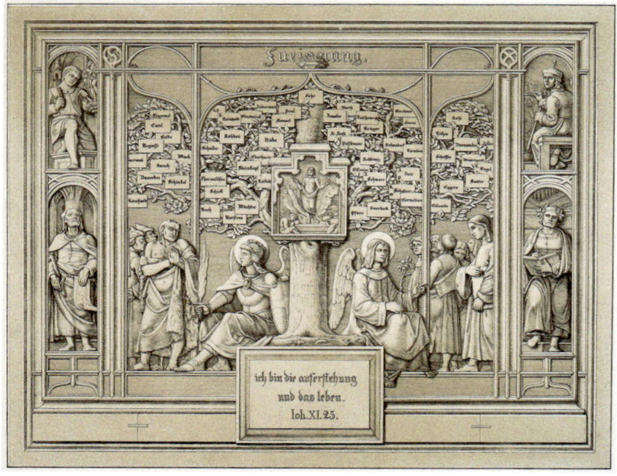

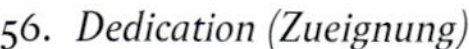

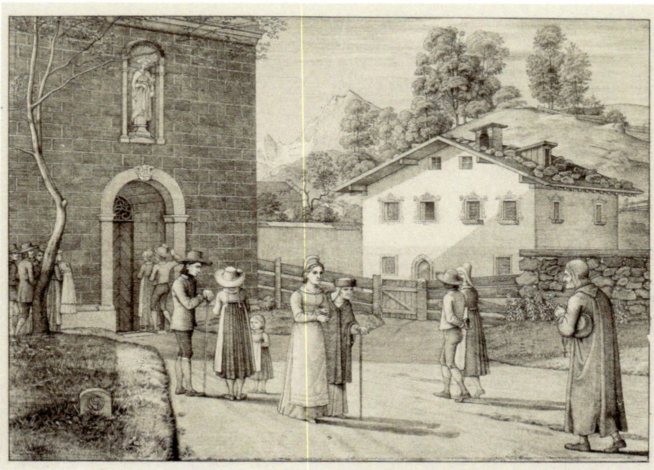

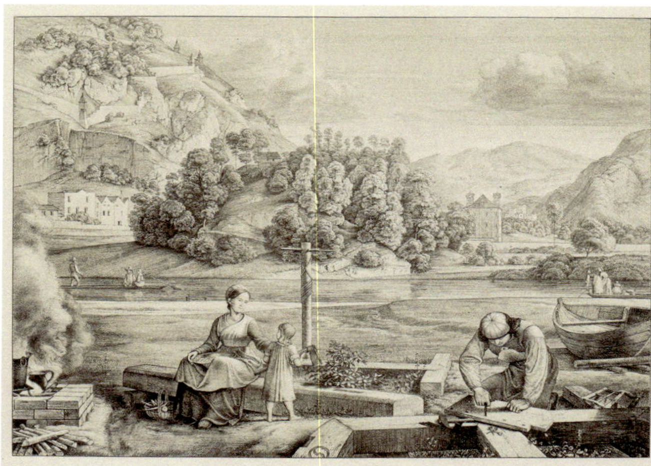

56. *Dedication (Zueignung)*

57. *Sunday: Going to Church in Berchtesgaden (Sonntag. Kircheneingang in Berchtesgaden)*

58. *Monday: Rosenecker Garden Outside Salzburg (Montag. Rosenecker Garten vor Salzburg)*

56–64

Ferdinand Olivier
DESSAU 1785–1841 MUNICH

Printed by Adolph Kunike
GREIFSWALD 1777–1838 VIENNA

Published by Ferdinand Olivier
DESSAU 1785–1841 MUNICH

Seven Places in Salzburg and Berchtesgaden (Sieben Gegenden aus Salzburg und Berchtesgaden), 1818–22, published 1823

Series of seven lithographs with dedication and keystone

Set in the Alpine towns of Salzburg and Berchtesgaden, Ferdinand Olivier's portfolio is rooted in Christian doctrine and reflects the Nazarene ideal of a national devotional art. Each lithograph is titled with a day of the week and a location Olivier visited during sketching trips in 1815 and 1817. The series begins on Sunday at a church to celebrate new life; a baby in a baptismal gown is visible on the far left. A funeral in a cemetery marks the last day of the week. During the intervening days, residents tend to fields and flocks, gather food from the land, and care for those in need.

The dedication and keystone that open and close the series feature the Gospel of John: A tree in the former bears the verse, "I am the resurrection and the life," along with the names of German artists Olivier respected, including his fellow Nazarenes. The verse "Blessed are those who have not seen and yet believe," engraved in the central shrine in the final print, unites the participants from all the scenes, who reappear in windows framed by decorative tracery.

Olivier's decision to set the series in the Bavarian Alps was significant; few artists had previously depicted the area, and Olivier hoped to share views of the awe-inspiring landscape with his compatriots. Through his multilayered images, Olivier introduced Salzburg and Berchtesgaden as uniquely German, idyllic Christian sites.

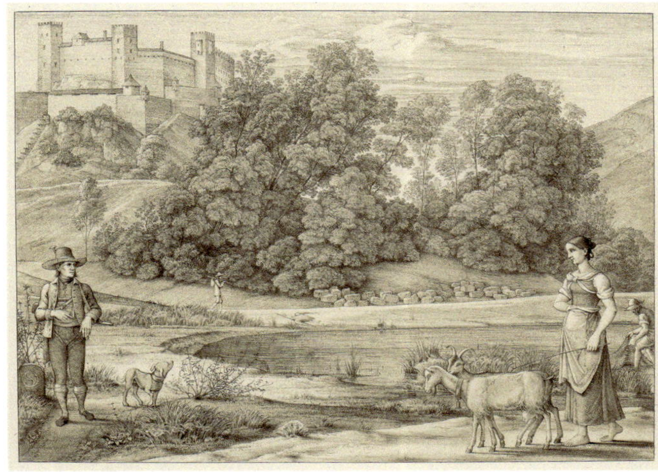

59. *Tuesday: Salzburg Castle from the South*
(Dienstag. Bergveste Salzburg von der Mittagseite)

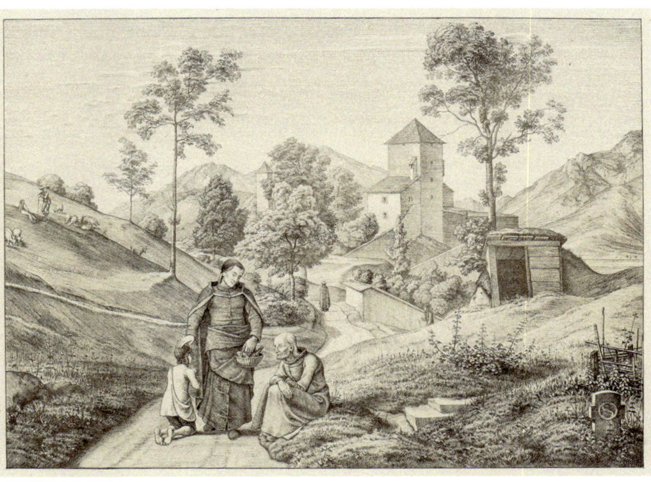

60. *Wednesday: Footpath on the Mönchsberg near Salzburg*
(Mittwoch. Fußpfad auf dem Mönchsberge bei Salzburg)

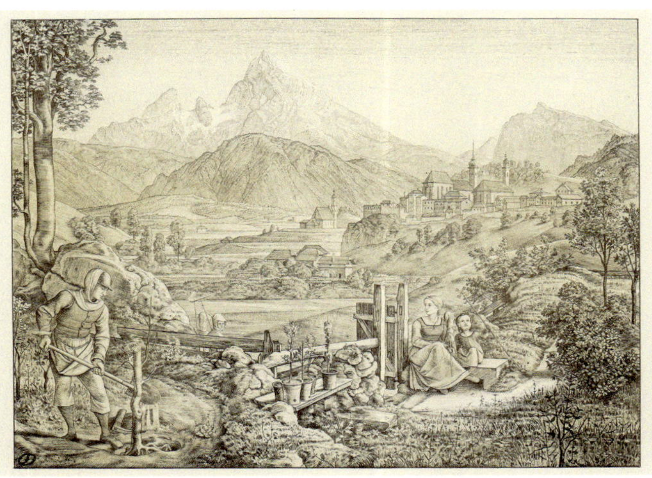

61. *Thursday: Berchtesgaden and the Watzmann*
(Donnerstag. Berchtesgaden und der Watzmann)

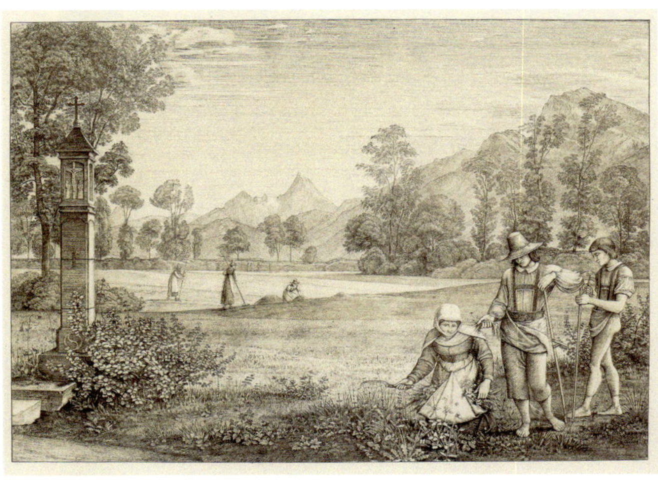

62. *Friday: Meadow Before Aigen near Salzburg*
(Freitag. Wiesenplan vor Aigen bei Salzburg)

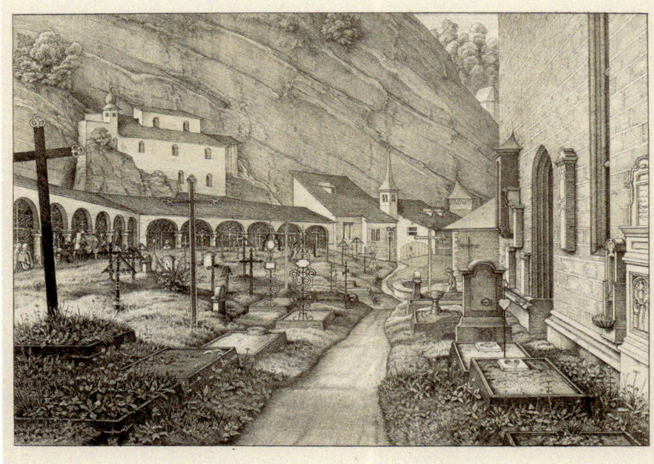

63. *Saturday: Graveyard of St. Peter's in Salzburg*
(Sonnabend. Gottesacker zu St. Peter in Salzburg)

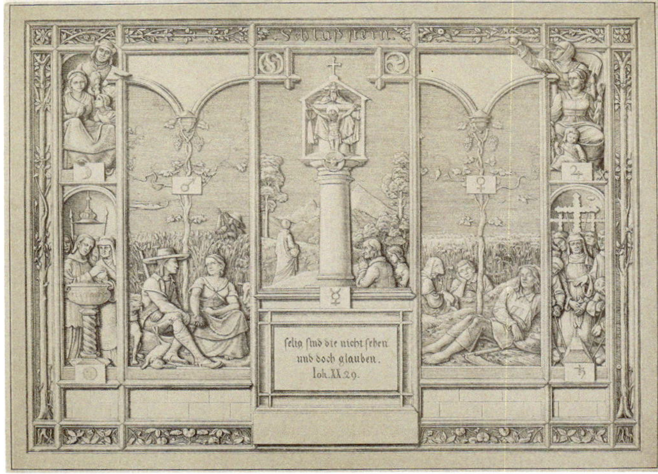

64. *Keystone (Schlussstein)*

65.

Ernst Fries

HEIDELBERG 1801–1833 KARLSRUHE

View of Salzburg and the Königssee, 1820

Brush and gray-brown ink over graphite on paper

The Salzburg region grew in popularity among travelers in the early nineteenth century. Many artists were attracted by the idea of a beautiful, lesser-known landscape located within the German Confederation. Ernst Fries spent his early career traveling around the German lands, and he visited Salzburg and Berchtesgaden in the summer of 1820 and September 1821. Although this sheet is undated, the delicate modeling is typical of drawings Fries made during his first trip. He sometimes divided his sketchbook sheets in half, allowing him to capture two views. In this case, he drew the distant Hohensalzburg Fortress at the top and Königssee Lake at the bottom. Faint vertical graphite lines suggest the artist intended to enlarge and paint these compositions, but no paintings resembling them exist. Fries lived in Italy from 1823 to 1827, where he befriended Ludwig Richter (see plates 68–73) and other German artists in Rome.

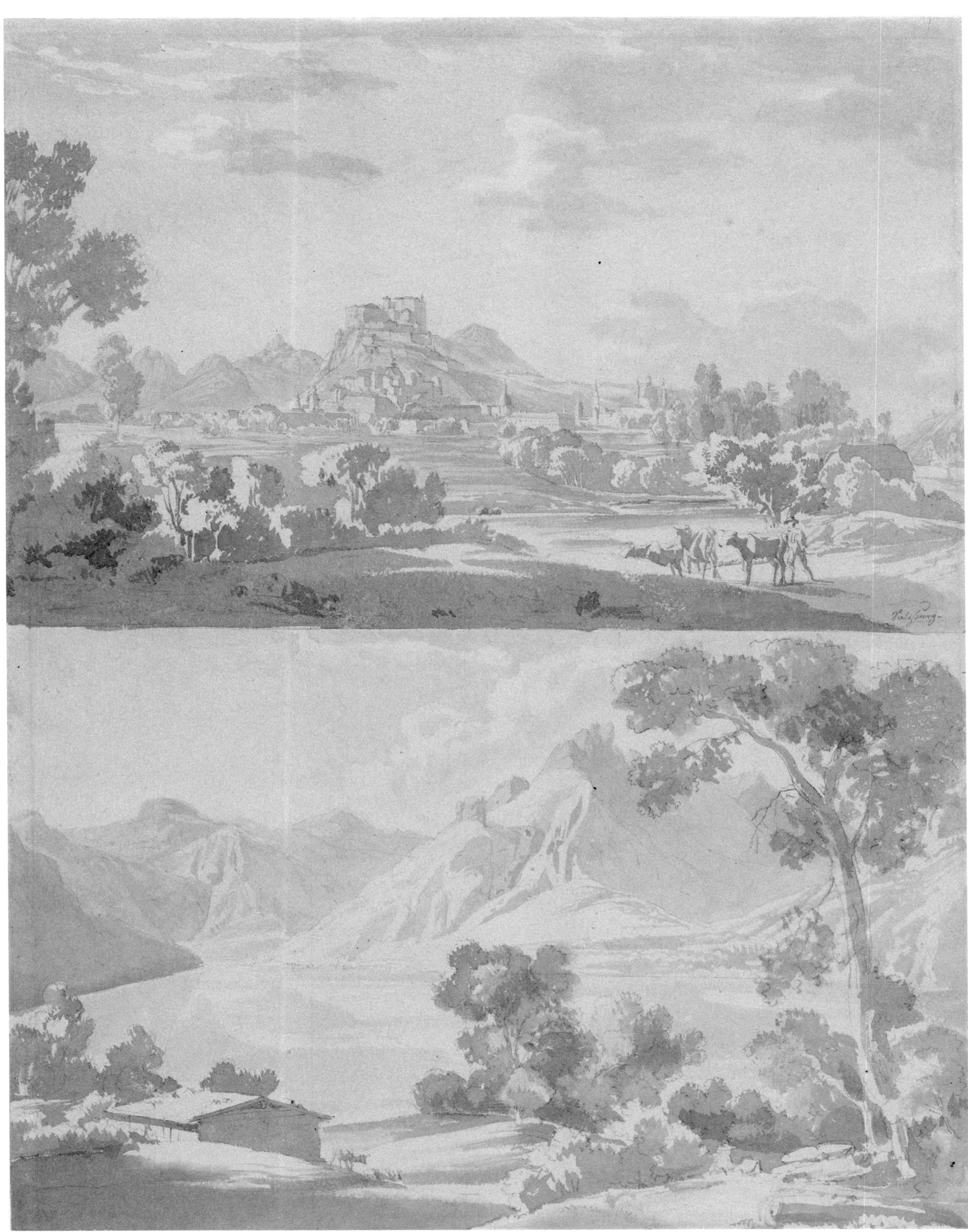

Salzburg

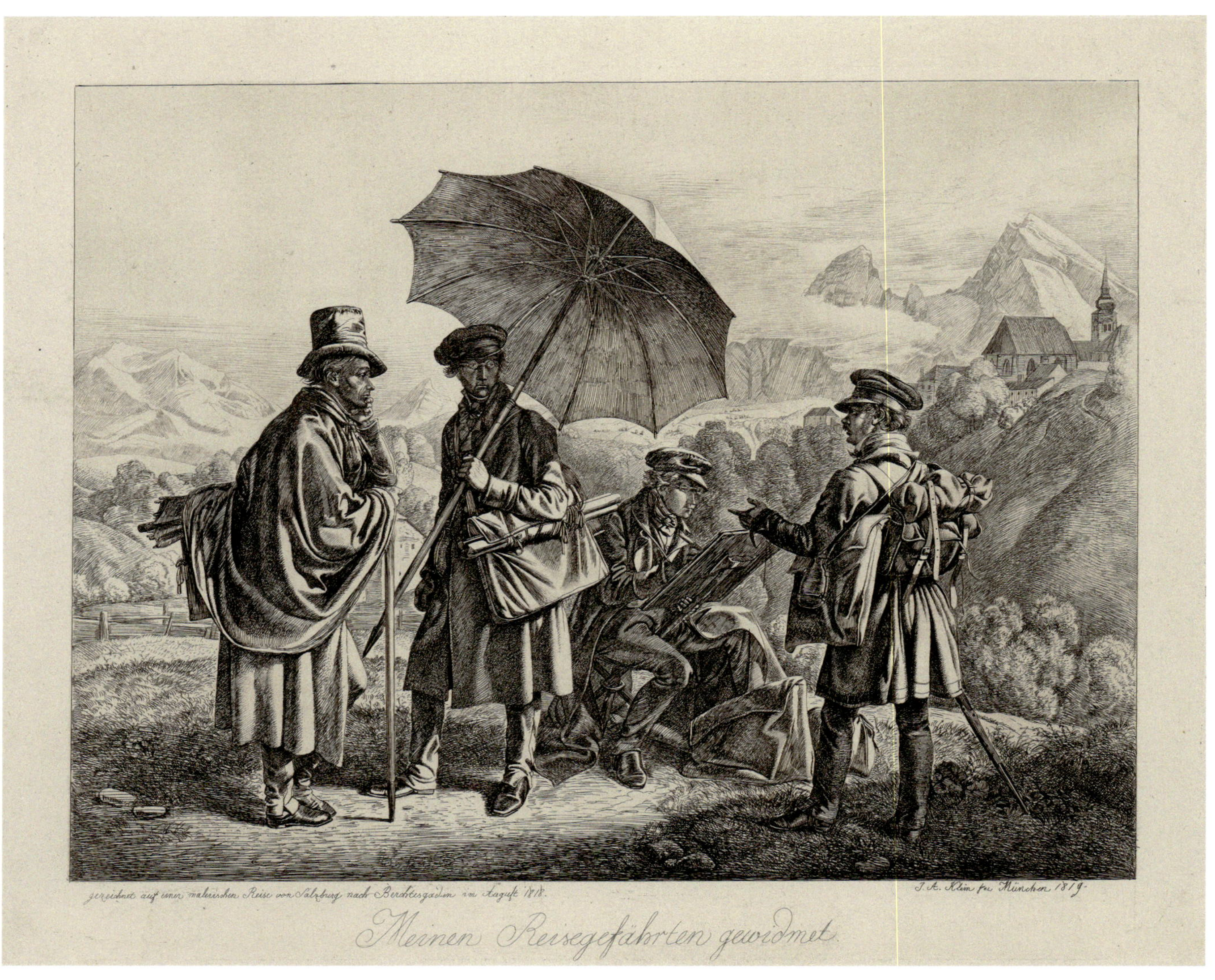

66.

Johann Adam Klein

NUREMBERG 1792–1875 MUNICH

The Artists on Their Journey (Meinen Reisegefährten gewidmet), 1819

Etching

This etching by Johann Adam Klein captures the type of sketching trip in the Alps that became typical for artists in the nineteenth century. Resting in a clearing with a view of the Watzmann mountain, brothers Friedrich and Heinrich Reinhold stand under Heinrich's umbrella, while Christian Erhard draws and Ernst Welker speaks to the group from the right. The scene, however, is largely fictional. A letter written by Heinrich Reinhold recounts that the artists spent their time in Berchtesgaden indoors. A five-day rainstorm left them unable to sketch the landscape, so they resorted to drawing each other at the inn. This print is based on two sketches Klein made during those drenching days, as well as one from a scenic location he visited after everyone went their separate ways. Klein's inscriptions below the image cite the picturesque trip in August 1818 and dedicate the print to his traveling companions.

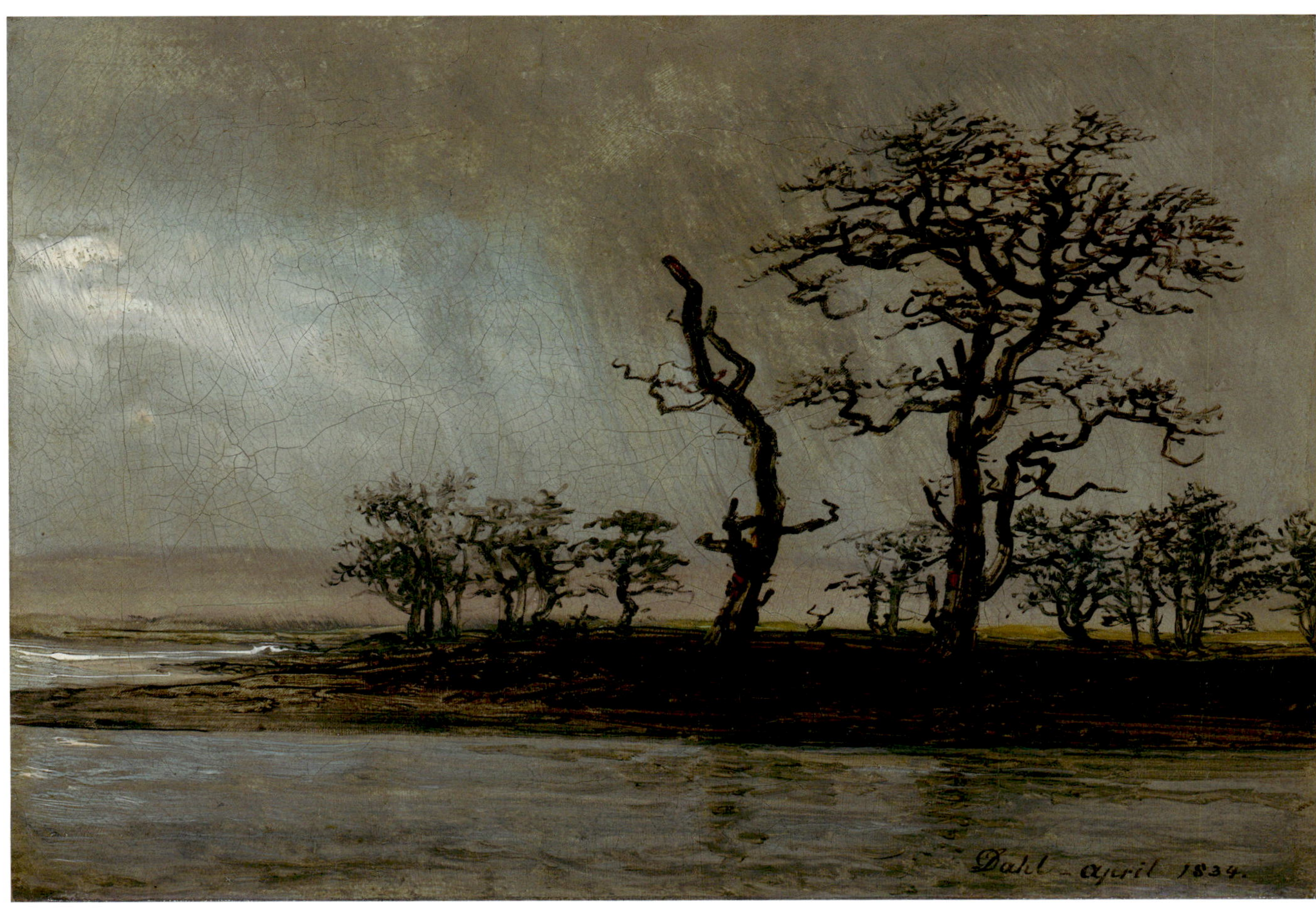

67.

Johann Christian Clausen Dahl
BERGEN 1788–1857 DRESDEN

*Trees by the River Elbe in the Rain
(Regenstimmung an der Elbe)*, 1834

Oil on canvas

Johann Christian Clausen Dahl painted many views of the Elbe River, which he could see from his window in Dresden. A ten-month trip to Naples and Rome in the winter of 1820 initiated his practice of creating small oil sketches like this one. During his time in Italy, he embraced the custom of painting outdoors and encountered work by French artists who focused on representing atmospheric effects. *Trees by the River Elbe* reflects this influence; broad strokes of gray paint behind the bare trees convey the falling rain, while white and lighter blue patches in the sky, reflected on the water as daubs of white, suggest a break in the clouds. These spontaneous compositions were a departure from the precisely detailed landscapes favored by German artists, and Dahl's work inspired some, including his methodical friend and housemate Caspar David Friedrich, to attempt their own oil studies.

68–73

Ludwig Richter
DRESDEN 1803–1884 DRESDEN

Published by Carl Gustav Boerner
KNAU 1790–1855 LEIPZIG

*Picturesque Views of the Environs of Rome
(Malerische Ansichten aus den Umgebungen
von Rom)*, 1832

Series of six etchings

Ludwig Richter based the etchings in this series on sketches he made years before in Italy while furthering his training. There, he met fellow artist Carl Gustav Boerner, who later established himself as an art dealer in Leipzig and commissioned Richter to create this print portfolio, as well as one representing Salzburg. The prints emphasize the region's idyllic and pastoral qualities, with rolling hills and groups of people interacting with each other and the landscape. The series may have evoked nostalgia in Richter for his life in Rome. In his autobiography, he recalled the youthful excitement he felt on his first morning in the city in 1824: "What would I see and experience here? Will the puzzling questions of art and life find a solution for me?"[1] Beyond Richter's personal connection to the depicted sites, Italian landscapes like these appealed to potential collectors' taste.

1. Heinrich Richter, ed., *Lebenserinnerungen eines deutschen Malers: Selbstbiographie nebst Tagebuchniederschriften und Briefen von Ludwig Richter* (Frankfurt: Johannes Alt, 1901), 133.

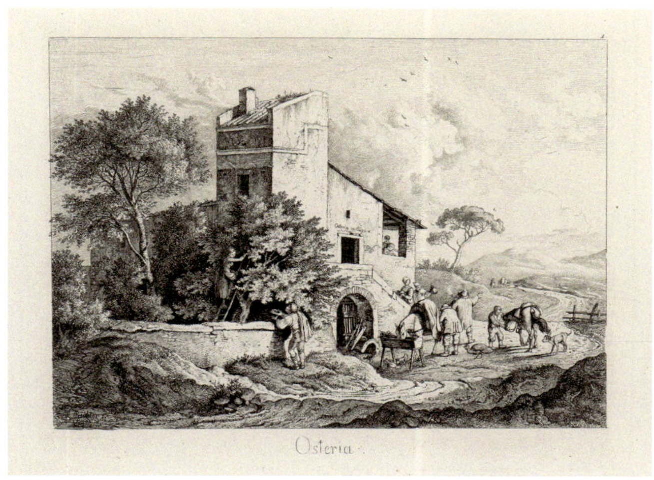

68. *Roadside Inn (Osteria)*

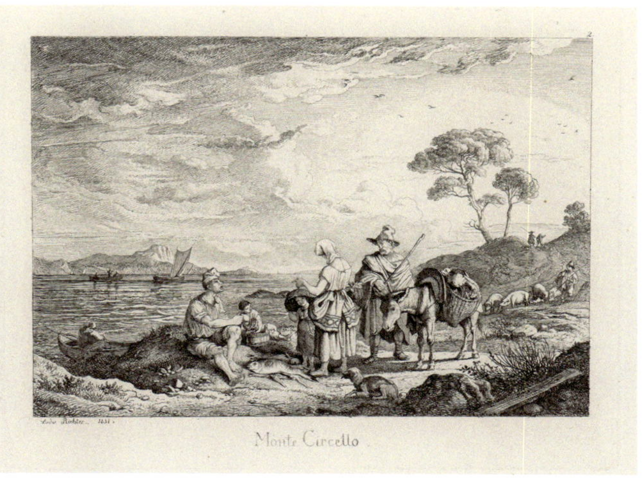

69. *Monte Circello*

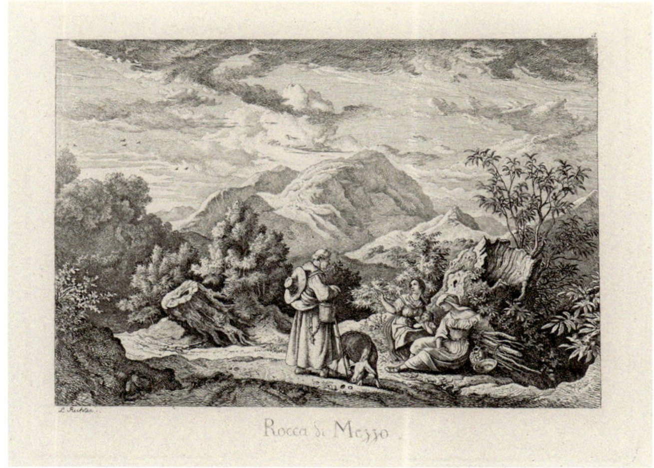

70. *Rocca di Mezzo*

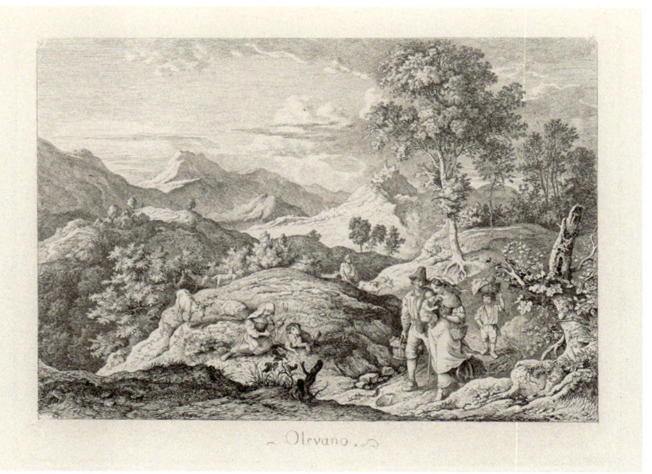

71. *Olevano*

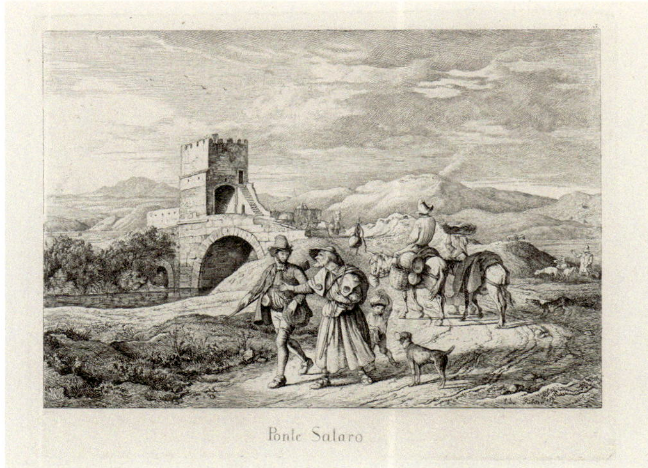

72. *Ponte Salaro*

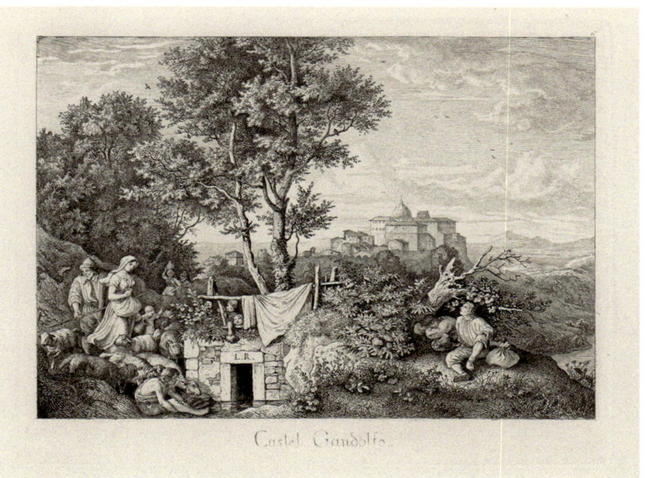

73. *Castel Gandolfo*

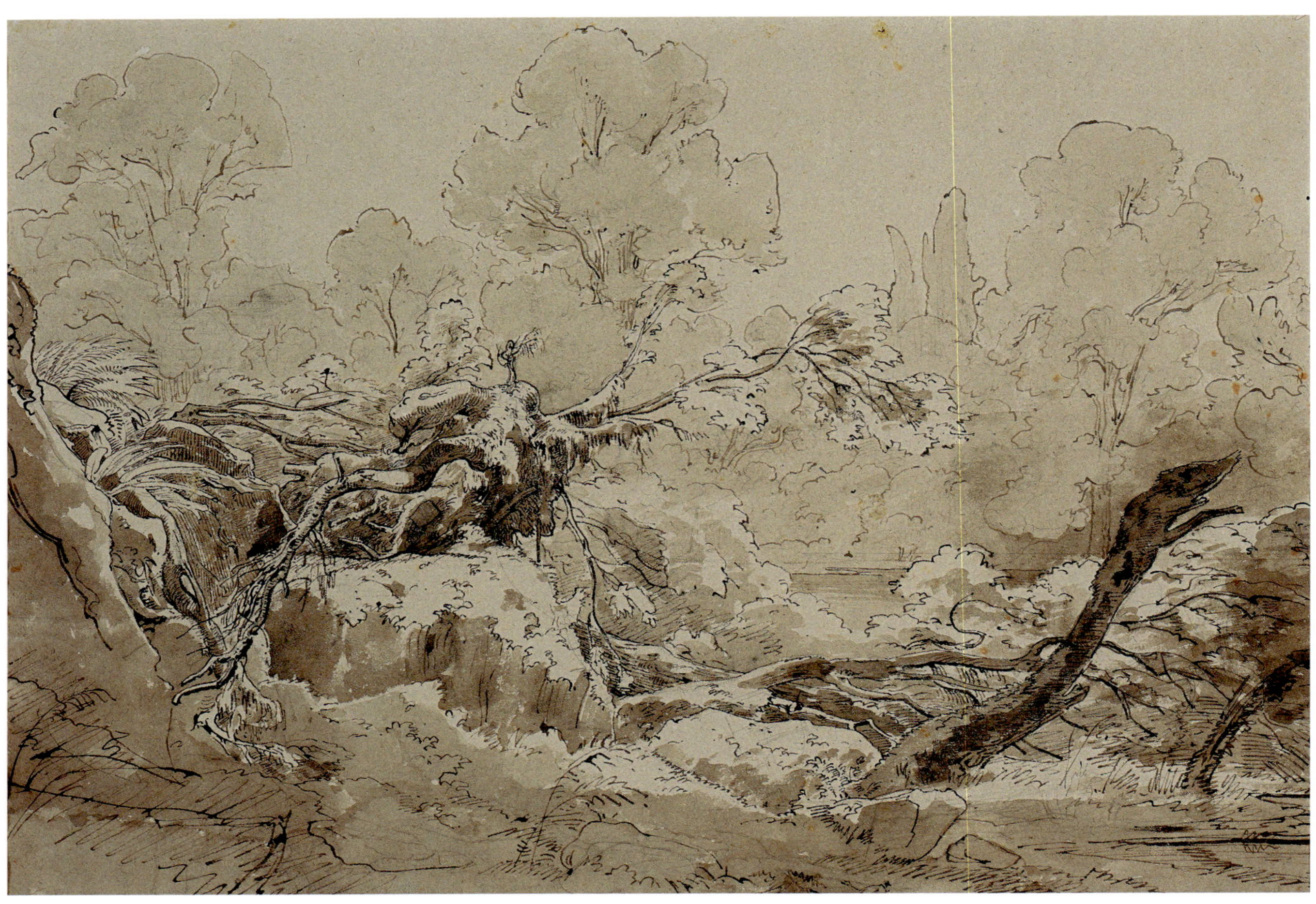

August Wilhelm Julius Ahlborn

In the Park of the Villa Chigi, Ariccia: Two Olive Trees on a Rock at a Brook (recto); *Fallen Tree Trunks and Overgrown Roots* (verso), ca. 1831

Pen and brown ink and wash over graphite on paper

Both drawings on this double-sided sheet picture the gardens surrounding the eighteenth-century Villa Chigi, a popular Italian destination among German artists in the 1820s and 1830s. August Wilhelm Julius Ahlborn's selection of locations within the park and his compositions convey a sense of Romantic drama and melancholy: Tangles of branches and roots, stripped bare by time or weather, stretch across the page; moss overtakes fallen trunks. Visible graphite lines throughout the drawing suggest that Ahlborn made a quick sketch at the location, then added pen and ink in his studio, perhaps attempting to bring more emotion to the scene.

Ahlborn trained as a landscape painter at the Berlin Art Academy and won the institution's prestigious Academy Prize in 1826, which allowed him to live in Rome for the next four years. The drawings he created there, like this one, informed many of his later paintings.

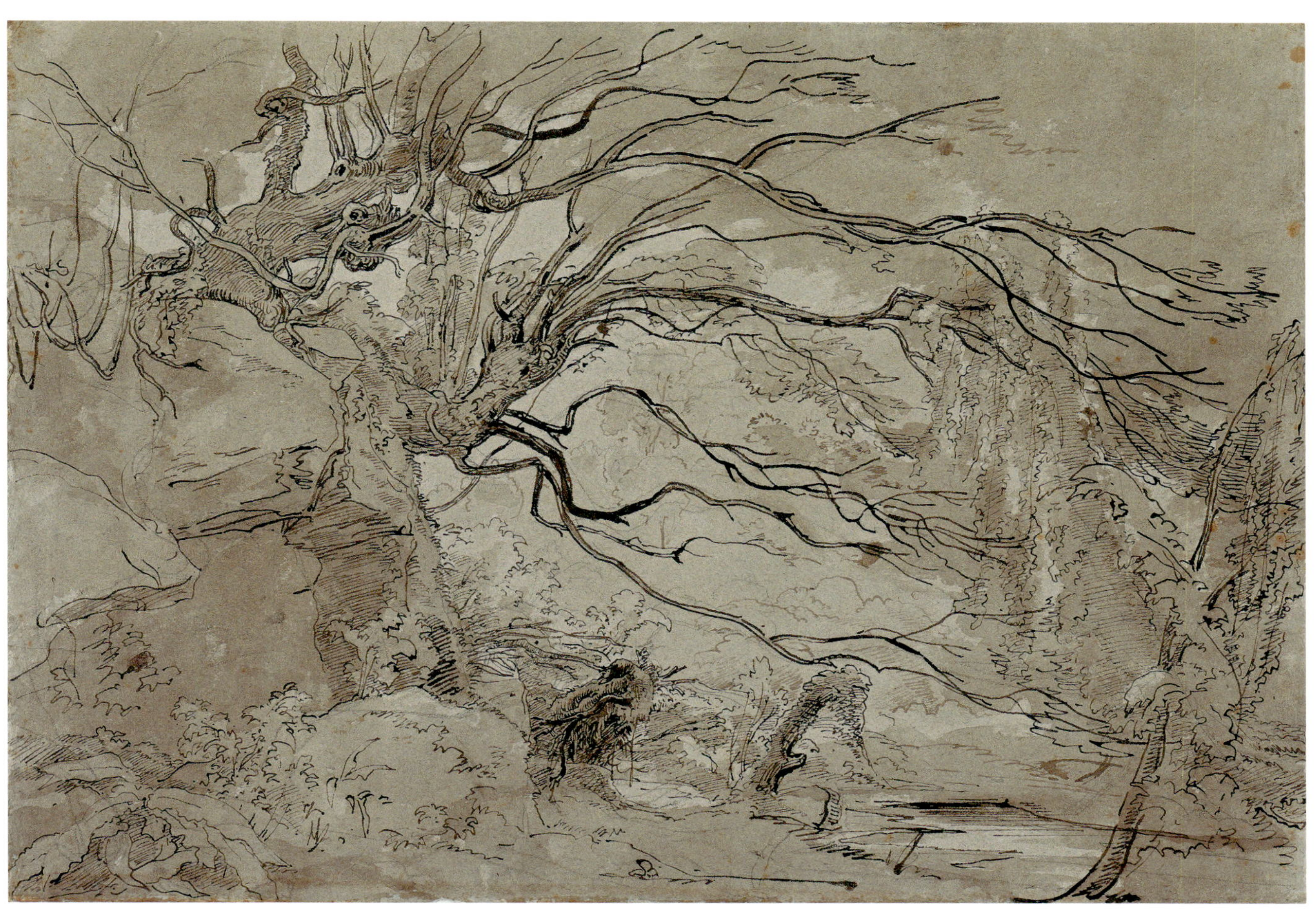

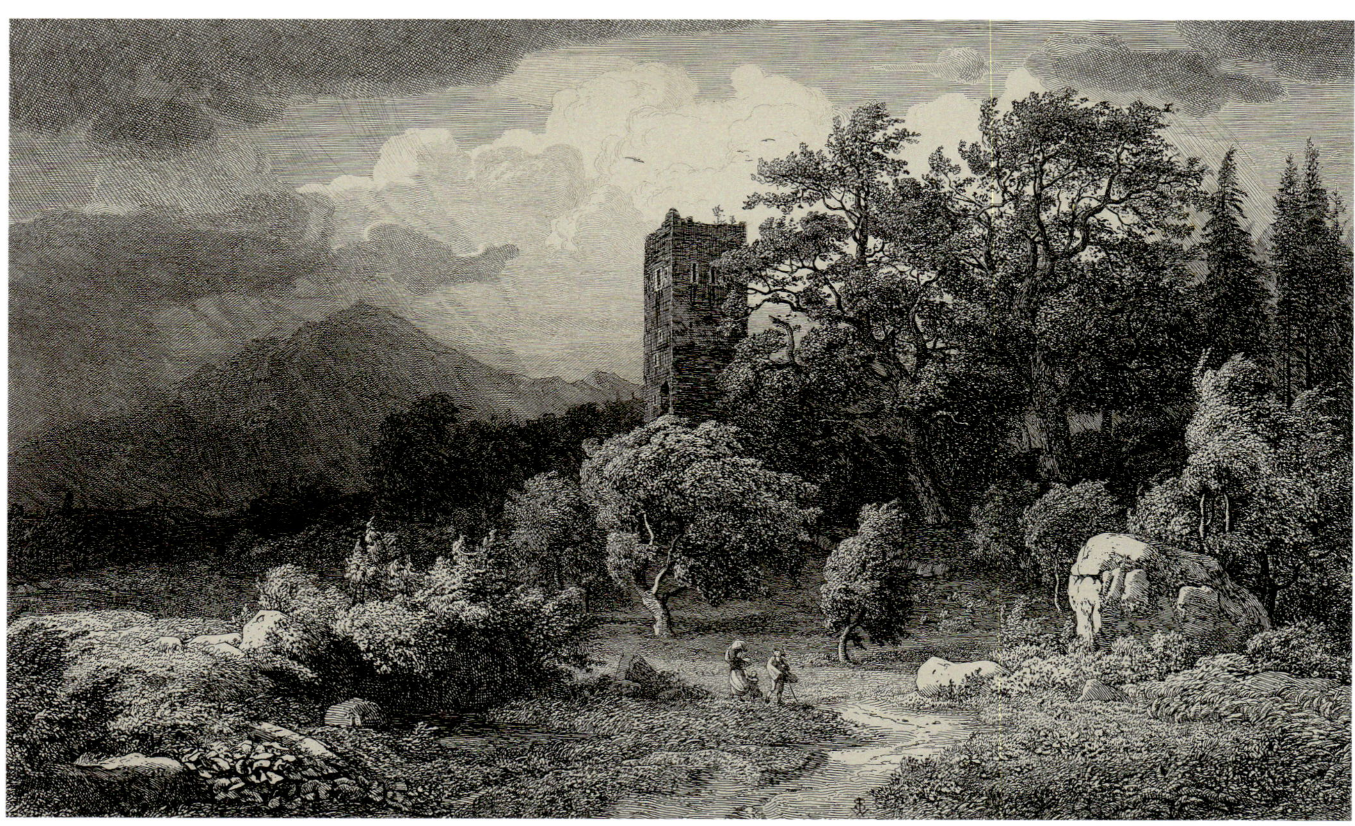

75.

Johann Wilhelm Schirmer
JÜLICH 1807–1863 KARLSRUHE

Ruined Castle near Meiringen (Burgreste bei Meiringen), ca. 1843

Etching, printed chine collé

This print depicts the Alpine village of Meiringen, which Johann Wilhelm Schirmer visited during trips to Switzerland in 1835 and 1837. The artist traveled extensively in search of dramatic sites to represent in his landscapes. Here, Castle Resti's thirteenth-century tower rises over this scene. In addition to capturing the location's peaks and ruins, Schirmer's print demonstrates the artist's interest in how weather affected the landscape. The figures at the center of the composition are caught in a storm, enduring the rain falling from dark clouds at the right and left. The smaller trees in the middle ground bend in the gale, their branches nearly touching the ground.

Schirmer drew upon well-established Romantic themes. In this image, gusting winds convey the sublime power of nature, while the crumbling castle serves as a reminder that time passes and societies decay.

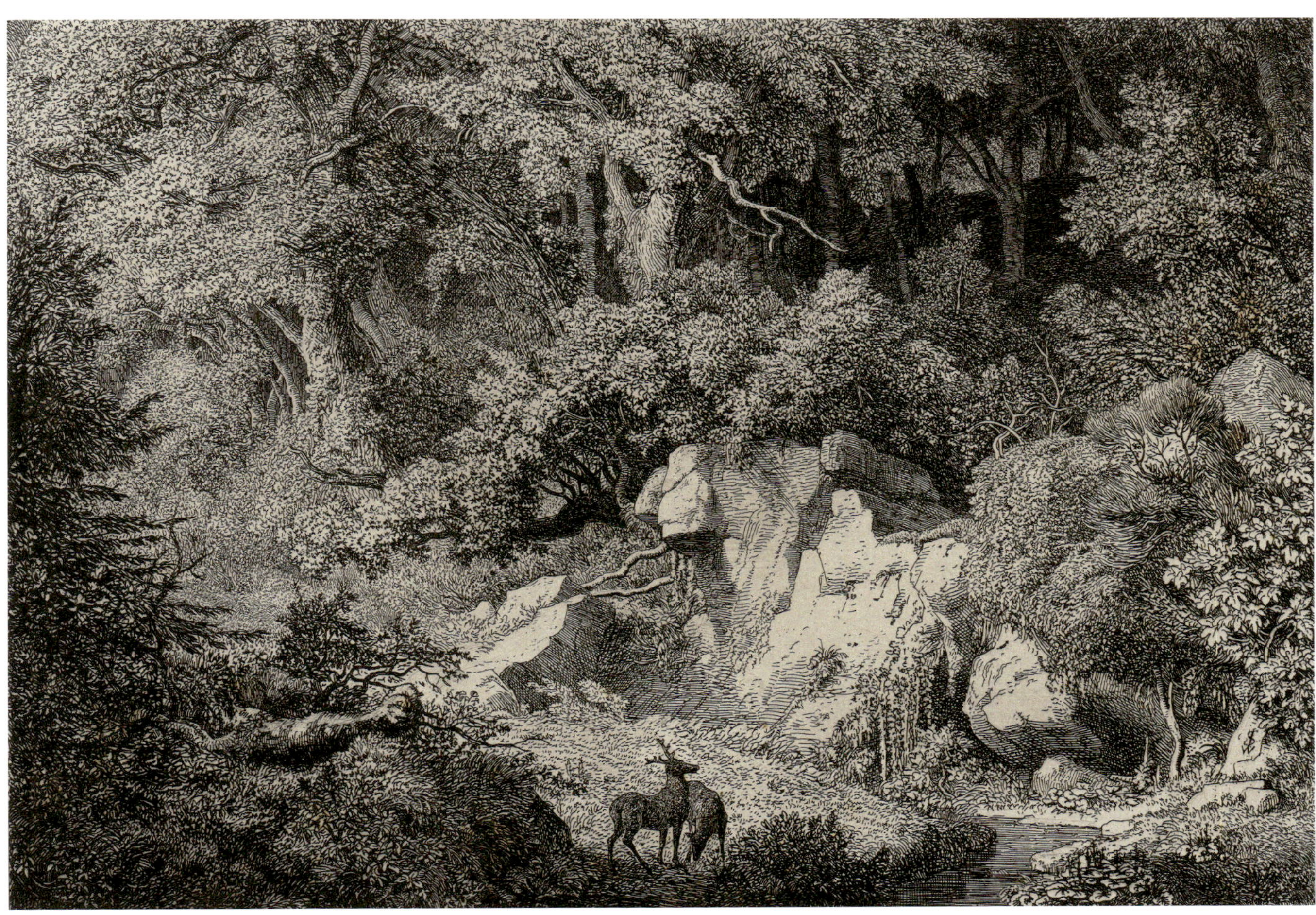

Johann Wilhelm Schirmer
JÜLICH 1807–1863 KARLSRUHE

In the Park Chigi (Aus dem Park Chigi), ca. 1840

Etching, printed chine collé

After his trips to Switzerland (see plate 75), Johann Wilhelm Schirmer visited several cities in Italy between 1839 and 1840. The park at Villa Chigi, southeast of Rome in Ariccia, had become a requisite stop for artists, and Schirmer's etching represents the popular site. Made slightly later than August Wilhelm Julius Ahlborn's sketch (plate 74), Schirmer's depiction emphasizes bucolic aspects of the grounds. A buck and doe stand just outside a patch of sunlight that illuminates a clearing next to a stream. The dense forest beyond creates a sense of depth and balances the brightness of the middle ground. Known for his highly detailed imagined scenes, Schirmer combined close observation of plants and trees with a composition intended to convey the idyllic atmosphere of the park.

Exhibition Checklist

Dimensions are listed with height first, width second. All works are from the collection of the Milwaukee Art Museum unless noted otherwise. In cases where the name of an artist's city of birth or death has changed since the nineteenth century, the more current form of the name is used. Nineteenth-century spellings of German words have been updated.

August Wilhelm Julius Ahlborn
(Hannover 1796–1857 Rome)
In the Park of the Villa Chigi, Ariccia: Two Olive Trees on a Rock at a Brook (recto); *Fallen Tree Trunks and Overgrown Roots* (verso), ca. 1831
Pen and brown ink and wash over graphite on paper
sheet: 15⅜ × 21⅝ in. (39.1 × 54.9 cm)
Purchase, René von Schleinitz Memorial Fund
M1994.368
(pl. 74)

Carl Blechen
(Cottbus 1798–1840 Berlin)
Figure Amidst the Ruins of a Gothic Abbey (Figur bei gotischer Ruine), ca. 1825
Pen and sepia ink and wash over graphite on paper
sheet: 6 × 7⅞ in. (15.2 × 20 cm)
Purchase, René von Schleinitz Memorial Fund
M1996.50
(pl. 15)

Guillaume Château
(Orléans 1635–1683 Paris)
After Nicolas Poussin
(Les Andelys 1594–1665 Rome)
The Israelites Gathering Manna in the Desert (Les Israélites recueillant la manne dans le désert), 1680
Engraving
plate: 17⅜ × 24⁹⁄₁₆ in. (44.1 × 62.4 cm)
sheet: 18¼ × 25⅛ in. (46.4 × 63.8 cm)
Gift of the Hockerman Charitable Trust
M1996.405

Daniel Nikolaus Chodowiecki
(Gdańsk 1726–1801 Berlin)
The Cabinet of a Painter (Cabinet d'un peintre), 1771
Etching
plate: 7¹⁄₁₆ × 9¹⁄₁₆ in. (17.9 × 23 cm)
sheet: 8³⁄₁₆ × 10⅜ in. (20.8 × 26.4 cm)
Purchase, Schuchardt Fund
M2019.114
(pl. 53)

Peter von Cornelius
(Düsseldorf 1783–1867 Berlin)
Engraved by Ferdinand Ruscheweyh
(Neustrelitz 1785–1846 Neustrelitz)
Published by Georg Reimer
(Greifswald 1776–1842 Berlin)
Illustrations for Goethe's "Faust" (Bilder zu Goethes Faust), 1813–18, published 1845
Series of ten engravings, printed chine collé, with title and dedication pages
Purchase, René von Schleinitz Memorial Fund and with funds from the Ralph and Cora Oberndorfer Family Trust

The Walk in the Garden (Der Spaziergang im Garten), 1813
plate: 16⅛ × 16¹¹⁄₁₆ in. (41 × 42.4 cm)
sheet: 24¹³⁄₁₆ × 30¾ in. (63 × 78.1 cm)
M2025.17.6
(pl. 27)

Gretchen Before a Statue of the Mater Dolorosa (Gretchen vor der Mater Dolorosa), 1816
plate: 19¹⁄₁₆ × 16⅛ in. (48.42 × 41 cm)
sheet: 30¾ × 24¹³⁄₁₆ in. (78.1 × 63 cm)
M2025.17.7
(pl. 28)

Valentin's Death (Valentins Tod), 1816
plate: 20¹³⁄₁₆ × 15⁹⁄₁₆ in. (52.9 × 39.5 cm)
sheet: 30¹³⁄₁₆ × 24¾ in. (78.3 × 62.9 cm)
M2025.17.8
(pl. 29)

Scene in the Cathedral (Szene im Dom), 1815
plate: 18¹³⁄₁₆ × 23¹⁄₁₆ in. (47.8 × 58.6 cm)
sheet: 24¹¹⁄₁₆ × 31⅛ in. (62.7 × 79.1 cm)
M2025.17.9
(pl. 30)

Journey to the Witches' Sabbath (Der Gang nach dem Brocken), 1813
plate: 17⅝ × 14½ in. (44.8 × 36.8 cm)
sheet: 31 × 24¾ in. (78.7 × 62.9 cm)
M2025.17.10
(pl. 31)

Vision at the Gallows (Die Erscheinung am Rabenstein), 1814
plate: 15⁷⁄₁₆ × 20⅞ in. (39.2 × 53 cm)
sheet: 24¹¹⁄₁₆ × 30⅞ in. (62.7 × 78.4 cm)
M2025.17.11
(pl. 32)

Gretchen in Prison (Gretchen im Gefängnis),
1815
plate: 15½ × 19¹³⁄₁₆ in. (39.4 × 50.3 cm)
sheet: 24¹¹⁄₁₆ × 30¹¹⁄₁₆ in. (62.7 × 78 cm)
M2025.17.12
(pl. 33)

Johann Christian Clausen Dahl
(Bergen 1788–1857 Dresden)
*Shipwreck on a Rocky Coast (Morning After
a Stormy Night) (Norwegische Seeküste
während eines Sturms)*, 1819
Etching with drypoint on brown-gray
paper
plate: 4⁹⁄₁₆ × 5⅞ in. (11.6 × 14.9 cm)
sheet: 6⅞ × 8¼ in. (17.5 × 21 cm)
Purchase, René von Schleinitz Memorial
Fund
M2024.17
(pl. 10)

*Trees by the River Elbe in the Rain
(Regenstimmung an der Elbe)*, 1834
Oil on canvas
5¼ × 7½ in. (13.5 × 19 cm)
Collection of Stephen and Elizabeth
Crawford
(pl. 67)

Cumulus Clouds (Kumuluswolken), 1845
Watercolor on paper
sheet: 3¹¹⁄₁₆ × 5⅞ in. (9.3 × 14.9 cm)
Collection of Stephen and Elizabeth
Crawford
(pl. 11)

Georg von Dillis
(Grüngiebing 1759–1841 Munich)
*The Rotting Trunk (Der modernde
Baumstamm)*, 1793
Etching
plate: 6⁹⁄₁₆ × 9⁷⁄₁₆ in. (16.7 × 24 cm)
sheet: 10⁵⁄₁₆ × 14¼ in. (26.2 × 36.2 cm)
Purchase, René von Schleinitz Memorial
Fund
M2022.29
(pl. 1)

Karel Dujardin
(Amsterdam 1626–1678 Venice)
The Shepherd Behind a Tree, ca. 1670
Etching
plate: 5⁷⁄₁₆ × 7¼ in. (13.8 × 18.4 cm)
sheet: 5¾ × 7⁹⁄₁₆ in. (14.6 × 19.2 cm)
Gift of Sanford Towart in memory of Dr.
David R. van Fossen
M2008.158

Albrecht Dürer
(Nuremberg 1471–1528 Nuremberg)
The Death of Mary (Der Tod der Mariens),
from the series *The Life of the Virgin
(Das Marienleben)*, 1510
Woodcut
Image and sheet: 11⁷⁄₁₆ × 8³⁄₁₆ in.
(29 × 20.8 cm)
Purchase, George B. Ferry Memorial
Fund
M1936.10

*The Madonna with the Pear (Die Jungfrau
mit der Birne)*, 1511
Engraving
Image and sheet: 6¼ × 4¼ in.
(15.9 × 10.8 cm)
Gift of Mrs. Albert O. Trostel, Jr.
M1970.91

Anselm Friedrich Feuerbach
(Speyer 1829–1880 Venice)
Mother and Child, 1858
Black chalk, watercolor, and white
heightening on paper
sheet: 16 × 10¾ in. (40.6 × 27.3 cm)
Purchase, René von Schleinitz Memorial
Fund
M1990.63
(pl. 51)

Caspar David Friedrich
(Greifswald 1774–1840 Dresden)
Block carved by Christian Friedrich
(Greifswald 1779–1843 Greifswald)
*Woman with a Raven at the Abyss (Die Frau
mit dem Raben am Abgrund)*, 1803
Woodcut
block: 6¾ × 4¹¹⁄₁₆ in. (17.2 × 11.9 cm)
sheet: 9¼ × 6⅞ in. (23.5 × 17.5 cm)
Purchase, René von Schleinitz Memorial
Fund
M2001.54
(pl. 8)

*Two Landscapes in Oberlausitz (Zwei
Landschaftsskizzen, 6. Juli 1810)*, 1810
Graphite on paper
sheet: 10⅛ × 14¼ in. (25.7 × 36.2 cm)
Purchase, René von Schleinitz Memorial
Fund
M1995.296
(pl. 54)

Ernst Fries
(Heidelberg 1801–1833 Karlsruhe)
View of Salzburg and the Königssee, 1820
Brush and gray-brown ink over graphite
on paper
sheet: 14⅜ × 10¾ in. (36.5 × 27.3 cm)
Purchase, René von Schleinitz Memorial
Fund
M1995.297
(pl. 65)

Joseph von Führich
(Chrastava 1800–1876 Vienna)
Engraved by August Gaber
(Koperniki 1823–1894 Berlin)
*The Bethlehemitic Path (Der Bethlehemi-
tische Weg)*, ca. 1865
Series of twelve woodcuts with
frontispiece
Gift of C. G. Boerner

Frontispiece
block: 8¹⁄₁₆ × 12⅛ in. (20.5 × 30.8 cm)
sheet: 14⅛ × 17¹³⁄₁₆ in. (35.9 × 45.2 cm)
M2022.45.13
(pl. 45)

Jesus as an Infant (Jesus als Säugling)
block: 8 × 12 in. (20.3 × 30.5 cm)
sheet: 14¹⁄₁₆ × 17¹¹⁄₁₆ in. (35.7 × 44.9 cm)
M2022.45.3
(pl. 46)

The Sacrifice of Jesus (Jesu Aufopferung)
block: 8¹⁄₁₆ × 11¹⁵⁄₁₆ in. (20.5 × 30.3 cm)
sheet: 14⅛ × 17¹³⁄₁₆ in. (35.9 × 45.2 cm)
M2022.45.7
(pl. 47)

The Flight of Jesus (Jesu Flucht)
block: 8¹⁄₁₆ × 11⅞ in. (20.5 × 30.2 cm)
sheet: 14¹⁄₁₆ × 17¾ in. (35.7 × 45.1 cm)
M2022.45.8
(pl. 48)

Jesus Walking (Jesus wandelnd)
block: 8¹⁄₁₆ × 11⅞ in. (20.5 × 30.2 cm)
sheet: 14¹⁄₁₆ × 17¾ in. (35.7 × 45.1 cm)
M2022.45.10
(pl. 49)

Jesus, a Fisher of Men (Jesus ein Fischer)
block: 8⅛ × 12³⁄₁₆ in. (20.6 × 31 cm)
sheet: 14⅛ × 17¾ in. (35.9 × 45.1 cm)
M2022.45.12
(pl. 50)

Jean-Baptiste Isabey
(Nancy 1767–1855 Paris)
Rome, the Campo Vaccino from the Top of the Coliseum (Rome, Le Campo Vaccino, pris du haut du Colisée), from the series *Journey in Italy (Voyage en Italie),* 1822
Lithograph
image: 6½ × 7⅝ in. (16.5 × 19.4 cm)
sheet: 10½ × 15¼ in. (26.7 × 38.7 cm)
Gift of Arthur J. Laskin in memory of Myron Laskin, Jr.
M2018.87

Tivoli, Interior of the Villa of Maecenas (Tivoli, un intérieur du Palais de Mécène), from the series *Journey in Italy (Voyage en Italie),* 1822
Lithograph
image: 6½ × 7⅝ in. (16.5 × 19.4 cm)
sheet: 10¼ × 14⅝ in. (26 × 37.2 cm)
Gift of Arthur J. Laskin in memory of Myron Laskin, Jr.
M2018.88

Franz Ittenbach
(Königswinter 1813–1879 Düsseldorf)
Queen of Heaven (Himmelskönigin), 1872
Oil on panel
39 × 22⁷⁄₁₆ in. (99 × 57 cm)
Purchase, René von Schleinitz Memorial Fund and with funds in memory of Betty Croasdaile and John E. Julien
M2015.37
(pl. 52)

Angelica Kauffman
(Chur 1741–1807 Rome)
Published by John Boydell
(London 1719–1804 London)
Seated Contemplative Girl (Sitzendes nachdenkendes Mädchen), 1766, published 1780
Etching and aquatint
image: 8⁵⁄₁₆ × 6½ in. (21.1 × 16.5 cm)
sheet: 9¹⁄₁₆ × 7⁹⁄₁₆ in. (23 × 19.2 cm)
Maurice and Esther Leah Ritz Collection
M2004.215
(pl. 7)

Johann Adam Klein
(Nuremberg 1792–1875 Munich)
The Artists on Their Journey (Meinen Reisegefährten gewidmet), 1819
Etching
plate: 9¹¹⁄₁₆ × 12 in. (24.6 × 30.5 cm)
sheet: 11⅛ × 13⅜ in. (28.3 × 34 cm)
Purchase, René von Schleinitz Memorial Fund
M2024.18
(pl. 66)

Ferdinand Kobell
(Mannheim 1740–1799 Munich)
Philosopher's Path near Heidelberg (Philosophenweg bei Heidelberg), 1780
Etching
plate: 9¾ × 7½ in. (24.8 × 19.1 cm)
sheet: 12¼ × 10 in. (31.1 × 25.4 cm)
Gift of George and Angela Jacobi in memory of Eugen Langenbach
M1997.80
(pl. 4)

Franz Kobell
(Mannheim 1749–1822 Munich)
Nocturnal Landscape with Two Figures, ca. 1807
Pen and brown ink and wash over graphite on paper
sheet: 13⅝ × 9³⁄₁₆ in. (34.6 × 23.3 cm)
Purchase, René von Schleinitz Memorial Fund
M1990.57
(pl. 9)

Joseph Anton Koch
(Obergiblen 1768–1839 Rome)
Landscape with Noah's Sacrifice (Landschaft mit Dankopfer Noahs), ca. 1823/25
Pen and brown ink and wash on paper
sheet: 15⅞ × 19⅞ in. (40.3 × 50.5 cm)
Collection of Stephen and Elizabeth Crawford
(pl. 38)

Landscape with Ruth and Boaz (Landschaft mit Ruth und Boas), 1823/25
Oil on canvas
33¼ × 43¼ in. (84.5 × 109.9 cm)
Gift of René von Schleinitz Memorial Fund, by exchange
M1999.117
(pl. 37)

Carl Wilhelm Kolbe the Elder
(Berlin 1759–1835 Dessau)
Cow in the Reeds (Die Kuh im Schilfe), ca. 1800/03
Etching
plate: 11¹⁵⁄₁₆ × 16½ in. (30.3 × 41.9 cm)
sheet: 16¹⁵⁄₁₆ × 22¹³⁄₁₆ in. (43 × 57.9 cm)
Purchase, René von Schleinitz Memorial Fund
M2001.171
(pl. 3)

Landscape with Clumps of Tall Oak Trees (Landschaft mit Gruppen hoher Eichen), ca. 1802
Etching
plate: 12¹⁵⁄₁₆ × 16¹⁵⁄₁₆ in. (32.9 × 43 cm)
sheet: 16⁵⁄₁₆ × 20⅝ in. (41.4 × 52.4 cm)
Purchase, René von Schleinitz Memorial Fund
M2022.26
(pl. 2)

Carl Friedrich Lessing
(Wrocław 1808–1880 Karlsruhe)
Landscape with Wanderers, 1837
Pen and brown ink and watercolor over graphite on paper
sheet: 6½ × 11¼ in. (16.5 × 28.6 cm)
Purchase, René von Schleinitz Memorial Fund
M1996.7
(pl. 55)

Claude Lorrain
(Chamagne 1604–1682 Rome)
The Cowherd (Le bouvier), 1636
Etching
plate: 5⅛ × 7⅞ in. (13 × 20 cm)
sheet: 7¾ × 10¹⁵⁄₁₆ in. (19.7 × 27.8 cm)
Gift of the Hockerman Charitable Trust
M2001.175

Heinrich Karl Anton Mücke
(Wrocław 1806–1891 Düsseldorf)
The Body of Saint Catherine of Alexandria Carried to Heaven by Angels (Der Leichnam der heiligen Katharina von Alexandrien, von Engeln zum Himmel getragen), ca. 1836
Watercolor with touches of gold and lead white on paper
sheet: 11¹⁄₁₆ × 16½ in. (28.1 × 41.9 cm)
Purchase, René von Schleinitz Memorial Fund
M1995.293
(pl. 40)

Published by Julius Buddeus
(active Düsseldorf 1830s–1852)
Angels Carrying the Body of St. Catherine to Mount Sinai (Engel tragen den Leichnam der heil. Katharina nach dem Berge Sinai), from the portfolio *Album of German Artists in Original Etchings (Album deutscher Künstler in Original-Radierungen)*, 1841
Etching
plate: 9¼ × 12¹³⁄₁₆ in. (23.5 × 32.5 cm)
sheet: 11⅛ × 15⅝ in. (28.3 × 39.7 cm)
Purchase, René von Schleinitz Memorial Fund
M1994.402
(pl. 41)

Eugen Napoleon Neureuther
(Munich 1806–1882 Munich)
The Morning After the Masquerade (Am Morgen nach dem Maskenfeste), 1840
Etching, printed chine collé
plate: 8⅛ × 11⁷⁄₁₆ in. (20.6 × 29 cm)
sheet: 13⅞ × 18¼ in. (35.2 × 46.4 cm)
Purchase, René von Schleinitz Memorial Fund
M2025.15
(pl. 42)

Printed by Carl Mayer
(Nuremberg 1798–1868 Nuremberg)
Maximilian I Presenting the Artists' Coat of Arms to Albrecht Dürer (Artists' Masquerade 1840) (Die Verleihung des Künstlerwappens an Albrecht Dürer durch Max I. [Maskenfest der Künstler 1840]), 1841–43
Etching
plate: 24 × 18¾ in. (61 × 47.6 cm)
sheet: 26¼ × 19⅞ in. (66.7 × 50.5 cm)
Purchase, René von Schleinitz Memorial Fund
M1996.256
(pl. 43)

Ferdinand Olivier
(Dessau 1785–1841 Munich)
Printed by Adolph Kunike
(Greifswald 1777–1838 Vienna)
House Altar, 1820
Lithograph
image: 7 × 16½ in. (17.8 × 41.9 cm)
sheet: 7⅛ × 16⅝ in. (18.1 × 42.2 cm)
Purchase, René von Schleinitz Memorial Fund and with funds from the Ralph and Cora Oberndorfer Family Trust
M2023.2
(pl. 36)

Printed by Adolph Kunike
(Greifswald 1777–1838 Vienna)
Published by Ferdinand Olivier
(Dessau 1785–1841 Munich)
Seven Places in Salzburg and Berchtesgaden (Sieben Gegenden aus Salzburg und Berchtesgaden), 1818–22, published 1823
Series of seven lithographs with dedication and keystone
Purchase, Marjorie Tiefenthaler Bequest

Dedication (Zueignung)
Lithograph without tint stone
image: 11⅛ × 14¹⁄₁₆ in. (28.3 × 35.7 cm)
sheet: 14⅝ × 20⅞ in. (37.2 × 53 cm)
Art Institute of Chicago, Clarence Buckingham Collection, 1996.341.1
(pl. 56)

Sunday: Going to Church in Berchtesgaden (Sonntag. Kircheneingang in Berchtesgaden)
Lithograph with tint stone and hand touching
image: 7¹¹⁄₁₆ × 10⅝ in. (19.5 × 27 cm)
sheet: 14⅛ × 20 in. (35.9 × 50.8 cm)
M1997.8.1
(pl. 57)

Monday: Rosenecker Garden Outside Salzburg (Montag. Rosenecker Garten vor Salzburg)
Lithograph with tint stone and hand touching
image: 7¾ × 10¹³⁄₁₆ in. (19.7 × 27.5 cm)
sheet: 14⅛ × 19⅞ in. (35.9 × 50.5 cm)
M1997.8.2
(pl. 58)

Tuesday: Salzburg Castle from the South (Dienstag. Bergveste Salzburg von der Mittagseite)
Lithograph with tint stone and hand touching
image: 7¾ × 10⅝ in. (19.7 × 27 cm)
sheet: 14⅛ × 20 in. (35.9 × 50.8 cm)
M1997.8.3
(pl. 59)

Wednesday: Footpath on the Mönchsberg near Salzburg (Mittwoch. Fußpfad auf dem Mönchsberge bei Salzburg)
Lithograph with tint stone and hand touching
image: 7⅞ × 10⅞ in. (20 × 27.6 cm)
sheet: 14⅛ × 20 in. (35.9 × 50.8 cm)
M1997.8.4
(pl. 60)

Thursday: Berchtesgaden and the Watzmann (Donnerstag. Berchtesgaden und der Watzmann)
Lithograph with tint stone
image: 8⅛ × 11 in. (20.6 × 27.9 cm)
sheet: 14⅛ × 20 in. (35.9 × 50.8 cm)
M1997.8.5
(pl. 61)

Friday: Meadow Before Aigen near Salzburg (Freitag. Wiesenplan vor Aigen bei Salzburg)
Lithograph with tint stone and hand touching
image: 7¾ × 10¾ in. (19.7 × 27.3 cm)
sheet: 14⅛ × 20 in. (35.9 × 50.8 cm)
M1997.8.6
(pl. 62)

Saturday: Graveyard of St. Peter's in Salzburg (Sonnabend. Gottesacker zu St. Peter in Salzburg)
Lithograph with tint stone
image: 7¾ × 11¹⁄₁₆ in. (19.7 × 28.1 cm)
sheet: 14⅛ × 20 in. (35.9 × 50.8 cm)
M1997.8.7
(pl. 63)

Keystone (Schlussstein)
Lithograph with tint stone
image: 10⅞ × 14¾ in. (27.6 × 37.5 cm)
sheet: 11 × 15 in. (27.9 × 38.1 cm)
M1997.8.8
(pl. 64)

Johann Friedrich Overbeck
(Lübeck 1789–1869 Rome)
Joseph Being Sold by His Brothers (Joseph wird von seinen Brüdern verkauft), 1817
Graphite on paper
sheet: 6½ × 7¾ in. (16.5 × 19.7 cm)
Purchase, René von Schleinitz Memorial Fund
M1997.78
(pl. 34)

Lithographed by Hans Jakob Oeri
(Kyburg 1782–1868 Zurich)
Published by Johann Velten
(Wetzlar 1784–1864 Karlsruhe)
Joseph Being Sold by His Brothers (Joseph wird von seinen Brüdern verkauft), 1826
Lithograph
image: 21¹⁵⁄₁₆ × 27⅜ in. (55.7 × 69.5 cm)
sheet: 25¹⁵⁄₁₆ × 31⅜ in. (65.9 × 79.7 cm)
Purchase, René von Schleinitz Memorial Fund
M2023.4
(pl. 35)

Lithographed by Nikolaus Hoff
(Frankfurt 1798–1873 Frankfurt)
Printed by Friedrich Carl Vogel
(Frankfurt 1806–1865 Venice)
Italia and Germania, 1830
Lithograph
image: 16¾ × 18⅝ in. (42.6 × 47.3 cm)
sheet: 20⁷⁄₁₆ × 22¹⁄₁₆ in. (51.9 × 56 cm)
Purchase, René von Schleinitz Memorial
Fund
M2025.14
(pl. 39)

Domenico Quaglio II
(Munich 1786/7–1837 Schwangau)
*Court in a Gothic Abbey (Gotischer
Klosterhof)*, 1808
Crayon manner lithograph
image and sheet: 12½ × 10½ in.
(31.8 × 26.7 cm)
Purchase, René von Schleinitz Memorial
Fund
M1996.38
(pl. 12)

Ludwig Richter
(Dresden 1803–1884 Dresden)
Published by Carl Gustav Boerner
(Knau 1790–1855 Leipzig)
*Picturesque Views of the Environs of Rome
(Malerische Ansichten aus den Umgebungen
von Rom)*, 1832
Series of six etchings
Purchase, René von Schleinitz Memorial
Fund

Roadside Inn (Osteria)
plate: 6¼ × 7¹⁵⁄₁₆ in. (15.9 × 20.2 cm)
sheet: 8⅞ × 11⁷⁄₁₆ in. (22.5 × 29.1 cm)
M1996.276
(pl. 68)

Monte Circello
plate: 6¹⁄₁₆ × 7¹⁵⁄₁₆ in. (15.4 × 20.2 cm)
sheet: 8⅞ × 11⁷⁄₁₆ in. (22.5 × 29.1 cm)
M1996.277
(pl. 69)

Rocca di Mezzo
plate: 6¹⁄₁₆ × 7⅞ in. (15.4 × 20 cm)
sheet: 8¹⁵⁄₁₆ × 11⅝ in. (22.7 × 29.5 cm)
M1996.278
(pl. 70)

Olevano
plate: 6 × 7¹⁵⁄₁₆ in. (15.2 × 20.2 cm)
sheet: 8⅞ × 11¼ in. (22.5 × 28.6 cm)
M1996.279
(pl. 71)

Ponte Salaro
plate: 6¹⁄₁₆ × 7¹³⁄₁₆ in. (15.4 × 19.8 cm)
sheet: 8¹³⁄₁₆ × 11⁷⁄₁₆ in. (22.4 × 29.1 cm)
M1996.280
(pl. 72)

Castel Gandolfo
plate: 6⅛ × 7⅞ in. (15.6 × 20 cm)
sheet: 8¹⁵⁄₁₆ × 11⁷⁄₁₆ in. (22.7 × 29.1 cm)
M1996.281
(pl. 73)

Johannes Riepenhausen
(Göttingen 1787–1860 Rome)
Raphael and La Fornarina, ca. 1833
Watercolor and ink over graphite on
paper
sheet: 9⁹⁄₁₆ × 7⁷⁄₁₆ in. (24.3 × 18.9 cm)
Purchase, René von Schleinitz Memorial
Fund
M1993.84
(pl. 44)

Philipp Otto Runge
(Wolgast 1777–1810 Hamburg)
Etched and engraved by Johann Adolph
Darnstedt (Auma 1769–1844 Dresden)
Etched and engraved by Ephraim
Gottlieb Krüger (Dresden 1756–1834
Dresden)
Etched and engraved by Johann Gottlieb
Seyfert (Dresden 1760–1824 Dresden)
Published by Friedrich Christoph
Perthes (Rudolstadt 1772–1843 Gotha)
Times of Day (Die Zeiten), 1803/05,
published 1807
Series of four etchings with engraving
Purchase, René von Schleinitz Memorial
Fund

Etched and engraved by Johann Gottlieb
Seyfert (Dresden 1760–1824 Dresden)
Morning (Morgen)
plate: 27⅞ × 18¾ in. (70.8 × 47.6 cm)
sheet: 31⅛ × 21½ in. (79.1 × 54.6 cm)
M1996.338.1
(pl. 23)

Evening (Abend)
plate: 28 × 18¹³⁄₁₆ in. (71.1 × 47.8 cm)
sheet: 31⁹⁄₁₆ × 21¹⁵⁄₁₆ in. (80.2 × 55.7 cm)
M1996.338.3
(pl. 25)

Etched and engraved by Johann Adolph
Darnstedt (Auma 1769–1844 Dresden)
Etched and engraved by Ephraim
Gottlieb Krüger (Dresden 1756–1834
Dresden)
Day (Tag)
plate: 28¹⁄₁₆ × 18¹³⁄₁₆ in. (71.3 × 47.8 cm)
sheet: 31⅝ × 21¹⁵⁄₁₆ in. (80.3 × 55.7 cm)
M1996.338.2
(pl. 24)

Night (Nacht)
plate: 28¹⁄₁₆ × 18¹¹⁄₁₆ in. (71.3 × 47.5 cm)
sheet: 31½ × 21¹⁵⁄₁₆ in. (80 × 55.7 cm)
M1996.338.4
(pl. 26)

Karl Friedrich Schinkel
(Neuruppin 1781–1841 Berlin)
*Gothic Courtyard, Classical Landscape with
a Fountain, Landscape Sketch (Gotischer
Hof, Klassische Landschaft mit Brunnen,
Landschaftsskizze)*, 1800
Etching
plate: 8 × 5 in. (20.3 × 12.7 cm)
sheet: 8¹⁄₁₆ × 5⅛ in. (20.5 × 13 cm)
Purchase, René von Schleinitz Memorial
Fund and with funds from the Ralph and
Cora Oberndorfer Family Trust
M2019.34
(pl. 13)

A Gothic Cathedral Behind Trees, 1810/15
Pen and gray ink and watercolor over
graphite on paper
sheet: 9¹¹⁄₁₆ × 8¹⁵⁄₁₆ in. (24.6 × 22.7 cm)
Purchase, René von Schleinitz Memorial
Fund
M1995.285
(pl. 14)

Johann Wilhelm Schirmer
(Jülich 1807–1863 Karlsruhe)
*The Forest with a Prowling Fox (Der Wald
mit dem schleichenden Fuchs)*, ca. 1829
Etching, printed chine collé
plate: 10½ × 15 in. (26.7 × 38.1 cm)
sheet: 17½ × 23⅜ in. (44.5 × 59.4 cm)
Purchase, René von Schleinitz Memorial
Fund
M1996.47
(pl. 16)

Churchyard (Der Kirchhof), ca. 1838
Etching, printed chine collé
plate: 10¾ × 8¾ in. (27.3 × 22.2 cm)
sheet: 8⅜ × 7¼ in. (21.3 × 18.4 cm)
Purchase, René von Schleinitz Memorial
Fund
M1996.44
(pl. 17)

In the Park Chigi (Aus dem Park Chigi),
ca. 1840
Etching, printed chine collé
plate: 9¾ × 12 in. (24.8 × 30.5 cm)
sheet: 7⅜ × 10½ in. (18.7 × 26.7 cm)
Purchase, René von Schleinitz Memorial
Fund
M1996.41
(pl. 76)

*The Hunter's Departure from the Forest
(Der Jäger Abschied vom Wald)*, ca. 1843
Etching, printed chine collé
plate: 8⅛ × 7¼ in. (20.6 × 18.4 cm)
sheet: 17⅝ × 12⅞ in. (44.8 × 32.7 cm)
Purchase, René von Schleinitz Memorial
Fund
M1996.43
(pl. 18)

The Mill near a Forest (Die Mühle am Wald),
ca. 1845
Etching, printed chine collé
plate: 11 × 15 in. (27.9 × 38.1 cm)
sheet: 21⅜ × 25⅞ in. (54.3 × 65.7 cm)
Purchase, René von Schleinitz Memorial
Fund
M1996.45
(pl. 21)

*Ruined Castle near Meiringen (Burgreste bei
Meiringen)*, ca. 1843
Etching, printed chine collé
plate: 7¾ × 11¾ in. (19.7 × 29.9 cm)
sheet: 21¼ × 26½ in. (54 × 67.3 cm)
Purchase, René von Schleinitz Memorial
Fund
M1996.42
(pl. 75)

*The Forest Brook with Storks (Der
Waldsturm mit den Störchen)*, 1845
Etching with touches of graphite
plate: 15⅞ × 12⅞ in. (40.3 × 32.7 cm)
sheet: 22⅝ × 14¾ in. (57.5 × 37.5 cm)
Purchase, René von Schleinitz Memorial
Fund
M1996.48
(pl. 19)

*The Forest Brook with Storks (Der
Waldsturm mit den Störchen)*, 1845
Etching, printed chine collé
plate: 15⅞ × 12⅞ in. (40.3 × 32.7 cm)
sheet: 22⅞ × 21⅝ in. (58.1 × 54.9 cm)
Purchase, René von Schleinitz Memorial
Fund
M1996.49
(pl. 20)

Forest Landscape with the Good Samaritan,
1856–57
Pen and ink with brown wash and black
chalk on paper
sheet: 15⅞ × 20¹¹⁄₁₆ in. (40.3 × 52.6 cm)
Purchase, René von Schleinitz Memorial
Fund
M1994.363
(pl. 22)

Max Josef Wagenbauer
(Öxing 1775–1829 Munich)
*Model Sheets for Landscape Draftsmen
(Vorlagen für Landschaft-Zeichner)*, 1805,
published 1823
Lithographs; bound volume
closed: 13⅝ × 10⅛ × ½ in. (34.6 × 25.7 ×
1.3 cm)
open: 13⅝ × 20⁵⁄₁₆ in. (34.6 × 51.6 cm)
Purchase, René von Schleinitz Memorial
Fund
M2022.27
(pl. 6)

Adrian Zingg
(St. Gallen 1734–1816 Leipzig)
*Blooming Thistle (Große Distel or Blühende
Distelpflanze)*, ca. 1810
Pen and ink and wash over graphite on
paper
sheet: 13⅛ × 8¹³⁄₁₆ in. (33.3 × 22.4 cm)
Purchase, René von Schleinitz Memorial
Fund
M1996.51
(pl. 5)

Index

This catalogue has been published on the occasion of the exhibition *Seeking Revelation: German Romantic Prints and Drawings*, presented at the Milwaukee Art Museum from June 19 to November 1, 2026.

The exhibition was realized with support from the following generous sponsors:

Supporting Sponsors:
Katharine and Sandy Mallin
Milwaukee Art Museum's Print Forum

Additional support provided by:

IFPDA FOUNDATION

Drs. Peter Drescher and Karin Madsen Drescher

The Milwaukee Art Museum extends its sincere thanks to the Visionaries for their support of the exhibition program:
Mark and Debbie Attanasio
Donna and Donald Baumgartner
Murph Burke
Bill and Sandy Haack
The Helmerich Trust
Kenneth and Alice Kayser
Joan Lubar and John Crouch
Jeff and Gail Yabuki

Library of Congress Control Number:
2025949616
ISBN 978-1-64657-053-9

Published by the Milwaukee Art Museum
700 North Art Museum Drive
Milwaukee, Wisconsin 53202
www.mam.org

Available through:
ARTBOOK | D.A.P.
75 Broad Street, Suite 630
New York, NY 10004
www.artbook.com

Produced by Marquand Books, Seattle
www.marquandbooks.com

Edited by Christina Dittrich
Designed by Ryan Polich
Typeset in Elfreth, Albertus Nova, and
   Wolpe Pegasus by Tina Henderson,
   Miko McGinty Inc.
Proofread by Jennifer Snodgrass
Indexed by David Luljak
Color management by I/O Color, Seattle
Printed and bound in China by Artron Art
   Group

Details
Cover front: Carl Wilhelm Kolbe the Elder, *Cow in the Reeds*, ca. 1800/03 (cat. p. 160)
Cover back: Johann Friedrich Overbeck, *Italia and Germania*, 1830 (cat. p. 162)
p. 2: Johann Wilhelm Schirmer, *The Hunter's Departure from the Forest*, ca. 1843 (cat. p. 163)
p. 4: Johann Christian Clausen Dahl, *Shipwreck on a Rocky Coast (Morning After a Stormy Night)*, 1819 (cat. p. 159)
p. 6: Franz Kobell, *Nocturnal Landscape with Two Figures*, ca. 1807 (cat. p. 160)
p. 9: Karl Friedrich Schinkel, *A Gothic Cathedral Behind Trees*, 1810/15 (cat. p. 162)
p. 10: Philipp Otto Runge, *Evening*, 1803/05, published 1807 (cat. p. 162)

Photography Credits
pp. 2, 4, 9, 10: Photo by Cleber Bonato
p. 6: Photo by John R. Glembin

Introduction and Acknowledgments
Figs. 1, 2: Maps designed by Amy Cannestra
Figs. 3, 6: Photo by John R. Glembin
Figs. 4, 5, 8, 9: Photo by Cleber Bonato
Fig. 7: bpk Bildagentur / Staatliche Museen zu Berlin, Nationalgalerie / Andres Kilger / Art Resource, NY

O'Rourke essay
p. 22: Photo by Cleber Bonato
Fig. 1: © Bavarian State Painting Collections
Fig. 2: © Anhaltische Gemäldegalerie Dessau/Photo: Dietmar Gunne
Fig. 3: Beinecke Rare Book and Manuscript Library Open Access
Figs. 4–7, 11: Photo by Cleber Bonato
Fig. 8: Image from the Biodiversity Heritage Library. Contributed by New York Botanical Garden, LuEsther T. Mertz Library. | www.biodiversitylibrary.org

Fig. 9: HIP / Art Resource, NY
Fig. 10: © Private Collection

Grewe essay
p. 70: Photo by John R. Glembin
Fig. 1: Courtesy of HathiTrust via Getty Research Institute
Fig. 2: bpk Bildagentur / National Museums in Berlin, National Gallery / Andres Kilger / Art Resource, NY
Figs. 3, 6, 7, 12: Photo by John R. Glembin
Fig. 4: © Ketterer Kunst GmbH und Co. KG, reproduced with kind permission
Figs. 5, 10, 13: Photo by Cleber Bonato
Fig. 8: Photo by Larry Sanders
Fig. 9: Städel Museum, Frankfurt am Main
Fig. 11: Courtesy of Neue Galerie Graz / Universalmuseum Joanneum
Fig. 14: © Generaldirektion Kulturelles Erbe Rheinland-Pfalz, Direktion Landesdenkmalpflege Mainz, Fotoarchiv, Sigmar Fitting, 2003

Otten essay
p. 122: Photo by Cleber Bonato
Fig. 1: Courtesy Staatliche Graphische Sammlung
Figs. 2, 3, 5, 6: Photo by John R. Glembin
Fig. 4: Städel Museum, Frankfurt am Main
Figs. 7, 9–14: Photo by Cleber Bonato
Fig. 8: © Bavarian State Painting Collections

Plates
1, 2, 4, 6, 7, 10–12, 14, 16–21, 23–33, 35, 36, 38–40, 42, 43, 45–50, 55, 65–73, 76: Photo by Cleber Bonato
3, 5, 8, 9, 13, 15, 22, 34, 41, 44, 51–54, 57–64, 74, 75: Photo by John R. Glembin
37: Photo by Larry Sanders
56: Art Institute of Chicago